The Library of Yiddish Classics is sponsored by the
Fund for the Translation of Jewish Literature
Series Editor: Ruth R. Wisse

▼   ▼   ▼

Tevye the Dairyman and The Railroad Stories
by Sholem Aleichem
translated and with an introduction by Hillel Halkin

The I. L. Peretz Reader
edited and with an introduction by Ruth R. Wisse

The Dybbuk and Other Writings
by S. Ansky
edited and with an introduction by David G. Roskies

▲

The Dybbuk
and
Other Writings

▼

LIBRARY OF YIDDISH CLASSICS

The Dybbuk

—— a n d ——

Other Writings

by S. Ansky

Edited and with an Introduction

by David G. Roskies

With translations by Golda Werman

SCHOCKEN BOOKS   NEW YORK

Copyright © 1992 by The Fund for the Translation of Jewish Literature

The present volume was made possible by a generous gift to the Fund for the Translation of Jewish Literature by Mr. and Mrs. Edwin M. Gale of Beaumont, Texas.

Grateful acknowledgment is made for permission to reprint the following previously published stories: "I Enlighten a Shtetl," which appears in this volume under the title "The Sins of Youth" is from *The Golden Tradition: Jewish Life and Thought in Eastern Europe*, edited by Lucy S. Dawidowicz (New York: Holt, Rinehart, and Winston, 1967; paperback: Schocken Books, 1985). Copyright © 1967 by Lucy S. Dawidowicz. Reprinted by permission of Henry Holt and Company. "Behind a Mask" is from *A Shtetl and Other Yiddish Novellas*, edited by Ruth R. Wisse (Detroit: Wayne State University Press, 1986). Reprinted by permission of Ruth R. Wisse.

Library of Congress Cataloging-in-Publication Data
An-Ski, S., 1863–1920.
[Selections. English. 1992]
The Dybbuk and other writings / by S. Ansky; edited and with an
introduction by David G. Roskies; with translations by Golda
Werman.
p. cm. — (Library of Yiddish classics)
1. World War, 1914–1918—Personal narratives, Jewish. 2. World
War, 1914–1918—Galicia (Poland and Ukraine) 3. An-Ski, S.,
1863–1920—Diaries. I. Roskies, David G., 1948–   . II. Werman,
Golda, 1930–   . III. Title. IV. Series.
PJ5129.R3A27   1992
839'.098309—dc20   91-52619
ISBN 0-8052-4111-6

רוטאַסיקל—
דאָס בוך געהערט לחלוטין צו דיר.
▼ ▼ ▼

Contents

▼

Acknowledgments

▼

The Dybbuk and Other Writings by S. Ansky is the third volume in the Library of Yiddish Classics published by Schocken Books. It serves as fitting sequel to Sholem Aleichem's *Tevye the Dairyman and The Railroad Stories*, translated with an introduction by Hillel Halkin (1987) and *The I. L. Peretz Reader*, edited by Ruth R. Wisse (1990). Though each volume can stand on its own, the Library taken as a whole will represent the very best that Yiddish literature has to offer. Within that whole, S. Ansky's contribution as Yiddish-Russian playwright, fiction writer, and memoirist will henceforth occupy its rightful place. And so, my first debt of thanks goes to Ruth R. Wisse, the series editor, who matched me up with Ansky's life and work. For this, and many other reasons, I dedicate the book to her.

The lion's share of the volume was translated by Golda Werman, including a new rendering of the famous *Dybbuk* itself. Her critical comments during our two-year collaboration also helped me ferret out what really worked in an English-language anthology. I owe a special thanks to Robert Szulkin, my beloved teacher, for translating an early sketch of Ansky's from the Russian, and to Michael Stern for his dedicated work under difficult time contraints. My thanks as well to Ruth R. Wisse and also to Henry Holt & Co. for permission to reprint copyrighted material.

Among the most memorable pieces in this volume is one translated by the late Lucy S. Dawidowicz. In addition to her many other achievements, Mrs. Dawidowicz was responsible for establishing the Fund for the Translation of Jewish Literature, which sponsors the translations in the Library of Yiddish Classics series. The present volume was made possible by a generous gift to the Fund by Mr. and Mrs. Edwin M. Gale of Beaumont, Texas.

Finally, it is my pleasure to thank Bonny Fetterman, senior editor of Schocken Books. The continued flourishing of the Library of Yiddish Classics is in no small measure due to her exacting standards and unflinching support.

D.G.R.

Introduction

▼

When Solomon Rappoport fled the Bolsheviks disguised as a priest and reached the German-occupied city of Vilna aboard a refugee train, he was a broken man. A lifetime of service to the revolutionary cause in his native land and abroad had been cut short by Lenin's seizure of power in January 1918. As a deputy to the All-Russian Constituent Assembly on the Socialist-Revolutionary ticket, Rappoport was now a fugitive. Worse still, the Bolsheviks impounded the treasures of the Jewish Ethnographic Museum in Petrograd on whose premises he had lived. The Moscow Art Theater's premiere performance of *The Dybbuk*—the indisputable masterpiece of the Jewish theater that would have culminated his literary career—was canceled due to Stanislavsky's illness and the political upheaval in Russia. Rappoport did not even salvage a copy of the play when he was forced to flee. Among other papers left behind was the manuscript of his four-volume war chronicle, *The Destruction of Galicia*. Now, from his sickbed in Vilna, where he lay stricken with diabetes and heart disease, Rappoport instructed future generations to study his life rather than to read his published and still unpublished works.

Yet there was no reason to choose between the man and his work. Having lived most of his life "on the border between two worlds," he made the subject of competing loyalties into the substance of his fiction, drama, essays and memoirs. The divided life and complex personality of Solomon Rappoport-Ansky offered a key to the evolution of the Jews—and of Jewish literature—in modern times.[1]

Born Shloyme-Zanvl ben Aaron Hacohen Rappoport in Marc Chagall's city of Vitebsk, Ansky was raised in the unusual confluence of two opposing streams of East European Orthodoxy. The historic center of Habad Hasidism (known today as Lubavitch), Vitebsk also boasted one of Jewish Lithuania's finest yeshivas. When not engaged in his own talmudic recitative inside the *besmedresh* (house of study), Shloyme-Zanvl could listen to the haunting contemplative melodies that emanated from the small hasidic *shtiblekh* (houses of prayer). The young man was reputed to be a Talmud prodigy.

These were boom years for the city, whose Jewish population jumped from fourteen thousand in the year of Rappoport's birth (1863) to twenty-four thousand when he left for good (1881). Some families, like the Zhitlowskys, struck it rich during this period of rapid expansion, whereas others, like the once wealthy Rappoports, suffered a severe reversal of fortune. Shloyme-Zanvl's mother was forced to run a tavern, while his father was always away on business. They lived in Podvinye, the poorer section of town, and could not afford the monthly three-ruble tuition to send Shloyme-Zanvl or his two sisters to the local gymnasium. So he was left to learn Russian from his well-heeled friend Chaim Zhitlowsky, the future philosopher of a Yiddish-based nationalism, and together they strayed from the straight and narrow.

It began with some amateur Yiddish journalism: an issue or two of the *Vitebsker gleklekh* (*The Little Bells of Vitebsk*) with Shloyme-Zanvl serving as local correspondent and Chaim writing fiction. A traveling Yiddish theater inspired fifteen-year-old Shloyme-Zanvl to write a melodrama about the evils of (his) heder education, but actor-director Jacob Adler was not impressed. Meanwhile, the two boys were busy reading. They read the militant works of the Hebrew Enlightenment, notably Moshe Leib Lilienblum's *Hattot Ne'urim* (*The Sins of Youth*, 1876). This autobiographical exposé of a tradition-minded father and his idealistic son was an epoch-making indictment of the whole of Jewish civilization. And they read the Russian nihilist manifestos of Pisarev alongside Chernichevsky's feminist and utopian novel, *What Is to Be Done?*

By the age of seventeen, Shloyme-Zanvl had lost his faith, had become a "critical realist," and was running a commune on the outskirts of town for poor boys who had left the yeshiva. He taught them mathematics and Russian and urged them on to "productive labor." A year later, Shloyme-Zanvl left home to preach the gospel in the heartland of Jewish obscurantism. This brief period spent in the hasidic shtetl of Liozno as an undercover agent for the enlightenment was a turning point. While subversive tactics remained a vivid and viable option throughout his life, the inaugural mission failed because he was flushed out by the Orthodox establishment. It marked the beginning of his estrangement from the seemingly hopeless cause of Jewish reform. Meanwhile, Rappoport decided to head north to seek opportunity in the city of Dvinsk (Daugaupils, Latvia). During a brief stop in the shtetl Osvey, he wrote home to his buddies in a mixture of Yiddish and Russian:

> Listen well—I'm earning twelve rubles giving private lessons. By Saturday night I'll have as much as fifteen. I should reach twenty by next week. Twenty-five to thirty are still a utopian dream. There's no society of freethinkers [here], no antagonism toward me [either]; nothing to remind me of the [heady] phrases and self-sacrifices. They're busy fleecing the *goy*, and that's that. I take the measure of the households where I go looking for lessons. It's awful how they treat me with such respect, even with love. But for all that, I don't even make enough for matches.

Trying to liberate himself from the bonds of love and bourgeois society, he apprenticed to a German bookbinder—the only "productive labor" for which he would ever be formally trained. Yet to pay for the matches, Shloyme-Zanvl went on tutoring Jewish boys and girls in Russian for several more years.

His growing estrangement from the Jews is difficult to gauge precisely. We know that his mother died around this time and that his father declined all offers to move in with his equally mobile and penurious son. (A photograph of them taken in Moscow is the sole memento of their relationship.) At one point, Rappoport junior moved outside the Jewish Pale of Settlement to the city of Tula, perhaps in the hope that there a Jew might make it into the university. Shloyme-Zanvl had an uncle in Tula who was a former Cantonist (child conscript in the czar's army). But if Ansky's fiction is to be believed, he refused to accept help even from these distant relatives, gave lessons instead, and starved.

Judging from his early Yiddish writings, young Rappoport was at war with the past. *The History of a Family* chronicled the economic and moral collapse of a "typical" Jewish family. The men, raised on a strict diet of prayer and Talmud study, were utterly passive. The women sacrificed themselves even to the point of prostitution. Except for a grandfather's stories and some old wives' potions, there was nothing in tradition that had any redemptive power whatsoever. Only hard, physical labor could change a man, provided it didn't kill him first. In the early 1880s, when *The History of a Family* was written, such frontal attacks on all the institutions of *yiddishkayt* were still rare in Yiddish fiction. Because no publisher would go near it, Rappoport finally placed his family chronicle in the Russian-Jewish periodical *Voskhod*, where it appeared under the pen name "Pseudonym" in 1884 in someone else's translation. So completely did the young author cover his tracks that when Jewish socialists at the end of the century needed suitable material to further the class struggle, they translated this novel back into Yiddish—not knowing that there was once a Yiddish original and that its author was alive and well somewhere in Paris.

By the time a highbrow Yiddish literature came into being under the generous and energetic auspices of one Solomon Rabinovich of Kiev (alias Sholem Aleichem), the battle lines were firmly drawn. Rappoport found him to be a "dry" bourgeois entrepreneur with a parochial program and a draconian editorial policy. The meetings between them in the summer of '89 bore no fruit, and volume two of Sholem Aleichem's literary miscellany contained nothing by Rappoport. But for a cameo appearance in I. L. Peretz's radical *Holiday Folios* in 1896 (this time apparently translated *into* Yiddish by a third party), Solomon Rappoport had severed all ties with the world of Yiddish—and Jewish—letters.

By 1887 he was living two thousand miles from home, in the southern city of Yekaterinoslav. Still precariously positioned "on the border between two worlds," he rented a room from a Jewish family, earned his keep by tutoring young Jews but threw his considerable energy into a vastly different educational venture. The Russian *narod*, the simple peasant folk, now occupied the center of Rappoport's moral imagination.

Typical of the Russian revolutionary movement as a whole, Rappoport was drawn to "the simple life of the *narod*, its naïveté, poverty, truth, its lack of malice," as he announced to Zhitlowsky. Many roads then led to the Russian "folk," foremost among them the path laid out by populist theoretician Peter Lavrov. An unpaid debt, he preached, weighed on the conscience of the privileged groups toward the millions of Russian workers of this generation and those of the past. According to Lavrov, the intellectuals had first to prepare themselves before they could wage successful propaganda among the masses. To this end, Rappoport set about educating himself on the life and reading habits of the peasants. He himself began reading to the illiterate peasants from the classics of modern Russian literature. What the "folk" read and what it was capable of absorbing became his abiding interest. The logical next step for a self-styled Jewish radical whose own people had no use for him was to become one with the "real" folk, the Russian *narod*.

But because the villages were by this time swarming with spies and police agents (wise to earlier attempts at infiltration from above), Rappoport found his niche among the miners of the Donets Basin instead. Every kind of misfit came to work in the mines. Backbreaking and debilitating, this hard labor was the great leveler of society. While shtetl fathers and especially mothers were constantly spying on the Russian tutor lest he undermine the morals of the young, here one could go about without an internal passport. The miners, who found the name Solomon Aronovich unassimilable, Russified Rappoport's name to Semyon Akimovich, and thus it remained on his calling cards until the day he died.

By accepting their name for him, Rappoport signified that he had also adopted their way of life, their "poverty, truth and lack of malice," as his own. Not only had he sacrificed his health in the three years he spent in the mines and lost most of his teeth to scurvy, but he also maintained his spartan surroundings, proletarian dress, and the practice of self-denial in all his subsequent travels—to St. Petersburg, Paris, Geneva, Moscow, Vilna and Warsaw. Meanwhile, his educational work among the miners convinced him that the intellectuals and the folk were utterly distinct cultural and psychological "types" and that to speak *for* the folk one necessarily had to be *of* them.

Semyon Akimovich was anxious for the radical intellectuals to hear his message. St. Petersburg was now the center of "legal populism" within Russia, home of agrarian socialist Nikolai Mikhailovsky and radical writer Gleb Uspensky. How exactly this twenty-eight-year-old veteran was catapulted directly from the southern mines to the charmed inner circle of the St. Petersburg intelligentsia (where no Jew could live without a residence permit) remains unclear. Apparently, the ever-vigilant czarist police finally flushed Semyon Akimovich out, threw him into solitary confinement, and sent him packing. (Rappoport later described his brief stint in prison but gave it no date.) It also appears that his published accounts of the miners' life had caught the eye of a local Russian editor who gave Semyon Akimovich a letter of introduction to Uspensky. Be that as it may, the Jewish narodnik was taken in by the famed Russian writer, and within months of his arrival in St. Petersburg, S. A. An-ski's *Sketches on Folk Literature*—the scholarly fruits of his labors in the Russian mines—was being serialized in a leading populist journal.

Now "S.A." could stand for Solomon Aronovich or Semyon Akimovich. But where did the "Ansky" (or "An-ski") pen name come from? Consistent with the split inside himself, Ansky told two competing versions of his life's story. The "Jewish" version had it that "Ansky" came from his mother's name, Anna. "I wanted to show Mother," he explained to his confidante and literary executor Rosa Monoszon, "who suffered so much on account of my seeking an alien path, that my connection to her, who symbolized my beloved past, was not only not severed but would actually be preserved and strengthened in my future work." The problem with this version is that Monoszon met Ansky twenty-three years after he first adopted this not-too-Jewish-sounding name; and besides, Anna had presumably died long before her son's literary debut. In contrast, there was Victor Chernov, who knew Ansky in Paris as a man completely divorced from Jews and Judaism. In the version Ansky recounted to his Russian comrade-in-arms, Uspensky got the credit for inventing the pen name out of whole cloth. The truth of both versions of the "Ansky" story is that without his prior—and profound—alienation from Jewish life and letters it is impossible to understand his later "return."

The only Jews with whom Ansky still maintained contact during his sojourn in St. Petersburg were his former Vitebsk buddies—especially Masha Reines and her cousin, Chaim Zhitlowsky. The latter, after marrying the daughter of a local Russian populist, headed for Switzerland to pursue his studies; so too did cousin Masha. So when Uspensky suggested to his Jewish protégé that he travel abroad to expand his intellectual horizons, Semyon Akimovich had an added incentive to leave. It was the first of many romantic debacles.

He headed for Paris, cradle of the revolution, and worked for a time as a bookbinder (alongside Rudolph Rocker, the famous German anarchist). But when Masha rejected his advances, Ansky was so crushed that he decided to return to Russia and convert to Christianity, thus eliminating the last barrier between himself and the Russian folk. Zhitlowsky, our only source for this remarkable episode (except for a scribbled note from Rappoport to Zhitlowsky, dated October 2, 1892), claims that he talked his friend out of so drastic an action, and the jilted lover did in fact return to Paris. There his life picked up when he met émigré philosopher Peter Lavrov, whose private secretary he became until the latter's death in February 1900.

Ansky's life in Paris was indistinguishable from that of other émigrés: another disastrous affair, this time with a Parisian woman named Jeanette; a bohemian life-style; heated debates to plan the revolution from afar. When Victor Chernov arrived from Russia, Ansky helped him establish the Socialist Agrarian League, reviving the old dream of mobilizing his beloved peasants. With the birth of the Socialist-Revolutionaries Party in 1902, founding member Semyon Akimovich adopted Z. Sinanni as his nom de guerre. The name meant "Anna's son."

There was now good reason for a Russian-Jewish radical to identify as the son of his people. The Jewish Labor Bund had been founded in 1897, and although it was aligned with his hated rivals, the Social Democrats, it raised the banner of revolution among Jewish workers. For a brief moment in time, Sinanni became the official poet of the General Jewish Labor Bund in Lithuania, Poland and Russia. The October 1902 issue of *Der arbayter* (published in London) featured "The Oath," still sung today as the Bund's official anthem, and the fiercely anti-Zionist and anti-religious hymn "To the Bund," which defiantly proclaimed:

> Messiah and Judaism—both have died,
> Another Messiah has come:
> The *Jewish Worker* (the rich man's victim)
> Raises the flag of freedom.

As this notorious stanza makes clear, it was the Bund's militant Marxism and internationalism that first attracted Ansky to its ranks, not its concern for the Jews. But the new Jewish politics in Russia, Europe, America, and Palestine, as historian Jonathan Frankel has shown, was now entering a period of nationalization.[2] Even the most hardened cosmopolitans from across the radical spectrum were asking themselves whether the Jews as a nation did not require their own strategy, platform, solution. Victor Chernov, Ansky's Russian comrade-in-arms, tried to convince him to take a more positive attitude to the Jewish national revival. So too, Zhitlowsky, with whom Ansky now began, tentatively, to correspond in the mother tongue, Yiddish. Ansky's populism, for all that it inspired his studies of Russian and, later, French folklore, was strictly universalist. In this he remained a true disciple of Lavrov. It would take a great deal of persuasion to convince Ansky that the Jews were also—let alone exclusively—worthy of his efforts.

Not until 1905—after meeting with Zionist youth groups in Geneva—did Ansky evince any sympathy for the Jewish nationalist cause. Almost overnight, however, he reclaimed his artistic stake in the lost world of the Jews. It happened when he read I. L. Peretz's collected writings in 1901. For the first time, he discovered a modern European sensibility expressing itself in Yiddish. As an immediate result of reading Peretz, Ansky went back to writing in that language, after a nineteen- or twenty-year hiatus. The voice of these early efforts—a mixture of satire and neoromanticism—was Peretz's through and through.

If Ansky had a lot of catching up to do in Yiddish, it was because Russian was by now his lingua franca and the only language in which he could bare his soul. But like other émigrés, his Russian, too, was stuck in a time warp. The aestheticism then taking hold of Russian arts and letters, for instance, left him cold. Making a virtue of necessity, Ansky returned to his own lived experience within the Haskalah movement of the 1870s. To his Russian audience, *Pioneers*, his chronicle of Jewish political radicalism, must indeed have read like tales of the Wild West. It told of young men who traded the Talmud in for Russian nihilist tracts and together with a very few women burned all the bridges behind them. Their tragicomic story of living in one language and dreaming in another bore a striking resemblance to Ansky's own.

Then, miraculously, his linguistic and political exile came to an end. The flash point in the liberation movement in Russia came on Bloody Sunday (January 9, 1905), when the czar's army opened fire on unarmed protesters led by Father Gapon, the outstanding labor leader in Russia. Gapon fled to Switzerland, where he was befriended by Semyon Akimovich, among others. Jointly they defended the Nationalities platform at revolutionary conclaves in Geneva, collaborated on anti-pogrom brochures in London, and returned, separately, to Mother Russia immediately upon the granting of political amnesty and freedom of the press in October. Gapon's career as liberator of his people ended soon thereafter in assassination. Ansky's career had just begun.

Much had changed in St. Petersburg since Ansky's departure thirteen years before. It was almost open season for plotting the downfall of the czarist regime. Aboveground, a network of Jewish cultural institutions was being established to preserve the facts and artifacts of Jewish folk culture and to disseminate knowledge thereof in the Russian language. Ansky was an intimate of the newly founded Jewish Historic-Ethnographic Society, the Jewish Literary Society, and the Russian-Jewish monthly *Evreiski Mir* whose literary editor he became. He was similarly close to the Society for Jewish Folk

Music, also based in St. Petersburg.³ For the first time, Ansky, who habitually lived hand to mouth, could make a living as a *Jewish* writer, journalist, lecturer. He now did the circuit throughout the Pale of Settlement, spreading the word about Jewish folklore and language, Yiddish literature and theater, about war, the folk, and the revolution. In the inaugural issue of the Historic-Ethnographic Society's journal, Ansky published his revelatory essay on Jewish ethnopoetics.

Now that he spanned the Russian and Jewish worlds like no one else among his contemporaries, he saw his way clear to an undivided life. Once and for all he hoped to achieve a synthesis between the folk and the intelligentsia, tradition and modernity, politics and culture. Meeting Peretz for the first time in St. Petersburg, Ansky was most impressed that the master did not carry himself like a traditional shtetl Jew at all. "In his whole demeanor—no hint whatsoever of *goles* [diaspora]!" he marveled. To erase the boundary between both worlds, Ansky married a Jewish woman, adopted Yiddish alongside Russian as his literary medium, and finally made an open confession to underscore the intensity of his "reconversion."

At a 1910 banquet in his honor at Mikhalevitsh's restaurant in St. Petersburg, Ansky expressed anguish for having once abandoned his people. "Bearing within me an eternal yearning toward Jewry," he confessed to his audience in Russian, "I nevertheless turned in all directions and went to labor on behalf of another people. My life was broken, severed, ruptured. Many years of my life passed on this frontier, on the border between two worlds. Therefore, I beg you, on this twenty-fifth year of summing up my literary work, to eliminate sixteen years."⁴

In fact, Ansky drew heavily upon his experience as a Russian populist and socialist to produce a modern artistic synthesis in his mature writing. If once he had toiled among the Russian folk to study their habits and to enlighten their minds, he now embarked on a large-scale exploration of the Yiddish-speaking "folk," of the old-timers who still lived in remote towns and villages preserving the old folkways in unadulterated form. The Jewish Ethnographic Expedition that Ansky conceived and directed from 1912 to 1914 proved to be an act of personal and national self-discovery, for he ascribed to Jewish folklore the importance of a new "Torah" of the masses. Just as the Written Torah had been the source of all prior Jewish creativity in a religious age, so now the gathered texts and artifacts created by the folk through centuries of trial and tribulation would be the wellspring of Jewish artists of the future. Ansky was at once the theoretician who interpreted the significance of Jewish folklore, the field-worker who gathered it, and the inspired artist who drew upon it in his work, most notably in *The Dybbuk*. Shifting the source of authority from above to below, much as the revolutionary movement had done in politics, Ansky located in the Jewish people the aesthetic and moral foundation of a modern Jewish culture.

His childless marriage soon ended in divorce, however, and the expedition was cut short by the "guns of August" 1914. Though now suffering from serious ailments, including a first bout of diabetes, Ansky, at age fifty-one, threw himself into the most arduous task of his career: the rescue of Jewish lives, livelihoods and legends in the occupied war zone.

On August 31, 1914, the Russian Second Army was defeated in eastern Prussia, but in Galicia, the Russians broke the enemy front, capturing its capital, Lemberg, on September 3. Guided by directives from St. Petersburg, now renamed Petrograd, and fueled by ethnic and religious hatred among the local Christian population, the Russian army wrought terrible vengeance upon the Jews, every one of whom was suspected of being a German spy. Despite military censorship and the eventual banning of Hebrew and Yiddish from the press and even from private letters, news began to trickle back to the home front about wide-scale pogroms, expropriations and the mass expulsion of Jews. A year later, the Russian hinterland was inundated with almost two hundred thousand of its *own* Jewish civilian population, sent into internal exile by order of the czar. Mobilizing all his contacts in the Russian press, in liberal and radical circles, and among the Jewish elite (who had previously supported his ethnographic project), Ansky spearheaded a massive relief effort on behalf of Galician and Russian Jews and then took his rescue mission into the war zone itself.

Never had his ability to straddle both worlds stood him in better stead. With his impeccable Russian, Ansky could unmask the hatred and stupidity emanating from within the ranks of his fellow countrymen, especially the intellectuals. With his Red Cross insignia, supplied by the All-Russian Union of Zemstvos, he could move freely through the military and medical establishment. With his firsthand knowledge of Jewish life and lore, he could penetrate the inner reaches of the Jewish psyche and bring direct aid to the most isolated of Jewish settlements. With his eye for symbolic detail, he could later recast this experience into a lasting memorial.

From then on, events moved rapidly. On the political front, the February Revolution brought a provisional government into power, with Ansky's Socialist-Revolutionaries playing a vital (though not always salutary) role. On the cultural front, Ansky appeared as the Nationalities representative on the presidium of the First All-Russian Theater Conference and read a lecture on biblical Purim plays; he gave readings of *The Dybbuk* in Yiddish and in Russian; saw the appearance of five volumes of his *Collected Works* in Russian; visited with Chagall in Chortkov, and shuttled between Petrograd and Moscow.

In the fateful January of 1918, Ansky was back in Petrograd. The Socialist-Revolutionaries had just won the first (and last) free election in Russia's history. When the Bolsheviks launched a terror campaign against the Constituent Assembly, the Socialist-Revolutionaries and Mensheviks called a huge counterdemonstration at the head of which walked the veterans of earlier revolutionary struggles, Ansky among them. As before on Bloody Sunday, Russian troops opened fire on the unarmed demonstrators; only this time the soldiers wore Bolshevik colors. That night (January 5), the Bolsheviks disrupted the assembly's meeting at the Taurida Palace. "All is lost!" cried Ansky over the telephone in the early hours of the evening to Roza Monoszon.

But perhaps not all was lost, for two months earlier he had sent greetings to the Central Zionist Bureau in Petrograd in honor of the Balfour Declaration. Ansky was not hedging his bets. He was gathering the sparks of holiness—as Khonon the young kabbalist in *The Dybbuk* might have put it—so as to hasten the redemption of the Jews.

Ansky's last two years of life—spent in exile, first in Vilna, then in Warsaw—served, if anything, to intensify his utopian dreams. With Vilna changing hands and pitched battles and pogroms raging in the background, Ansky's voice was heard above the fray as a rallying cry of hope and solidarity. He helped establish the Vilna Union of Writers and Journalists, arguing almost alone for the inclusion of Jewish writers in non-Jewish languages. As the Bolsheviks advanced on the city, the young Jewish communist leader Shimele-vitsh was killed in a riot—and Ansky delivered the eulogy. Ansky saw him as an exemplar of Jewish idealism, just as he had earlier applauded Vladimir Jabotinsky's efforts to found the Jewish Legion. During the various military occupations of Vilna, it was Ansky who interceded to save Jews (among them, the noted Yiddish critic Shmuel Niger) from execution. In the breathing space between one occupation and the next, he chain-smoked; organized the Vilna Historic-Ethnographic Society (later named after him); delivered lectures in defense of the traditional heder; and announced the establishment of a new Jewish political party that combined a socialist, Zionist, Yiddishist, and Hebraist platform. The crux of his utopia lay in achieving a "national-personal autonomy."

But Vilna was no safe haven for aging dreamers. No sooner did the Polish Legion take the city from the Bolsheviks, in April 1919, than it poured out its wrath on the Jews. The final blow for Ansky was the murder, among fifty-five others, of playwright A. Vayter and the desecration of his body. Depressed by such a surfeit of Jewish martyrdom, the fifty-six-year-old Ansky moved to Warsaw, where he died, on November 8, 1920, from a complication of pneumonia.

Had the Socialists-Revolutionaries stood their ground against the Bolsheviks, Semyon Akimovich might have been buried in Petrograd, alongside the martyrs and makers of the Russian Revolution. His universalist dream might thus have been vindicated. Instead, Solomon Rappoport-Ansky died surrounded by the same Lithuanian Jews among whom he had been born and raised. The Vilna Troupe honored his memory by finally staging *The Dybbuk*—to immediate and lasting acclaim—and the Vilna Jewish intelligentsia pooled its meager resources to rush an Ansky memorial volume into print. Shloyme-Zanvl ben Aaron Hacohen Rappoport was buried in the Warsaw Jewish cemetery, alongside two other architects of the Yiddish cultural renaissance. An impressive tombstone, unveiled in 1925, marked the gravesite of S. Ansky, I. L. Peretz, and Jacob Dinezon. Remarkably, it still stands there today.

This anthology, then, the first of its kind, tells the story of Ansky's homecoming. Since it was his search for the lost folk—rather than for lost faith—that brought the prodigal son home, it is altogether fitting to begin with the most dramatic episode of his adult life: the discovery of folklore as the wellspring of Jewish cultural renewal. It was Ansky's singular achievement to become both prophet and chief practitioner of Jewish ethnography in Eastern Europe.

The term "ethnopoetry," which Ansky introduced into the field of folklore studies, marks a turning point in Jewish literary culture.[5] Whereas the first generation of Enlighteners, fired by enthusiasm for scientific rationalism, viewed folklore as the seat of ossified traditions, Ansky argued that it was the repository of progressive values: It is through folklore that biblical monotheism reached its most refined level, celebrating the power of the spirit over the violence and tribalism that still tainted the biblical narrative. Ansky distinguished between the principle of struggle characteristic of all folk creation and the principle of *spiritual* struggle characteristic of Jewish folk creation. His interpretation of the Jewish folk spirit proved highly influential in the political thinking of the Jewish Labor Bund and in shaping the liberal sensibility of Yiddish writers and artists.

Despite its obvious appeal to estranged Jews of every stripe, this grand theory was based, for want of any other sources, on a single collection of Yiddish folk songs (published in 1901) and another of Yiddish proverbs (1908). Ansky had to draw the remainder of his data from Yiddish and hasidic storybooks that were hardly an accurate reflection of what the "real" folk actually believed. This didn't stop him from trying his hand at writing "stories in the folk vein," but the result was a poor and highly tendentious imitation of Peretz. Fortunately, the Old Narodnik could not be satisfied studying a folk culture secondhand, or even studying it "at a distance." "No," Ansky wrote emphatically to Zhitlowsky in America, "Yiddish tales, legends and the like must be collected among old folks who carry the past with them in unadulterated form." Only in the thick of Jewish life, the scene of his own rebellion, could the lost treasures be found.

Thus, the Jewish Ethnographic Expedition, bearing the name of Baron Naftali Horace Günzburg, was launched on July 1, 1912. It was Ansky's brainchild. Though still short the twenty-three thousand rubles he needed to see the project through to the end, Ansky had already assembled a stellar group of scholars and energetic young field-workers. By the end of the first year in the field, the expedition had grown in Ansky's eyes into "a survey of Jewish life on a national scale, if not larger." Before it was cut short by the outbreak of the war, here is what the expedition had amassed:

> 2,000 photographs
> 1,800 folktales and legends
> 1,500 folk songs and mysteries (i.e., biblical Purim plays)
> 500 cylinders of Jewish folk music
> 1,000 melodies to songs and *niggunim* without words
> countless proverbs and folk beliefs
> 100 historical documents
> 500 manuscripts
> 700 sacred objects acquired for the sum of six thousand rubles

Ansky experienced a form of religious exaltation at unearthing these unimagined treasures. He gave poignant expression to his sense of homecoming and revelation in the preface to *The Jewish Ethnographic Program* (1914). "The Oral Tradition," he wrote, "consisting of all manner of folklore—stories, legends, parables, songs, witticisms, melodies, customs and beliefs—is, like the Bible, the product of the Jewish spirit; it reflects the same beauty and purity of the Jewish soul, the same modesty and nobility of the Jewish heart, the same loftiness and depth of Jewish thought." What he actually found, then, not only confirmed the folk in its spiritual grandeur but also raised its folklore to the status of a new Torah. And when he appealed to the conscience of his fellow intellectuals to preserve Jewish folklore in the name of the people's suffering, he was following in the footsteps of his beloved teacher Peter Lavrov:

> Jewish life has undergone an enormous upheaval during the last fifty to sixty years and the losses in our folk creations are among the most unfortunate victims of this change. With every old man who dies, with every fire that breaks out, with every exile we endure, we lose a piece of our past. The finest examples of our traditional lives, our customs and beliefs, are disappearing; the old poetic legends and the songs and melodies will soon be forgotten; the ancient, beautiful synagogues are falling to ruin or are laid waste by fire and there the most precious religious ornaments are either lost or sold, often to non-Jews; the gravestones of our great and pious ancestors have sunk into the ground, their inscriptions all but rubbed out. In short, our past, sanctified by the blood and tears of so many innocent martyrs, is vanishing and will soon be forgotten.[6]

For Ansky, identifying Jewish folklore as a new "Oral Tradition" was no mere conceit. Here, at last, was the bridge between present and past, the intellectual and the folk, this world and the next.

The volume itself—the only published fruit of his labors—was a detailed questionnaire (2,657 questions in all) posed to informants on the Jewish life cycle. Here, for example, are some of the questions pertaining to death and dying:

> Is there a belief among you that if a dying man's bed contains iron his death throes will thereby be prolonged?
> Is there a belief among you that when the soul departs it

is forbidden to stand opposite the dying man's bed, because that is when the Angel of Death appears wielding a sword?

Why [upon a person's death] must one spill out all the water from his house and all the surrounding houses?

Do you know any stories about a corpse that was left unattended and disappeared?

How does one ask forgiveness of the dead? Who is the first to ask forgiveness? What is one accustomed to say? Does one ask forgiveness of a dead child? Do strangers also come forward to ask forgiveness?

Is it your custom to carry the coffin slowly past the synagogue but quickly past the church?

Is it your custom for the beadle of the Burial Society to precede the coffin and cry out: "Charity saves from death"?

Is there a belief among you that when the last shovel hits the earth the dead man forgets everything?

Do you believe that when you meet a dead man you should strike him a blow in an offhand manner in order to make him disappear?

Do you know any stories about a dead person being brought before a rabbinical court?[7]

The Oral Tradition, then, was not a system of beliefs but a cluttered account of everyday life—and death. As such, this treasure trove of folk life and lore could draw other nations closer to the Jews. In particular, Ansky argued at a board meeting of the Jewish Ethnographic Expedition on November 24, 1913, hasidic tales and legends were the best possible means of acquainting non-Jews with the aesthetic and ethical dimensions of Jewish culture.[8]

He knew whereof he spoke, for questionnaire in hand, Ansky had already conceived *The Dybbuk*. The romantic plot, the mystical setting and the historical landscape were all born en route from one godforsaken shtetl to another. He claims to have met the prototypes of the star-crossed lovers Khonon and Leah at a Friday night meal in the home of a wealthy Hasid. The study house in Gorlice provided the setting for the opening act. The holy tombstones from the time of the Chmielnicki massacres in the mid-seventeenth century pointed out to him by numerous shtetl informants suggested an historical analogue to the young couple cut down in the prime of life. And the folktales about dybbuks that he collected in the field offered a "realistic" way of bringing all the strands of the story together. Through a stunning orchestration of Jewish folk motifs and mystical lore, Ansky rescued for a secular (and largely non-Jewish) audience a most compelling version of a life that was about to vanish.

No Jewish drama was ever more popular—or controversial. The Yiddish production put the Vilna Troupe on the map and formed the basis of the 1937 Yiddish film classic, filmed on location in Poland. Habimah, the Hebrew repertory company founded in Moscow, made theater history with its expressionist decor and grotesque staging, which it has since preserved as a living memorial. The unprecedented furor over a mere "folk play" soon had professional critics in Poland and Palestine up in arms. "Pseudo-art!" screamed the title of M. Vanvild's book-length diatribe against the Yiddish production, its philistine audience, and its deluded admirers.[9] In Tel Aviv the recently imported Hebrew production was put on trial in 1926 and "convicted" of being a pastiche of "legendary, realistic and symbolist" elements. But even this elite group of Zionist critics, writers and public figures had to acknowledge that the play's folk elements struck a responsive chord in the audience. Would that "the new life in Erets Israel and our cultural reawakening" could do the same![10] Ansky's appeal was just the opposite: he had taken the "old life" and torn down all the boundaries—between Torah and taboo, the rebbe and the rebel, mysticism and modernity—only to put them back together again.

Billed as a "dramatic legend," *The Dybbuk* is a highly stylized work. Ansky never conceived of it as folklore-in-the-raw. The characters speak a cadenced, learned (that is to say, super-Hebraicized) Yiddish.[11] He deliberately situates his Hasidim not out-of-doors, as Peretz had done, but inside an "ancient wooden synagogue, its walls blackened with age." The authentic Habad melodies that ethnomusicologist Joel Engel had collected are as much a part of the decor as the mystical opening song, the "old embroidered ark hangings," and the "thick memorial candle." Nothing as redolent of study house folklore and hasidic fantasy had ever been assembled on a Yiddish stage before.

Ansky introduced a rich layering of literary and folkloristic motifs that give the play an authentic, "mystical" feel even as it turns traditional narratives to secular, dramatic, ends. All the play's major dichotomies—between rich and poor, the sacred and profane, life and death—are introduced by the synagogue regulars known as *batlonim* (idlers) as they casually swap stories about the competing hasidic dynasties. Holding the disparate strands together is the mysterious Messenger, who actually owes his existence to a last-minute suggestion by director Stanislavsky.[12] Functioning as a kind of Greek chorus, the Messenger alone perceives the hidden links between opposing worlds—how violating the balance between rich and poor would affect the balance between the sacred and profane, and so on. These multiple and intersecting motifs confounded Ansky's critics but have delighted his audiences.

The play's central motif, of course, is that of the dybbuk itself. A dybbuk, in Jewish lore, is an evil spirit or the restless soul of a dead person that resides in the body of a living human being. It can usually be expelled by magical means. Now in his reading of Yiddish storybooks, Ansky may well have come across the *Tale of an Exorcism in Koretz* (Prague, ca. 1665) or may have heard a comparable tale recounted to him in his travels. He might then have been struck by how active and sympathetic a character the possessed heroine of the story was, and how the male spirit, by contrast, was portrayed as a vulgarian trickster, while the exorcist himself, one Rabbi Borukh Kat, did not perform any magic at all.[13] Yiddish tales of exorcism, he might have noticed, now tended to be more true to life and were attached to real people and places. In a skeptical age like that of his own, moreover, the folk itself had begun to cast doubt on the reality of dybbuks and on the wonder worker's ability to work any wonders.[14] But whether in storybooks or in the field, whether an object of faith or subject to doubt, there was never a dybbuk who was in love with the woman he possessed. The victim was always chosen at random —by virtue of her maidenhood or, alternatively, because of her susceptibility to sin. No story before Ansky's had ever told of a dybbuk who was a lover in disguise.

By the time *The Dybbuk* unfolds, roughly in the 1860s, only someone of the hasidic persuasion could still exorcise demons, for Hasidism had given Jewish mysticism a new lease on life in Eastern Europe.[15] And of all the figures of early Hasidism, none was more attractive to Ansky, concerned with salvaging the beauty and mystery of Jewish folk religion, than Nahman of Bratslav (1772–1810), a storyteller of great renown. And so, to set the stage for the zaddik's entrance at the beginning of act III, Ansky has the Messenger deliver a soliloquy on the longing of the world's heart for the mountain spring. Identified as a "mystic teaching of Reb Nahman of Bratslav," the speech is an almost verbatim quote from the "Tale of the Seven Beggars" (1810). Ansky enlists "the just man" of the parable (who was one of many cloaks for Reb Nahman himself) to introduce the Rebbe of Miropolye, the play's great mediator between this world and the next. But whereas in its original context, the parable expressed Reb Nahman's paradoxical faith in an absent God, the parable as retold by the Messenger alludes to the sexual longing between the living and the dead.

Dybbuks and hasidic parables were not all that Ansky turned to very earthly purposes. Upon entering, the zaddik Reb Azrielke begins to expound on the theme of ascending levels of holiness based on the Mishnah (Kelim 1:6–9). The thrust of the Mishnah is to establish the absolute otherness of the high priest entering the Holy of Holies on Yom Kippur day—something so awesome that only God alone can witness it. Reb Azrielke, however, proceeds to allegorize each detail and thereby to subvert its original intent: "Every piece of ground on which a person stands when he raises his eyes to Heaven is a Holy of Holies; everyone created in the image of God is a high priest; every day in a person's life is Yom Kippur; and every word which a person speaks from his heart is God's name."

The hasidic masters were well known for taking esoteric rabbinic and kabbalistic doctrines and cutting them down to psychological size. That too was part of their appeal for Ansky the dramatist and modern storyteller. But would a zaddik whose flock considered him a combination high priest and prophet himself espouse the supreme holiness of each individual and of every human utterance? Only if the rebbe, in turn, were portrayed as a man of very human dimensions, plagued by doubts about his own intercessionary powers. This trend to radically democratize the hasidic movement owes much more to I. L. Peretz than to any of the informants whom Ansky interviewed on his ethnographic travels.

Peretz had led the way in the secular appropriation of Hasidism and in using a religious setting to explore issues of sin and unrequited sexuality (notably in his play *Chained to the Synagogue Vestibule*, which Ansky had translated into Russian in 1909). Ansky, the idealist, replaced Peretz's tragic plot with a pair of star-crossed lovers who rebel against bourgeois marriage and ultimately prevail. Ansky's original twist on this well-worn formula, as critic Gershon Shaked has shown, is to introduce a prior set of marital vows made not between the lovers but prenatally, as it were, by their respective fathers.[16] Ansky conjures up the dense world of Jewish folk belief to convince his audience that irrational forces are more logical than rational ones; that since the two lovers cannot live without each other, Khonon has to break the metaphysical bonds and enter Leah's body at the canopy. Any attempt to circumvent this primal bond—however legally justified—is bound to fail. No wonder that the combined efforts of the charismatic leader Reb Azrielke (in act III) and the rabbinical judge Rabbi Shimshon (in act IV) cannot set things right again. And no wonder that flesh-and-blood Hasidim angrily boycotted the performances of Ansky's *Dybbuk* in Poland. The manifold religious elements in the play had come to serve antireligious ends.

The power of *The Dybbuk*, however, cannot be explained solely in terms of its use and abuse of prior literary and folkloristic sources. Conceived before the war and completed after the Bolshevik seizure of power, the play is also an outgrowth of that period of monstrous upheaval, when Ansky saw the Jewish spirit struggling to maintain itself against forces of overpowering destruction. Even the tragedy of his own childless marriage found symbolic expression in the last, moving, moments of the play. Then as now, audiences who knew no Yiddish and had never set eyes on a Hasid could come away inspired by the story of Khonon and Leah. Alone and in the face of all odds, these young rebels had restored the moral and metaphysical order by sacrificing their own earthly pleasures and desires.

The Dybbuk, like almost everything else translated here, was originally intended for a Russian audience. Indeed, the present volume could just as easily be placed within a Library of Russian-Jewish Classics as of Yiddish Classics. It is not too much to say that Ansky's most Jewish works are his most Russian. It was "in the Russian language," he once wrote, that "I would discover the beauty of the poetry that lies buried in the old historical foundations and traditions" of Judaism. The very culture that had seduced him away from home and caused a clean break with the past was the culture that later provided Solomon Rappoport-Ansky with a map of return.

To unravel Ansky's life and letters from the outside in, following him out to the Russian- and back to the Yiddish-language sphere, one must look to his sketches and stories. Drawing heavily on autobiography, they provide stark and authentic insights into the conflict between generations that strained Jewish society to the breaking point. There he dramatizes the "heresies" of his youth, the double life of the "non-Jewish Jew," and the ironic balance of aging revolutionaries, with a unique combination of warmth and detachment. Ansky was the first in a distinguished line of modern Jewish writers to draw the process of homecoming against a landscape that was at once psychological and historical.

Native ground for Ansky the young populist was decidedly not the synagogue or study house. It was the tavern. Ansky's literary medium was not the folktale or the mystical reverie; it was the naturalistic "sketch" (called *ocherk* in Russian): an exhaustive study of society's outcasts and the genre perfected by his mentor, Gleb Uspensky. Here, spitting, swearing, boozing, and brawling are the measure of truthfulness. And here, the tenacity of the folk is embodied not by Malke and her granddaughter Khanke (Hannah), the two Jewish women who run the tavern, but by a gentile souse named Axinya.

Unique in Jewish literature, Ansky's "In the Tavern" (1883–86) makes a gentile woman the central consciousness of the narrative (roughly a third of which is excerpted here). It is through Axinya's eyes that readers are asked to judge the behavior of her drinking partners, whether Jewish or gentile, highborn or low. The pawning of her kerchief inaugurates a day of heavy drinking for all the Whirlpool regulars, just as her revival through song introduces a brief respite in the general debauchery. Without glossing over the tensions between gentiles and Jews by resorting to stereotype or apologetics—as routinely practiced by his contemporaries, whether they wrote in Yiddish, Hebrew, or Russian—Ansky presents the real interaction between the Jews who dispense the vodka and the Russians who pawn their stolen goods and the shirts off their backs to drink it. For Axinya, a "fallen" woman, these exploitative relationships are part of the accepted pecking order in postfeudal Russia. Thus did twenty-year-old Solomon Rappoport turn his mother's tavern into a whirlpool-in-miniature.

Effectively to gauge the distance traveled by the twenty-year-old rebel, one need only compare "The Sins of Youth" (written in 1910) with that postcard dashed off to his buddies soon after he fled the shtetl of Liozno for the city of Dvinsk. For the author of the postcard, the older generation could do no right, whether they sicked the police on him or smothered him with love. The adult writer, in marked contrast, titled his (Russian-language) memoir "The Sins of Youth and the Sins of the Old," thus spreading the blame evenly across the generations. By 1910, moreover, when the St. Petersburg elite marked Ansky's literary anniversary, rewriting his personal past had become a subtle yet powerful way for him to claim a place for his youthful rebellion (and that of others) in the annals of Jewish heroism. The Zionist leadership, after all, was itself a gallery of former heretics, internationalists and bohemians who became champions of their people. Ansky was more intent upon rescuing the few healthy shoots of Jewish radicalism than on exposing the roots of his alienation. So he returned to that formative experience of his eighteenth year in order to prove that the shtetl had, in fact, been

handful of women) how to negotiate the new frontier. Perhaps
[t]he next generation, fated to wage a still more dangerous war on
[t]he border between the Jewish and Christian worlds, would learn
[fr]om their struggle and their failure.

As someone who himself once flirted with apostasy, Ansky became
[lit]erature's great connoisseur of Jewish self-hatred. His writings
[co]ntain a veritable gallery of self-hating Jews from all walks of life
[an]d of every revolutionary stripe. He portrays a renegade yeshiva
[st]udent named Itsikovitsh who is forced to recant, then runs off to
[co]nvert; while Geverman, another one of the *Pioneers* (1904–5), is
[sto]pped from converting by his mother's pleas. Or there is "Fiedka"
[(1]910), the twenty-five-year-old bon vivant who, for all his regaling
[th]e ladies and his powerful Russian friends with anti-Semitic jokes,
[ca]n never escape the mark of his Jewishness. Ansky occasionally
[wa]xes sentimental, as in his portrait "Two Martyrs"—one a former
[ca]ntonist who suffers *for* his Jewishness and the other, an intellectual,
[wh]o suffers *from* it. But in "Go Talk to a Goy!" (1912) Ansky draws
[a b]ittersweet lesson from the subject of apostasy.

The story's title, *A goyisher kop* (Gentile brains in Yiddish), carries
[an] ironic punch: spoken by someone who is reasserting his Jewish
[ide]ntity after years in the revolutionary camp, it reveals a man who
[has] switched allegiances once too often. In the "good ol' days" of
[the] revolutionary struggle, Silberzweig went by the name Afanasi.
[Cou]ld it be—the reader is left wondering—that his current embrace
[of] Judaism is also an act of expediency? By letting Silberzweig-
[Afa]nasi narrate the bulk of the story, Ansky pits two models of
[rev]olutionary action against each other: one (here represented by a
[self]-hating Jew) for whom the ends always justify the means, and
[the] other (represented by a lapsed Christian comrade, and a woman
[to b]oot) for whom even an assumed identity carries moral im-
[plic]ations.

[H]is last major work, "The Tower in Rome" (1920), brings every-
[thin]g together. Dedicated to the memory of I. L. Peretz, it uses
[alle]gory, myth, and Jewish historical legend to plot a future on the
[ruin]s of the past. This time no one could accuse Ansky of cribbing
[from] preexisting sources. The closest model was the medieval Jewish
[apoc]alypse *Sefer Zerubbabel* with its very confusing cast of characters.[17]
[Ans]ky's version of the End of Days was woven out of whole cloth.
[A]nsky no longer proclaims the death of God and his Messiah.
[Inste]ad, he resurrects Peretz as an aged stargazer privy to the secrets
[of Je]wish survival. The apocalyptic landscape of war and revolution
[now] becomes a map of redemption. Key to the world's salvation

his first base of operations, just as Lilienblum's *The Sins of Youth*, an
Enlightenment tract, had been his first Bible. If Ansky could present
himself as the one Jewish narodnik and nihilist who found his way
home again, then perhaps he had not strayed that far to begin with.

As a consequence of the radical and early break he had made
with his own past, Ansky was one of the first of his generation to
look back with mixed emotion at the lost world of shtetl culture. If
the dates he supplied in the Russian editions of his work are reliable,
he spent the better part of his 1892 sojourn in St. Petersburg writing
about a young alienated Jew who discovered something humane,
authentic, and even sublime in the world he had left behind. Some
of these lessons were more painful than others.

Happy to be living far from his "fanatical" parents, the twenty-
year-old hero of "Hunger" is nonetheless afraid to ask the Jewish
grocery store owner for credit because she suspects him of being a
Jew. Would that his anti-Semitic landlady, who harbors no such
suspicions, could be milked for more than a free samovar of boiling
water! The greater his hunger, the more painfully clear are the
moral failings of his high-minded, blue-blooded, Russian radical
friends. Caught between his own radical ideals and Jewish self-hate,
the hero almost martyrs himself for the cause. He is saved in a state
of delirium by seeking the haven of his relatives. Here the hero finds
succor for his body in an aunt's gefilte fish and succor for his soul
in the bosom of distant family and friends.

So there is still room in the shtetl for a prodigal son. But what
about the loner and naysayer who lives in the very midst of a
traditional society? Such a one is the Hebrew schoolteacher, nicknamed Mendl Turk, who gets it into his head to support the enemy
camp in Russia's war with the Turks. The meaning of Mendl's
passion for politics is a matter of perspective. The shtetl views Mendl
as a stubborn, wrongheaded Jew who had simply misread the
messianic signs. As for the worldly young narrator, on one of his
frequent sojourns in a Lithuanian shtetl, he reads the papers and
therefore sees the geopolitical meaning of things. (The "real" Ansky
was still safely ensconced in the Vitebsk yeshiva during the Russo-
Turkish War.) For him, Mendl is a living exemplar of shtetl insularity,
a quixotic type born and bred in the house of study. But from the
perspective of radical ethnographer Semyon Akimovich, who was
busy studying what the folk read, how they misread it, and how they
instinctively rebelled against the wars fought in their name, Mendl
upholds the principle of absolute justice over the exercise of brute
force. Unfortunately, his is not a faith that can overturn the system.

Only the illiterate folk who worked the mines of the Donets Basin could do that. The Jews of the shtetl, in contrast, were Talmudists and dreamers who had nothing better to do than pit their absolute faith against the equivocal facts of history.

Underscoring the comic discrepancy between the shtetl intellectuals and the Russian *narod* is the narrator's childhood reverie situated midway into the story. Its purpose is to heighten the contrast between the real and the ideal. The shtetl sublime of haunting hasidic melodies and traditional storytelling that a child experiences in the bewitching hour between afternoon and evening prayers is irretrievably locked in the narrator's memory. It bears no resemblance to the absurd goings-on among the study house regulars of his present shtetl. And besides, the songs, stories and twilight are hardly more than the aesthetic trappings of Judaism. Semyon Akimovich was still far from acknowledging a Jewish folklore that could creatively distill the lost world of tradition.

Yet who could have imagined back then, when the *Kulturkampf* in Jewish Eastern Europe known as the Haskalah had just begun, that one generation after Lilienblum vast numbers of Jewish youth would no longer choose to continue the struggle within the border of Jewry? What exactly had gone wrong? Why—if modernity had finally vanquished its foe—did the Haskalah come out looking so bad? Why—if the *Kampf* had succeeded beyond anyone's expectations—had the *Kultur* not reaped the expected rewards?

According to Ansky's superb novella "Behind a Mask" (1909), the main legacy of the Haskalah has been the transformation of the shtetl into a battlefield, complete with headquarters, paramilitary maneuvers, intelligence and codes. His most bellicose fiction on the Haskalah theme, the novella contains the memorable (semiautobiographical) portrait of a young rebel named Krantz.

Krantz boasts the highest credentials among the members of his commune. As a rabbi's son he can easily slip back into the role of piety and talmudic learning. Part of his assignment is, therefore, to make contact with a secret cell of enlightened radicals in the distant town of Bobiltseve. "When *he* puts on a mask," exclaims Shekhtl of the cell's leader, "it's a real mask all right!" On the eve of his first contact with the cell, Krantz has every reason to await success.

> Going over in his mind the many incidents and conversations of the day, he buried his head in the pillow and giggled madly. Had anyone told him that in fact he had spent the day cheating and lying with more malice and

treachery than a thief, Krantz would simply hav[e] incredulous, so intoxicated was he by the artistry performance.

Too bad for Krantz that he never internalizes the na[tive] verdict of his behavior. But Leivick, his entrée into him in his proper place: "I just don't trust the big-[city]" Leivick begins.

> They love scandal. They want to show off their
> and their wit, to put something over on the p[eople]
> they don't know how to work in the dark, with
> energy. What's worse, they love to write long,
> letters about everything that ought to be kep[t]
> and their letters have a habit of falling into th[e hands]
> of the rabbi or the head of the yeshiva. And th[e]
> constant need to stuff their pockets with radi[cal pam-]
> phlets. . . .

As a tutor, Leivick continues his diatribe, all Krant[z] "a couple of boys and girls to read and write," but the light, he can learn everything there is to know mentor." Leivick claims to have covered the whole [curric-] ulum of the gymnasium in two years, "while prete[nding to study] the Talmud."

What the backwoods shtetl of Bobiltseve has t[o teach is] what every big-city organizer ignores only at his [peril: the or-] dinary tenacity of the folk, exemplified by Leivick['s mastering] the foreign curriculum on his own, and by Shekhtl['s mother,] who will stop at nothing to win back her son. In [the gallery of] archetypal Jewish mothers, none is more resourc[eful.]

At story's end, Krantz has won the battle but [lost his war. His] true identity exposed, his friends routed from [town] by Krayne, Krantz just manages to save his own s[kin. Nor] makes contact with the cell leader, either. By de[nying the reader a] rousing finale, so basic a feature of earlier mas[kilic fiction, Ansky] issued a highly ambivalent verdict on the Haska[lah as a] whole. The movement could destroy, but it coul[d not build. It set] young men loose from their traditional homes an[d freed them from the] claims of the Jewish collective, but it did not sec[ure that traditional] home either from external attack or from intern[al subversion. For Ansky] the Haskalah was a testing ground, teaching Jew[s] from "duplicity, fraud, and deceit" is the solidarity of the seventieth nation among the nations of the world. No earthly power can ever destroy the sorely tested People of the Book so long as they still direct their prayers heavenward. That is the stargazer's prophecy on the eve of his demise. And that was Ansky's final assessment after all attempts to force the hand of the Messiah had failed.

That S. Ansky, the "critical realist" and revolutionary activist, could arrive at such a redemptive reading of Jewish history after all he had seen is truly remarkable. For no other Jewish writer and intellectual had had such immediate and prolonged exposure to the devastation wrought by the First World War upon the life and sanctity of his fellow Jews. Rather than shaking the foundations of his newfound faith in the Jewish people, the war strengthened Ansky's resolve. So profound was his reidentification with the Jews that he mobilized a massive relief work on their behalf, took on the entire military and Jewish establishment in the process and, sick as he already was, personally delivered the donated funds to his brethren in the occupied war zone. He also kept a diary, which later formed the basis of a work unique in the annals of war, *The Destruction of Galicia*.[18]

One of Ansky's greatest literary achievements, this four-volume chronicle records his travels through some of the same Jewish areas he had once combed as a gatherer of folklore, now torn by the occupying armies of World War I. Galician Jews were especially vulnerable because for a hundred and fifty years they had lived apart and aloof from the Jews of czarist Russia. Now, with the collapse of the Austro-Hungarian Empire, they had lost their protector, the beloved Franz Josef, and were at the mercy both of the Russian invaders from without and the native Christian populations who saw the war as an opportunity to settle some old scores. Ansky, a Russian Jew, negotiated freely among Polish anti-Semites posing as protectors of the Jews; Russian military officials, journalists, and raw recruits; and among Jews of every stripe—including a privileged audience with the Gerer Rebbe himself, the leader of ultraorthodox Jewry. Out of his engaged relief work and his informed inquiries, he produced a new kind of history that was at once analytical and full of pathos.

The original four-volume work, which he had planned to publish in Russian, Yiddish, and Hebrew, makes clear that Ansky did not return to Galicia merely to record what was happening or even to go on with his ethnographic work (though he did succeed in rescuing many hundreds of religious and historical artifacts). His primary mission was to bring money and relief to a tribe of the Jewish nation that had been cut off from all other means of support. The present selection—the longest thus far available in English—preserves the relentless impact of Ansky's original version while bringing his symbolic reading of events to the fore. Just as Ansky had long come to see his own life as paradigmatic, he now struggled to perceive the larger, transhistorical pattern of Jewish national destruction and rebirth.

Ansky would doubtless have rejoiced to see a collection of his writings appear in translation at precisely the moment when the Jews of Russia were standing once more at the historic crossroads, free at last to choose their path to a "national-personal autonomy." He would have cheered on those of his aging brethren who were trying to master modern Hebrew (as he himself had tried to do) and to negotiate the foreign landscape of their ancestral homeland. He would also have encouraged those Soviet Jews who still believed they could make good the failed promises of the Russian Revolution to the Jewish people. It was *his* party, after all, that had championed national rights. Above all, it would have pleased him to know that besides the riveting—and downright inspirational—story of his life, he had also left behind a literary legacy of varied and formidable proportions.

DAVID G. ROSKIES
New York City, 1991

▲

The Dybbuk,

o r

Between
Two Worlds:

A DRAMATIC LEGEND IN FOUR ACTS

Dedicated to the sacred memory of my friend A. Vayter

CHARACTERS

▼

SENDER

LEAH, his daughter

FRADE, her old nurse

GITTEL, her friend

BASSIA, another friend

MENASHE, Leah's bridegroom

NAHMAN, his father

REB MENDL, Menashe's rabbi/
teacher

THE MESSENGER

REB AZRIELKE from Miropolye, a
zaddik (hasidic sage)

MIKHOEL, his *gabbai* (assistant)

REB SHIMSHON, the rabbi of
Miropolye

FIRST RABBINICAL JUDGE

SECOND RABBINICAL JUDGE

MEYER, *shammes* (caretaker) of
the Brinitz synagogue

KHONON ⎫ students in
HENEKH ⎬ the Brinitz
OSHER ⎭ Yeshiva

FIRST BATLEN ⎫ dreamers and
SECOND BATLEN ⎬ scholars
THIRD BATLEN ⎭ maintained by
the community

FIRST HASID

SECOND HASID

THIRD HASID

FOURTH HASID

AN OLD WOMAN

A WEDDING GUEST

A POOR HUNCHBACK

A POOR MAN ON CRUTCHES

A POOR LAME WOMAN

A POOR WOMAN WITH ONE HAND

A POOR BLIND WOMAN

A POOR TALL, PALE YOUNG
WOMAN

A POOR YOUNG WOMAN WITH A
CHILD IN HER ARMS

HASIDIM, YESHIVA STUDENTS,
MEMBERS OF THE COMMUNITY,
STOREKEEPERS, WEDDING
GUESTS, BEGGARS, CHILDREN

ACT I

▼

The synagogue in Brinitz

Total darkness. Before the curtain is raised, a soft, mystical chant is heard, as if from afar:

Why, oh why did the soul plunge
From the upmost heights
To the lowest depths?
The seed of redemption
Is contained within the fall.

The curtain rises slowly, revealing an ancient wooden synagogue, its walls blackened with age. Two wooden posts support the roof; an old brass lamp hangs from the center of the ceiling above the pulpit, which is covered with a dark cloth. A long bench stands against the rear wall under the small windows, which open into the women's gallery. In front of it is a long wooden table on which books are scattered; two half-melted candles set in clay candlesticks are burning near a pile of books. To the left of the table is a narrow door leading to the rabbi's private room. A cabinet filled with books stands at the far end of the wall. The Holy Ark containing the Torah scrolls stands at the center of the right wall between two windows; to its left is the cantor's reading stand, on which a thick memorial candle is burning. The entire length of the wall is lined with benches and bookstands. A large tile stove stands against the left wall; near it is a long bench and a table covered with books, as well as a wash basin and a towel hanging from a ring. Next to the wide door leading to the street is a chest; above it the eternal light is burning in a niche in the wall.

Henekh, sitting near the cantor's platform, is bent over a bookstand completely absorbed in a sacred text. Five or six yeshiva students are half-reclining in various postures of weariness around a table near the front wall studying

Talmud in a low, dreamy chant. Meyer is bent over the pulpit sorting the bags which contain prayer shawls and phylacteries. The three Batlonim are seated around the table at the left wall; they are lost in a world of their own as they sing and gaze into space. The Messenger lies on the bench near the stove, his backsack under his head. Khonon stands meditatively with his hand resting on the upper edge of the bookcase.

It is evening; a mystical atmosphere pervades the synagogue; shadows lurk in the corners.

THE THREE BATLONIM   (*Finish the song*)
      Why, oh why did the soul plunge
      From the upmost heights
      To the lowest depths?
      The seed of redemption
      Is contained within the fall.

(A long pause; all three sit motionless, transfixed, in a dreamlike world)

FIRST BATLEN (*In the manner of a storyteller*)   Reb Dovidl of Talna, may his merits protect us, had a golden chair on which was carved: "David, King of Israel, lives forever." (*Pause*)

SECOND BATLEN (*In the same manner*)   Reb Yisroel of Rizhin, of blessed memory, lived like a monarch. An orchestra of twenty-four musicians played at his table and when he traveled his carriage never had less than six horses.

THIRD BATLEN (*With enthusiasm*)   And they say that Reb Shmuel of Kaminka wore golden slippers. (*Entranced*) Golden slippers!

THE MESSENGER (*Sits up and speaks calmly and thoughtfully*)   The holy Reb Zushe of Annipol was poor all his life; he wore a peasant's blouse tied with a rope around his waist and had to beg for alms. Yet his good deeds were no less worthy than those of the rebbe of Talna or the rebbe of Rizhin.[1]

FIRST BATLEN (*Annoyed*)   Please don't take offense at what I say, but you don't even know what we're talking about and yet you intrude. When we speak about the greatness of the Talner rebbe or of the Rizhiner rebbe do you suppose that we refer to their wealth? Rich men are nothing special; the world is filled with them. But you must understand that the golden chair and the orchestra and the golden slippers are profoundly significant vehicles; they contain the deepest secrets.

THIRD BATLEN   That's obvious! Who can't see that for himself?

SECOND BATLEN   Those who have their eyes open see it. It is said that when the rebbe of Apt met the rebbe of Rizhin for the first time he threw himself on the ground and kissed the wheels of his carriage. And when he was asked why, he shouted: "Fools! Don't you see that this is the holy chariot of the Lord?"[2]

THIRD BATLEN (*Enraptured*)   Aah—aah—aah!

FIRST BATLEN   The point is that the golden chair was not a chair, the orchestra was not an orchestra, and the horses were not really horses. They were all shadows and reflections which served as garments, cases to enclose their greatness.

THE MESSENGER   True greatness requires no adornment.

FIRST BATLEN   You are mistaken! True greatness must be suitably bedecked.

SECOND BATLEN (*Shrugging his shoulders*)   Their greatness and might are beyond measure!

FIRST BATLEN   Their power was very great. Do you know the story of Reb Shmelke of Nikolsburg and his whip? Listen, it's worth a hearing. Once a poor man had a dispute with a certain rich man whom everyone feared because of his close connections with the court. Reb Shmelke was asked to settle the case, and after hearing both sides he ruled in favor of the poor man. Offended, the rich man declared that he would not abide by the judgment. Reb Shmelke spoke to him calmly: "You *will* honor the judgment. When a rabbi gives an order, the order must be obeyed." This made the rich man angry and he began to shout: "I don't give a fig for you *or* for your rabbinical judgments." Reb Shmelke pulled himself up to his full height and thundered back: "You will carry out the order immediately! If you do not I will use the whip." At this the rich man lost all control and in a frenzy he screamed insults and curses at the rabbi. Without another word Reb Shmelke opened the drawer of his desk and out jumped the Primordial Serpent, who immediately wrapped himself around the rich man's neck.[3] What an uproar there was! The rich man shrieked and cried for mercy: "Help, Rebbe, forgive me! I will do everything you say, only take away the snake!" To which Reb Shmelke answered: "You must admonish your children, and your children's children, to obey the rebbe and to fear his whip." Then he removed the snake from the rich man's neck.

THIRD BATLEN   Ha, ha, ha! That was quite a whip! (*Pause*)

SECOND BATLEN (*To the first one*)   You must be wrong. It couldn't possibly have been the Primordial Serpent. . . .

THIRD BATLEN   What are you saying? Why not?

SECOND BATLEN   Very simple. Reb Shmelke of Nikolsburg would never have invoked the Primordial Serpent; it is the Evil One, it is Satan himself, may the merciful God preserve us. (*He spits*)

THIRD BATLEN   Well, you can be sure that Reb Shmelke knew what he was doing!

FIRST BATLEN (*Hurt*)   I don't understand you! I tell you about an event which occurred in a public place, which was witnessed by scores of people, and yet you claim that the incident could not possibly have taken place. Do you think it is all idle talk?

SECOND BATLEN   Not at all! But I don't believe that incantations and kabbalistic letter combinations can call up the Evil One. (*He spits*)

THE MESSENGER   The Devil can be summoned only by uttering the mighty double name of God whose flame dissolves the highest mountain crests and melts them into the deepest valleys. (*Khonon lifts his head and listens intently*)

THIRD BATLEN (*Apprehensive*)   But what about the danger in using the holy name?

THE MESSENGER (*Thoughtfully*)   The danger is . . . that the vessel might shatter because of the great intensity of the spark's longing for the flame. . . .

FIRST BATLEN   There is a wonder worker in my shtetl who can perform the most astounding miracles. He can start a fire with one spell and make it vanish with another. He can see at a distance of one hundred miles. He can draw wine from the wall with his bare fingers. He once confided to me that he knows the spells for making a golem, for bringing back the dead, for making himself invisible, for calling up evil spirits . . . even the Devil! (*He spits*) I have it from his very own lips.

KHONON (*Who has been standing motionless, listening intently with his head cocked, walks to the table and turns his glance first to the Messenger and then to the First Batlen, as he says in a pensive, dreamy voice*)   Where is he? (*The Messenger never takes his eyes off Khonon*)

FIRST BATLEN (*Surprised*)   Who?

KHONON   The wonder worker.

FIRST BATLEN   Where would he be? In my shtetl, of course, if he is still alive.

KHONON   Is it far from here?

FIRST BATLEN   The shtetl? Yes, very far, a long distance away, deep in Polesia!

KHONON   How long does it take to walk there?

FIRST BATLEN   To walk? A good month, perhaps more. . . . (*Pause*)

Why do you ask? Do you want to go to him? (*Khonon says nothing*) The shtetl is called Krasne, the wonder worker is Reb Elkhonon.

KHONON (*Amazed, speaks to himself*) Elkhonon. El Khonon . . . the God of Khonon.

FIRST BATLEN (*To the Batlonim*) I tell you, he is an incomparable miracle worker! One day, in broad daylight, he attempted to. . . .

SECOND BATLEN (*Interrupting*) Enough of this kind of talk at night! And in a holy place, too. We might unintentionally utter a spell or an incantation which could bring about a catastrophe, God forbid . . . such things have happened, may the merciful God preserve us. (*Khonon exits slowly as everyone watches him; pause*)

MESSENGER Who is that young man?

FIRST BATLEN A yeshiva student. (*Meyer closes the gate in front of the pulpit and approaches the table*)

SECOND BATLEN A first-rate scholar. A genius!

THIRD BATLEN A brilliant mind! He knows five hundred pages of Talmud by heart!

MESSENGER Where does he come from?

MEYER From somewhere in Lithuania. He was considered the outstanding student at the yeshiva and was granted rabbinical ordination. And then, without any warning, he disappeared; for an entire year no one knew where he was. Some said he had gone to perform the penance of exile, to afflict his body in order to shorten our exile from the holy land. He returned a changed person; he is lost in his own thoughts, he fasts from one Sabbath to the other, he performs endless ablutions. . . . (*In a quieter tone*) They say he studies Kabbalah.

SECOND BATLEN (*Quietly*) In town they say the same thing . . . they've even started to ask him for charms, but he refuses.

THIRD BATLEN No one knows who he is. You can never tell, he might even be one of the great ones. But it would be dangerous to watch him too closely. . . . (*Pause*)

SECOND BATLEN (*Yawning*) It's late . . . time to go to sleep. . . . (*To the first Batlen, with a smile*) What a pity that your wonder worker who draws wine from the bare walls isn't here . . . I'd give anything for a good drink right now. I haven't had a bite of food all day!

FIRST BATLEN For me it's more or less a fast day, too. I only had a single occasion to recite the blessing on food today, and that was early this morning when I had a bite to eat after prayers.

MEYER (*Half whispering, with a content expression*) Just have a little patience. I think we will soon be toasting each other with good brandy. Sender has gone to arrange a match for his only daughter and if he signs the wedding agreement he will surely provide us with the best.

SECOND BATLEN Eh! I don't believe he will ever make up his mind. He has met with prospective bridegrooms three times already and always returned empty-handed. Either the young man doesn't appeal to him, or the family background isn't good enough, or the marriage dowry is too small . . . it's wrong to be so demanding!

MEYER Sender has a right to be choosy. He's a rich man, he comes from a good family, and his only daughter is beautiful and clever, may no evil eye harm them. . . .

THIRD BATLEN (*With feeling*) I'm very fond of Sender! He is a good Hasid and has the soul of the Miropolyer Hasidim.

FIRST BATLEN (*Coldly*) I'm not denying that he's a good Hasid. But he could have arranged for his only daughter's marriage in a better way.

THIRD BATLEN What do you mean?

FIRST BATLEN In the old days when a rich person from a good family sought a suitable match for a daughter, the financial situation and social status of the parents were far less important than the young man himself; it was the groom's qualities alone that interested him. He would go to one of the famous yeshivas, give the principal a sizable donation, and leave it up to him to choose the best of the scholars who studied with him. Sender could have done the same.

THE MESSENGER He might even have found a suitable bridegroom here in this yeshiva.

FIRST BATLEN (*Surprised*) What makes you think so?

THE MESSENGER I'm only speculating.

THIRD BATLEN (*Snappily*) Well, well, let's not gossip, especially about one of our own. Matches are made in heaven. (*The door is flung open and an old woman, holding two small children by the hand, rushes in*)

OLD WOMAN (*Runs to the Holy Ark with the children, sobbing*) Oh, woe is me, God of the universe, help me! (*Approaches the Ark*) Dearest children! Let us open the Holy Ark and embrace the Torah scrolls until our tears work a cure in your mother! (*She opens the Ark, thrusts her head inside, and in a melancholy chant begins*) God of Abraham, Isaac and Jacob, behold my affliction! Look upon the sorrow of these dear little children and do not take their young mother from them. Holy scrolls of the Torah, plead for a wretched widow!

Blessed Fathers, dear Mothers, run to God and pray for mercy. Beg Him to keep the tender sapling from being uprooted, the fledgling bird from being cast from her nest, the gentle lamb from being separated from the flock! . . . (*Hysterical*) I will leave no stone unturned . . . I will split the very heavens . . . I will not move from this spot until you give me back my precious jewel!

MEYER (*Goes to her, holds her gently, and speaks to her softly*) Hannah Esther, shall I gather ten men for a minyan to recite Psalms?

OLD WOMAN (*Takes her head out of the Ark, looks bewildered at first, and then speaks abruptly*) Oh! Yes, of course, gather a minyan to recite psalms! But hurry, hurry! Every minute is precious. For two days now the poor girl has been lying speechless, struggling with death.

MEYER I'm off to get ten men this minute. (*In a pleading tone*) But they ought to be paid for their trouble . . . they are very poor.

OLD WOMAN (*Searching her pocket*) Here is a gilden. Make sure that they do everything that they are supposed to!

MEYER A gilden . . . that makes only three groschen for each man . . . it's not much.

OLD WOMAN (*Doesn't hear him*) Come children, let's go to the other synagogues. (*Departs quickly*)

THE MESSENGER (*To the third Batlen*) This morning a woman opened the Holy Ark and prayed for her daughter who has been in labor for two days and still has not given birth. Now a woman opened the Holy Ark to pray for her daughter who has been wrestling with death for two days.

THIRD BATLEN So? What are you getting at?

MESSENGER (*Thoughtfully*) When the soul of a person who has not yet died is destined to enter the body of a person who has not yet been born, a struggle takes place. If the sick person dies, the child will come into the world alive. If the sick person recovers, the child will be born dead.

THIRD BATLEN (*Surprised*) Ah! Man is so blind that he doesn't even see what is happening right next to him!

MEYER (*Approaches the table*) Well, God has provided us with drinks. We will recite psalms and toast *lekhayim* afterward and God, in His mercy, will restore the sick woman to health.

FIRST BATLEN (*To the students who sit around the large table, drowsing*) Gentlemen! Who is ready to recite psalms? There's a cake for everyone after you've finished. (*The students get up*) We'll go into the small room. (*The three Batlonim, Meyer, and all the yeshiva students except for Henekh go into the rabbi's private room and soon the sad chant of "Blessed is the man" is heard;*[4] *the Messenger remains seated at the smaller table, never lifting his eyes from the Holy Ark; a long pause; Khonon enters)*

KHONON (*Very sleepy and deep in thought, walks with apparent aimlessness to the Holy Ark, and notices with surprise that it is open*)   The Holy Ark open? Who opened it? For whom was it opened in the middle of the night? (*Looks into the Holy Ark*) The Torah scrolls lean against each other in silence. They contain all the secrets and allusions, all the possible combinations of words from the six days of creation to the end of the generations of man. And how difficult it is to learn the secrets and the allusions, how very difficult! (*He counts the Torah scrolls*) One, two, three, four, five, six, seven, eight, nine scrolls . . . they add up to the numerical value of *emes,* 'truth.' And every scroll has four wooden handles that we call the trees of life . . . again thirty-six! Not an hour goes by that I don't come across that number. I don't know what it means, but I feel that it contains the essence of the matter, the truth that I seek. Thirty-six is the numerical value of the letters in Leah's name. Khonon adds up to three times thirty-six. But Leah also spells 'not God,' not through God. (*Shudders*) What a terrible thought! Yet how it draws me.

HENEKH (*Lifts his head and looks at Khonon*)   Khonon! You walk about as if you were asleep.

KHONON (*Moves away from the Ark; walks slowly toward Henekh; stops, lost in thought*)   Mysteries, allusions without end, yet I see no straight path before me. (*Short pause*) The shtetl is called Krasne, the wonder worker Reb Elkhonon. . . .

HENEKH   What did you say?

KHONON (*As if waking from a trance*)   I? Nothing . . . I was thinking out loud.

HENEKH (*Shaking his head*)   You have plunged too deeply into Kabbalah, Khonon. Not once have you studied the sacred texts with us since your return.

KHONON (*Puzzled*)   Not studied the sacred texts? Which texts?

HENEKH   What kind of a question is that? Talmud, the commentaries, you know yourself which texts.

KHONON (*Still not comprehending*)   Talmud? . . . the commentaries . . . not studied? Talmud is cold and dry . . . the commentaries are cold and dry. (*Suddenly alert; speaks with animation*) Beneath the world there is another world exactly like ours; it has fields and forests, seas and deserts, towns and villages. Stormy winds blow through the fields and deserts, great ships sail the seas, fear haunts the dense forests, and there is thunder. Only one thing is missing: a heaven above from which lightning can flash and from which the sun can blaze. Talmud is like that. It is profound, it is sublime. But it shackles you to the earth, it keeps you from soaring to the heights. (*Ecstatically*) And Kabbalah! Kabbalah tears the soul from its earthly bonds! It lifts man to the highest spheres and opens up the heavens so that he can see inside. It leads straight to Paradise, it draws you to the Infinite, it opens a corner of the great curtain. (*Falls*) My strength . . . is failing.

HENEKH (*Earnestly*) True, all true. But you're ignoring the danger in these ecstatic flights, the possibility of losing one's grip and falling into the abyss. Talmud lifts the soul, but it does so gradually, in degrees; it guards man like a faithful watchman who never slumbers or sleeps. It embraces man like a shield and keeps him from straying off the straight-and-narrow path. But Kabbalah! Do you remember what the Talmud says? (*In the Talmud chant*) "Four entered Paradise: Ben Azzai, Ben Zoma, Akher and Rabbi Akiba. Ben Azzai looked around and died. Ben Zoma looked around and lost his reason. Akher cut down the plants and lost his faith. Rabbi Akiba alone entered in peace and departed in peace."[5]

KHONON Don't try to frighten me with what happened to them. We don't know how or why they went to Paradise. They may have stumbled because they went only to observe and not to be purified. We know that others entered after them—the holy Ari, the holy Baal Shem Tov—and they did not stumble.

HENEKH Are you comparing yourself to them?

KHONON I'm not making comparisons. I go my own way.

HENEKH And what is your way?

KHONON You wouldn't understand.

HENEKH I would understand. My soul, too, is drawn to the upper regions.

KHONON (*Thinks a while*) It is the function of the righteous zaddik to purify man's soul, to rip away its sinful sheath and restore it to its original perfection. The task is difficult because "sin crouches at the door." As soon as one soul is purified, another soul with even deeper sins takes its place. No sooner is one generation moved to repent than another, more stiff-necked than the last, appears. And the generations grow weaker and weaker and their sins more monstrous—and the righteous zaddikim are scarcer and scarcer.

HENEKH So what should be done?

KHONON (*Quietly, but emphatically*) We need not wage war against sin, we need only to purify it. Just as a goldsmith refines gold in a flame or a farmer threshes the chaff from the wheat, so must we cleanse sin of its dross until nothing but holiness remains.

HENEKH (*Amazed*)   Holiness in sin? Where did you get such an idea?

KHONON   Everything in God's creation contains a spark of holiness.

HENEKH   God did not create sin; that was the work of Satan!

KHONON   And who created Satan? It was God. Satan is the opposite of God, and, as one of His aspects, he contains a holy spark.

HENEKH (*Shaken*)   Holiness in Satan! I don't believe it! I can't understand it! Let me think. (*Lowers his head and presses it between his hands on the reading stand; pause*)

KHONON (*Approaches, bends his head toward him, and speaks with a shaking voice*)   Which sin is the most powerful? Which sin is the hardest to conquer? The sin of lust for a woman, right?

HENEKH (*Without lifting his head*)   Yes.

KHONON   But if the sin is purified in the heat of a strong flame this vilest uncleanness is transformed into the greatest holiness, to the "Song of Songs," (*Breathlessly*) the "Song of Songs." (*Stands upright and in a voice filled with rapture he sings quietly*) "Behold thou art fair, my beloved, behold thou art fair. Thy eyes are doves looking out from under thy brows. Thy hair is like a flock of goats scampering down Mount Gilead. Thy teeth are like a flock of sheep newly bathed in which there is none missing, all are twinned." (*Meyer comes out of the rabbi's room. A quiet knock is heard and the main door opens hesitantly. Leah enters, leading Frade by the hand; Gittel follows. They stand at the doorway*)

MEYER (*Very surprised to see them; speaks in a gracious, flattering tone*)   Look who's here. Reb Sender's daughter, Leah.

LEAH (*Shyly*)   Don't you remember that you promised to show me the old embroidered Ark hangings? (*The instant he hears Leah's voice Khonon stops singing and stares at her intently; throughout, he either fixes his gaze on her or shuts his eyes in ecstasy*)

FRADE   Show them to her Meyerke, show her the oldest and most beautiful hangings. Leah'le has promised to embroider one for her mother's *yortsayt*. She will use gold thread to work little lions and eagles onto the costliest velvet, just as they used to do in the old days. And when the hanging is fixed in front of the Holy Ark, her mother's pious soul will rejoice in Paradise. (*Leah looks about timidly, notices Khonon, and immediately lowers her eyes, remaining in that fixed position for the entire time*)

MEYER   Oh! With the greatest pleasure! Of course, absolutely! I will go this very moment and bring you the oldest and most beautiful hangings. (*Goes to the chest near the entrance to the synagogue and takes out some hangings*)

GITTEL (*Clutching Leah's hand*)   Leah'le, aren't you afraid to be here at night?

LEAH   I have never been in a synagogue at night, except on *Simchas Torah* when everything is lit up and festive in celebration of the end of the Torah cycle and the beginning of the new one. But now, how sad it is, how very sad!

FRADE   My dear girls, the synagogue is always sad because the dead come to pray at midnight and leave their sorrows behind.

GITTEL   Grandma, please don't speak about the dead. I'm afraid!

FRADE (*Without hearing her*)   And every morning, when the Almighty weeps for the destruction of the Temple, His holy teardrops fall into the synagogue. That is why the walls of old synagogues are always damp.

LEAH   How very old this synagogue is! It didn't seem quite so old from the outside.

FRADE   Yes, my daughter, it is very old. They say that it was found completely intact under the ground. How many times has this town been razed, how often has it been burnt to the ground— and yet the synagogue always survived. Only once the roof caught fire but hundreds of doves flew by and beat their wings until they extinguished the flames.

LEAH (*Not hearing, as if to herself*)   How sad it is here, yet how filled with love! I don't want to leave. I want to throw myself against these tear-stained walls and embrace them; I want to ask them why they are so sad, so silent and gloomy. I want . . . I don't really know what I want; I only know that my heart aches with pity.

MEYER (*Brings the hangings to the pulpit and spreads one out*)   This one is the oldest; it is over two hundred years old. We hang it up only on Passover.

GITTEL (*Delighted*)   Look, Leah'le, isn't it magnificent? Two lions embroidered in gold thread on thick brown velvet cloth, holding a star of David between them, with two trees with doves in the branches standing on either side! These days you cannot even get this kind of thread and such heavy velvet.

LEAH   Even the curtain is filled with sadness and tenderness. (*Caresses and kisses it*)

GITTEL (*Takes Leah's hand; quietly*)   Look over there, Leah'le—a young man is staring at you. See how strangely he fixes his gaze on you!

LEAH (*Lowers her eyes even further*)   He is a yeshiva student . . . Khonon . . . he used to eat at our house.

GITTEL   His eyes look as if he were beckoning you toward him. He probably wants to come closer but doesn't dare.

LEAH   I wonder why he is so pale and drawn. He must have been ill.

GITTEL   He isn't really sad. See, his eyes are bright.

LEAH   His eyes always sparkle—they are so brilliant! And he becomes quite breathless when we talk—and so do I. After all, it is not proper for a young woman to speak to a young man.

FRADE   (*To Meyer*)   May we kiss the Torah scrolls, Meyerke? How can we pay a visit as God's guests without kissing the holy Torah?

MEYER   Of course, you kiss the Torah, of course! Come! (*He goes to the Ark, Gittel follows, then Frade and last Leah; Meyer takes the scroll out of the Ark and holds it toward Frade to kiss*)

LEAH   (*As she passes Khonon she pauses a moment and says quietly*)   Good evening, Khonon . . . you are back?

KHONON   (*Breathless*)   Yes.

FRADE   Come to kiss the Torah scrolls, Leah'le! (*Leah goes to the Holy Ark, Meir holds the scroll for her to kiss; she embraces it and presses her lips close, kissing it with passion*) Enough, my child, enough! A brief kiss is all one may give the scroll. Torah scrolls are written in black fire on white fire! (*Suddenly frightened*) Oh, it is late, very late! Come, girls, come home quickly! (*They leave quickly; Meyer closes the Ark and follows them out*)

KHONON   (*Stands for some minutes with his eyes closed and then begins to sing verses from the "Song of Songs" again, continuing from the point at which he had stopped*)   "Thy lips are like a scarlet thread, thy lips are comely. Thy temples are like pomegranates beneath thy veil."

HENEKH   (*Lifts his head and looks at Khonon*)   Khonon! What are you singing? (*Khonon stops singing, opens his eyes and looks at Henekh*) Your earlocks are wet. Have you been to the ritual bath again?

KHONON   Yes.

HENEKH   During your ablutions do you recite incantations? Do you follow the rituals prescribed in the *Book of Raziel*?[6]

KHONON   Yes.

HENEKH   And you are not afraid?

KHONON   No.

HENEKH   And you fast from one Sabbath to the next? Don't you find it difficult?

KHONON   It is harder for me to eat on the Sabbath than to fast all week. I have lost all desire for food. (*Pause*)

HENEKH   (*Intimately*)   Why are you doing all this? What do you hope to gain?

KHONON (*As if speaking to himself*)   I want . . . I want to seize a clear and brilliant diamond . . . to dissolve it in tears and to draw it into my soul! I want to seize the rays of the third Temple, the third divine emanation. I want . . . (*Suddenly very distraught*) Yes! There are still two barrels of gold coins which I must get for the one who can count only gold coins.

HENEKH (*Appalled*)   What are you saying? Khonon, please, be careful. You are on a dangerous course . . . what you long for cannot be acquired by holy means.

KHONON (*Provocatively*)   And what if not by holy means? What if not by holy means?

HENEKH (*Very frightened*)   I'm afraid to listen to you! I'm afraid to be near you! (*Leaves hurriedly; Khonon remains in his place, a defiant expression on his face; Meyer comes in from the street; the first Batlen comes out of the rebbe's private room*)

FIRST BATLEN   I've recited eighteen psalms, the number signifying life; that's quite enough. We can't be expected to recite the entire Book of Psalms for a single gilden. But there's no talking to the others . . . once they get started, they don't stop. (*Osher hurries in, excited*)

OSHER   I've just met Borukh the tailor; he happened to be in Klimovka while Sender was negotiating the terms of his daughter's marriage contract and he heard that he did not come to an agreement with the prospective groom's parents. Sender demanded ten years' support for the young couple, and they only offered five. So they went their separate ways.

MEYER   This is the fourth time such a thing happened to him!

THIRD BATLEN   What bad luck!

THE MESSENGER (*To the third Batlen, smiling*)   You said yourself that marriages are made in heaven.

KHONON (*Stands upright, in extreme ecstasy*)   Once again the victory is mine! (*Sits down on the bench and remains seated with a rapturous expression on his face*)

THE MESSENGER (*Opens his travel bag and takes a lantern out*)   Time for me to go.

MEYER   What's your hurry?

THE MESSENGER   You know that I'm a messenger. I bring important messages and rare treasures from one nobleman to another. So I must be off. My time is not my own.

MEYER   Why don't you stay at least until daybreak?

THE MESSENGER   It's a long way to daybreak, and I have far to go. I will leave at midnight.

MEYER   It's pitch black outside.

THE MESSENGER   I won't get lost . . . I have a lantern. (*Remains standing. The second and third Batlonim and the yeshiva students come out of the rabbi's private room*)

SECOND BATLEN   Mazel tov! May God grant the sick woman a speedy recovery.

EVERYONE   Please God, Amen!

FIRST BATLEN   Now we should buy some brandy and cake for the gilden.

MEYER   It's all taken care of. (*Takes a bottle and some cakes out of the bosom of his coat*) Let's go into the vestibule and drink *lekhayim*. (*The door opens wide and Sender enters; he is very happy; his coat is unbuttoned and his hat is pushed to the back of his head; three or four men follow him*)

MEYER AND THE BATLONIM (*Together*)   Ah, Reb Sender, welcome back!

SENDER   I happened to be riding past the synagogue so I decided to drop in and see how you're all doing. (*Notices the bottle in Meyer's hand*) I expected to see everyone deep in study or discussing a problem in the Talmud—and what do I find? The whole group about to drink a toast in honor of some occasion or other! Ha, ha, ha! Typical Miropolyer Hasidim!

THIRD BATLEN   Will you have a drop with us, Reb Sender?

SENDER   You fool! I will provide the drinks myself, and good liquor, too. Wish me mazel tov! My daughter is betrothed, in a good hour, please God. (*Khonon jumps up, distraught*)

EVERYONE   Mazel tov! Mazel tov!

MEYER   But we heard that you could not come to terms with the groom's father, and that the match was off.

THIRD BATLEN   We were so sorry to hear it.

SENDER   The match was very nearly off, but at the last moment the groom's father agreed and we signed the betrothal papers.

KHONON   Betrothal? Betrothal? What happened? How is it possible? (*In complete despair*) So they didn't help—not the fasts, not the ablutions, not the mortifications of the flesh, not the kabbalistic spells! Were they all for nothing? What now? Is there nothing left to do? (*Clutches at his breast, straightens up, and with an expression of ecstasy on his face*) Ah—ah—ah! The great twice-proclaimed name is revealed to me! I . . . see it! I . . . I . . . I have won!! (*Falls*)

THE MESSENGER (*Opens the lantern*)   The fire has gone out. I must relight the lamp. (*Ominous pause*)

SENDER   Meyer, why is it so dark in here? Why don't you light the candles? (*Meyer lights the candles*)

THE MESSENGER (*Goes quietly to Sender*)   You came to terms with the groom's father?

SENDER (*Turns to him with surprise, somewhat frightened*)   Yes. . . .

THE MESSENGER   It has been known to happen that parents make promises and fail to honor them. Often it is even necessary to go to a rabbinical court for a judgment. One must be very careful.

SENDER (*Frightened, to Meyer*)   Who is this man? I don't know him.

MEYER   He is a stranger, a messenger.

SENDER   What does he want from me?

MEYER   I don't know.

SENDER (*Calming himself*)   Osher, run over to my house and tell them to prepare a spread—liquor, preserves, and other good things. Go quickly! (*Osher hurries out*) We'll just wait here and talk while they set the table. . . . Has anyone heard news of our rebbe? A story? A miraculous event? Every gesture of his is more precious than pearls.

FIRST BATLEN (*To Meyer*)   Put away the bottle. It will come in handy tomorrow. (*Meyer puts it away*)

THE MESSENGER   Let me tell you a parable of the rebbe's. Once a rich but stingy Hasid visited the rebbe. Taking him by the hand, the rebbe led him to the window and asked him to describe what he saw through the pane. "I see people in the street," the Hasid said. Then the rebbe took his hand again and led him to a mirror. "Now what do you see?" he asked. "I see myself," the Hasid answered. "Do you understand? Both the window and the mirror are made of glass; but as soon as you cover the glass with a small amount of silver you no longer see others but only yourself."

THIRD BATLEN   Ah! Ah! Sweeter than honey.

FIRST BATLEN   Holy words!

SENDER (*To the Messenger*)   Ha? What? Are you trying to provoke me?

THE MESSENGER   God forbid.

SECOND BATLEN   Let's sing a joyful song. (*To the third Batlen*) Sing the rebbe's special melody! (*The third Batlen begins to sing a soft, mystical tune; all join in*)

SENDER (*Jumps up*)   Let's dance! Everyone join in! You don't think that Sender will marry off his only daughter without dancing and rejoicing? What kind of Miropolyer Hasidim are we? (*Sender, the three Batlonim, and Meyer place their hands on each others' shoulders and in a circle, their eyes rolled up in an expression of ecstasy, they sing a repetitive tune while they move slowly in place. Sender breaks out of the circle, happy*) And now a lively dance. Everybody, come!

THIRD BATLEN   Gentlemen! All of you! Come here! (*Several young men join in*) Henekh! Khonon! Where are you? We're waiting for you to join our dance!

SENDER (*A little perturbed*)   Ah! Khonon! My Khononke should be here. Where is he? Bring him here now!

MEYER (*Sees Khonon lying on the floor*)   He's sleeping, there on the floor.

SENDER   Wake him, wake him up!

MEYER (*Shakes him, in a frightened voice*)   He won't wake up! (*Everyone comes close, bends over him, tries to rouse him*)

FIRST BATLEN (*Cries out in fright*)   He's dead!

THIRD BATLEN   Look! The *Book of Raziel* has fallen from his hand. (*All are in a state of shock*)

THE MESSENGER   He has been damaged—beyond repair.

(*Curtain*)

ACT II

▼

A street in Brinitz, three months later

A square in Brinitz. Left—an old wooden synagogue in the ancient architectural style. In front of the synagogue, somewhat to the side, a mound of earth with a gravestone bearing the inscription: "Here lie the holy and pure bride and groom who were martyred for their faith in the year 5408 [1648 C.E.]. Rest in peace." Beyond the synagogue, a lane with a few small houses. Right—Sender's house, large, wooden, with a porch. Beyond the house, a wide gate leading to the courtyard. Farther on, an alley with a row of shops which merge into the backdrop. On the right side of the backdrop, next to the shops, an inn and a large garden which is attached to the nobleman's mansion. A wide road leads down to the river. On the other side of the river on the high bank, a cemetery with gravestones; to the left a bridge over the river, a mill, and somewhat closer a bathhouse and the poorhouse. In the distance, a thick forest.

The gates to Sender's courtyard are wide open and long tables extend from the yard onto the square. Around the tables, which are laden with food, poor men and women, cripples, children, and old people eat hungrily. Servants come out of the house with platters of food and baskets of bread which they bring to the tables.

Women sit in front of the shops and houses, knitting stockings while they watch what is happening at Sender's house. Men of all ages come out of the synagogue with their prayer shawls and phylacteries in hand; some enter the shops and the houses, others stand talking in small groups. Sounds of music, dancing, and loud conversation are coming from Sender's house.

It is evening. The Wedding Guest, an elderly man in a satin kaftan, his hands tucked behind him in his belt, stands in the middle of the street in front of the synagogue. The Second Batlen stands near him.

WEDDING GUEST (*Looks around the synagogue*) You have a splendid synagogue . . . beautiful and large. God's spirit is upon it. It must be very old.

SECOND BATLEN Yes, it is. The old people say that even their grandfathers couldn't remember when it was built.

WEDDING GUEST (*Sees the gravestone*) And what is this? (*Goes closer and reads*) "Here lie the holy and pure bride and groom who were martyred for their faith in the year 5408." A martyred bride and groom?

SECOND BATLEN When that enemy of the Jews, Chmielnicki, may his name be blotted out, came to our town with his Cossacks and slaughtered half the Jews, he killed a bride and groom just as they were being led to the wedding canopy.[7] They were buried in one grave on the very spot on which they were murdered, and their grave has been called "the holy grave" ever since. (*In a whisper, as if telling a secret*) Each time the rabbi performs a wedding ceremony he hears sighs coming from the grave. In order to bring comfort and cheer to the buried bride and groom, it has long been a custom in our town to dance around the grave after every wedding.

WEDDING GUEST An excellent custom! (*Meyer comes out of Sender's courtyard and approaches*)

MEYER (*Excitedly*)   What a feast! Never in all my days have I seen a meal for the poor like this one.

WEDDING GUEST   It's no wonder! Sender is marrying off his only daughter.

MEYER (*With enthusiasm*)   Everyone got a portion of fish, a slice of roasted meat and a *tzimmes* of sweetened carrots, too. And before the feast they served brandy and cakes! It must have cost a fortune. I can't even imagine the sum!

SECOND BATLEN   Leave it to Sender—he knows what he's doing. If one isn't too generous to an invited guest, there's no great harm in it. At the worst he will grumble and pout. But if one fails to do one's duty by the poor, the danger is great indeed. Who knows? The person in rags may really be poor or be someone else entirely—a holy man or even one of the thirty-six righteous for whom the world is preserved.

MEYER   Perhaps even Elijah the Prophet. He always comes disguised as a pauper.

WEDDING GUEST   It is not just the poor who must be treated with care. You never know who anyone is, or who he was in a previous life, or what brought him back into the world. (*The Messenger appears from the left lane, his sack on his shoulders*)

MEYER (*Sees the Messenger and goes to him*)   Peace be with you. You've returned to us.

THE MESSENGER   I've been sent back.

MEYER   You've come at a good time—just in time for a rich man's wedding.

THE MESSENGER   Everyone in the area is talking about it.

MEYER   Did you, by any chance, see the groom's family on the road? They're late.

THE MESSENGER   The groom will come in good time. (*Goes to the synagogue; the Wedding Guest, Second Batlen and Meyer go into the courtyard; Leah, in her wedding dress, is visible from behind the tables, dancing with one poor old woman after another; others crowd around her; those who have finished dancing go into the square and stand in groups*)

A WOMAN WITH A CHILD (*Pleased*)   I danced with the bride.

A LAME WOMAN   So did I. I took her around and danced with her. Hee, hee!

THE HUNCHBACK   Why is the bride only dancing with women? I'd like a chance to hold her, too, and swing her around. Heh, heh, heh!

(*Laughter among the poor; Frade, Gittel and Bassia appear on the porch*)

FRADE (*Uneasy*) Oh my, oh my! Is Leah'le still dancing with the poor folks? She's sure to get dizzy. Girls, bring her here. (*She sits on a bench; Gittel and Bassia go to Leah*)

GITTEL You've danced enough for now, Leah'le. Come!

BASSIA Your poor head must be spinning. (*She and Gittel take Leah by the hand and lead her off*)

POOR WOMEN (*Surround Leah and shout in pleading, whining voices*) She hasn't danced with me yet. Am I not as good as the others?

I've been waiting a whole hour for her to dance with me!

Now it's my turn. I'm supposed to dance with her after Elke finishes.

She danced about ten times with that crippled Yakhne and not even once with me! I don't have any luck. (*Meyer comes out of the yard and stands on a bench*)

MEYER (*Loud and in the voice of a wedding jester*)

Reb Sender invites you to come one and all
And bids you to wait at the granary wall
Where he will distribute to everyone there
A ten-groschen coin, so be of good cheer.

POOR PEOPLE (*Run into the yard, pushing one another and shouting excitedly*) Ten groschen! Ten groschen! (*The square empties; only Leah, Gittel, Bassia and a half-blind old woman remain*)

HALF-BLIND OLD WOMAN (*Grabs Leah*) I don't want the gift, I only want you to dance with me. Spin me around just once. I haven't danced for forty years! But oh, how I danced when I was young, how I danced! (*Leah puts her arms around the old woman and dances with her; the old woman won't let go, pleading*) More! More! (*They dance, the old woman gasping for breath and screaming*) More! More! (*Gittel pulls the old woman into the yard with force; she returns and she and Bassia lead Leah to the porch and seat her on a bench; the servants remove the tables and lock the gate*)

FRADE You're as white as a sheet, Leah'le. Are you tired?

LEAH (*Eyes closed, head thrown back, speaks as if in a trance*) They held me, they surrounded me, they pressed themselves against me and pushed their cold, dry fingers into my flesh. My head was spinning, I grew faint. And then someone lifted me high into the air and carried me away—far, far away. . . .

BASSIA (*Frightened*) Leah'le, see how they've soiled and wrinkled your dress! What will you do now?

LEAH (*Trancelike, as before*)　If you leave the bride alone before the wedding evil spirits come and take her away. . . .

FRADE (*Frightened*)　What kind of talk is that, Leah'le? You must never mention the demons by name. They are everywhere around us; they hide in every hole, they lurk in every corner, watching and listening for someone to let slip one of their evil names. Then they leap out and throw themselves on the person. Tfu! Tfu! Tfu! (*She spits*)

LEAH (*Opens her eyes*)　They are not evil. . . .

FRADE　You must not believe that. If you believe that of one of the evil ones, he becomes spiteful and begins to do his tricks.

LEAH (*With conviction*)　Grandma, we are not surrounded by evil spirits but by the souls of people who have died before their time. It is they who watch every move we make and listen to everything we say.

FRADE　God help you, child! What are you talking about? Souls? What souls? Pure, undefiled souls fly up to heaven and find their eternal rest in Paradise.

LEAH　No, Grandma, they are here with us. (*In a different tone*) A person is born to live a long life. But if he dies before his time, what happens to his unlived life, his joys and his sorrows, the ideas he did not have time to develop, the deeds he had no chance to do? What happens to the children who were to have been born to him? Where are they? Where? (*Thoughtfully*) Once there was a young man with a lofty soul and a profound intelligence—a long life lay before him. And then, in an instant, his life was cut down; strangers came to bury him in foreign soil. (*Sorrowfully*) What happened to his unlived life, his unspoken words, his unuttered prayers? Grandma, when the flame of a candle is snuffed out, you can relight it and it burns to the end. So how can the uncompleted life of a person be stamped out forever? How can it?

FRADE (*Shakes her head*)　It's forbidden to think these thoughts, my child. God, in His wisdom, shapes the course of all things; we are blind and know nothing. (*The Messenger, unnoticed by her, comes close and stands behind her and Leah*)

LEAH (*Doesn't hear; speaks with conviction*)　No, Grandma, a human life cannot be lost. When a person dies before his time his soul returns to complete the span of life which he was given on earth, to finish the work he began, to feel the joys and sorrows he did not live to know. (*Pause*) Grandma, you told me that at midnight dead souls pray in the synagogue. They come to say the prayers they could not recite in their lives. (*Pause*) My mother died young, before she could fulfill her destiny. I will go to the cemetery today and ask her to lead me to the bridal canopy together with my father. And she will come; and afterward she will dance with me. So it is with all souls who were taken from this world before their time. They are with us but we don't see them or feel their presence. . . . (*Hushed*) Grandma, if one concentrates very hard, it is possible to see them and hear their voices and even know their thoughts. I know. (*Pause; points to the grave*) I have known this holy grave of the bride and groom who are buried here since I was a child. Awake and asleep I have often felt them with me; they are as close to me as my own flesh and blood. (*Thoughtfully*) A young and handsome couple on their way to the bridal canopy, looking forward to a long and beautiful life together, and in a flash all was over—evil people with axes hacked the bride and groom to death. They were buried in one grave so that they would be together for all eternity. And at every wedding, as we dance around their grave, they join in the festivities. (*Gets up and goes to the grave; Frade, Gittel and Bassia follow her; Leah raises her hands high*) Beloved bride and groom, I invite you to my wedding! Come and stand beside me under the canopy! (*A cheerful wedding march is heard; Leah screams in terror and almost falls*)

GITTEL (*Catches her*) What frightened you so? The groom has just arrived and they are greeting him with music at the entrance of town.

BASSIA (*Excited*) I'm going out there to get a look at him.

GITTEL I want to go, too. Then we'll come back to tell you what he looks like. Do you mind?

LEAH (*Shakes her head*) No.

BASSIA She's embarrassed. Don't be ashamed, little fool. We won't tell a soul. (*Leave hurriedly; Leah and Frade return to the porch*)

FRADE The bride always asks her friends to steal out and catch a glimpse of the groom; then they tell her what he looks like, whether he's dark or fair.

THE MESSENGER (*Goes closer*) Bride.

LEAH (*Shudders and turns around*) What do you want? (*Inspects him closely*)

THE MESSENGER The souls of the dead do return to the world, but not as disembodied spirits. There are souls which must go through several incarnations before they are finally purified. (*Leah listens with close attention*) Sinful souls return to earth in animals, in birds, in fish, and even at times in plants; they cannot achieve purification through their own efforts but must wait for a zaddik, a holy man, to free them and make them pure. And then there are souls who enter the body of a newborn child and purify themselves through their own deeds.

LEAH (*Trembling*)   Don't stop, please. Tell me more!

THE MESSENGER   There are also souls who belong nowhere, who find no peace anywhere; they take possession of another person's body in the form of a dybbuk, and in this way they achieve their purification. (*He leaves; Leah is astounded; Sender comes out of his house*)

SENDER   Why are you sitting here, my dear daughter?

FRADE   She was entertaining the poor people whom you invited to the special feast. She danced with them so much that now she has to rest.

SENDER   Yes! Bringing cheer to the poor is a good and pious deed! (*Looks up to the sky*) It's late. The groom and his parents have arrived. Are you ready?

FRADE   She still has to go to the holy ground.

SENDER   Go, my child, go to your mother's grave. (*Sighs*) Cry your heart out there and invite your mother to the wedding. Tell her that I want her to be by my side when we lead our only daughter to the wedding canopy. Tell her that I have kept all my promises to her, fulfilled all her dying wishes. My life has been entirely devoted to you; I brought you up to be a good and virtuous Jewish woman. And now I give you in marriage to a fine scholar and a God-fearing young man, from a fine family. (*He wipes his tears; with lowered head he returns to the house; pause*)

LEAH   Grandma, when we are at the cemetery, may I invite others besides my mother?

FRADE   Only close relatives. You should invite your grandfather, Reb Ephraim, and your aunt, Mirele.

LEAH   I want to invite someone who is not related to me.

FRADE   You may not do that, dear child. If you invite a stranger you might insult the others and they may harm you.

LEAH   He isn't really a stranger. He was like a member of the family when he was at our house.

FRADE (*In a low, frightened voice*)   Oh, my child, I am afraid! They say he died a terrible death. (*Leah cries quietly*) Don't cry, you can invite him, only don't cry. I will take the sin on myself. (*Suddenly remembers*) But I have no idea where his grave is, and it's not right to ask.

LEAH   I know where it is.

FRADE (*Astonished*)   How do you know?

SENDER (*Uneasy*)   Where is Leah? Where is Frade? Why haven't they returned from the cemetery yet? Has something happened to them, God forbid?

GITTEL, BASSIA   We'll go to meet them. (*Leah and Frade enter hurriedly in the left lane*)

FRADE   Hurry, hurry my child! We're very late. Why did I listen to you? Now I fear that something dreadful will happen, God forbid.

SENDER   Oh, there they are. What kept you so long? (*Women come out of the house*)

WOMEN   Bring the bride in to light the candles. (*They bring Leah into the house*)

FRADE (*Quietly to Gittel and Bassia*)   She fell into a faint—it was all I could do to revive her. I'm still shaking.

BASSIA   Well, she's fasting and that makes her weak.

GITTEL   Did she cry long at her mother's grave?

FRADE (*Shakes her hand*)   Don't ask what happened there; you're better off not knowing. I'm still trembling! (*A chair is placed near the door; Leah is brought out and sits on it; music is heard; Nahman, Menashe, Reb Mendl, and the groom's parents enter, left lane; Menashe carries a veil in both hands and places it on Leah's head and over her face; the Messenger leaves the synagogue*)

LEAH (*Tears off the veil, jumps up, pushes Menashe away, and cries out*)   You are not my bridegroom! (*Great confusion; all stand around Leah*)

SENDER (*Shaking*)   My daughter, my dear daughter! What is it?

LEAH (*Tears herself away, runs to the grave, spreads her arms*)   Holy bride and groom, protect me! Save me! (*She falls; people run to her and lift her up; she looks around wild-eyed and cries out, not with her own voice but with that of a man*) Ah! Ah! You have buried me! But I have returned to my promised bride and will not leave her! (*Nahman goes to Leah; she shouts at him*) Murderer!

NAHMAN (*Shaking*)   She is mad!

THE MESSENGER   A dybbuk has entered the body of the bride. (*Great confusion*)

(*Curtain*)

ACT III

▼

Reb Azrielke's home in Miropolye, two days later

Miropolye, in a large room at the home of Reb Azrielke, the zaddik; right, a door leading to the other rooms; in the middle of the front wall, a door to the street; benches on both sides of the door; windows in the wall; left, along most of the wall, a long table covered with a white cloth and piled with sliced white bread, ready for the blessing which begins a meal; at the head of the table, an armchair; at the right wall, next to the inner door, a small Holy Ark and a reading stand; in front of these a small table, a sofa, several chairs.

Saturday night, not long after evening prayers; Hasidim in the room; Mikhoel, the synagogue beadle, stands near the table and divides the white bread on plates; the Messenger sits near the Holy Ark, surrounded by a group of Hasidim; some sit by themselves, studying texts; first Hasid and second Hasid stand near the small table in the center of the room; from the inner room a quiet chant is heard: "God of Abraham, Isaac and Jacob."

FIRST HASID The stranger tells the most amazing wonder tales . . . they're really shocking . . . I'm afraid to listen to them.

SECOND HASID What do you mean?

FIRST HASID They're full of subtle, almost incomprehensible allusions. I'm not sure, but I think they are the mystic teachings of Reb Nahman of Bratslav.[8]

SECOND HASID The older Hasidim are listening to him so there's probably nothing to worry about. (*They join the circle around the Messenger*)

THIRD HASID Tell us another tale!

THE MESSENGER It's late. There's no time.

FOURTH HASID Don't worry, the rebbe won't come out for a while.

THE MESSENGER (*Narrates*) At one end of the world stands a high mountain and on the mountain there is a large rock from which a clear spring flows. And the heart of the world is found at the other end of the world; everything in the world has a heart and the world itself has one very large heart. And the heart of the world gazes continuously at the clear stream, never tiring of the sight. And though it never ceases thirsting for the stream and is drawn to it with the greatest longing and desire, it cannot come close. For as soon as the heart of the world moves, it loses sight of the clear stream on the mountaintop; and if the heart of the world does not see the stream for even a moment, it dies. And at that instant the world begins to die, too. And the clear stream has no lifetime of its own but lives on the time given to it by the heart of the world. And the heart gives it only one day. And when the day comes to an end the clear stream sings to the heart of the world. And the heart of the world answers the clear stream with a song. And their singing spreads over all the world, and shining threads flow out of the songs and spread to the hearts of every living thing and connect one heart with the other. And one just man who is favored of God wanders through the world and gathers the shining threads from the hearts of all living beings and weaves them into time. And when he has woven a full day of time he gives it to the heart of the world, and the heart of the world gives it to the clear stream. And so it lives another day.

THIRD HASID   The rebbe is coming. (*All stand in silence; Reb Azriel, a very old man in a white caftan and a fur-trimmed hat, comes out of the door, right*)

REB AZRIEL (*Walks slowly and in deep thought to the table and sits down heavily on the sofa; Mikhoel places himself to his right; the Hasidim seat themselves around the table; the older Hasidim sit on the benches, the younger ones stand behind them; Mikhoel distributes the white bread; Reb Azriel lifts his head and begins singing in a soft, quavering voice*)

This is the feast of King David, the Messiah.[9] (*All answer, recite the blessing over the bread, and begin softly to sing a sad and mystic melody without words; pause; Reb Azriel sighs deeply, rests his head on both hands, and sits a while deep in thought; a frightening stillness prevails; Reb Azriel lifts his head and begins in a soft, quavering voice*) It is told about the Baal Shem, may his merits preserve us: (*Short pause*) Once some German acrobats came to Mezhibezh to perform in the streets; they stretched a rope across the river and one of them balanced himself on it and walked to the other side. People came running from all over town to see this wonderful feat. Even the holy Baal Shem Tov stood with the crowd and watched the man walk on the rope across the river. His students, surprised to see him there, asked why he had come to see this trick, and he answered them as follows: "I came here to observe how a person crosses a deep abyss. And as I watched I thought: if a person were to put as much effort into developing his soul as he does into training his body, how many and what deep abysses would his soul be able to traverse on the slender thread of life." (*Sighs deeply; pause; the Hasidim look at each other enraptured*)

FIRST HASID Sublime!

SECOND HASID Marvelous!

THIRD HASID Unmatched!

REB AZRIEL (*Quietly to Mikhoel who bends toward him*) There is a stranger here.

MIKHOEL (*Looks around*) He's a messenger, apparently a student of Kabbalah.

REB AZRIEL What message does he bring us?

MIKHOEL I don't know. Shall I send him away?

REB AZRIEL No, of course not. We must receive strangers with honor. Offer him a seat. (*Mikhoel, somewhat surprised, brings the Messenger a chair; no one pays attention; Reb Azriel looks at one of the Hasidim who is singing a melody without words; pause; Reb Azriel continues*) God's world is holy and great.[10] The holiest land in the world is Israel. The holiest city in Israel is Jerusalem. The holiest place in Jerusalem was the Temple, and the holiest spot in the Temple was the Holy of Holies. (*Short pause*) There are seventy nations in the world, and among them the people of Israel is the holiest. And the tribe of Levi is the holiest of the twelve tribes of Israel, and among the Levites the holiest are the priests. And among the priests the holiest is the High Priest. (*Short pause*) There are 354 days in the year, and among them the holy days are sacred. And the Sabbath is holier than the holy days. And the holiest of all the holy days, the Sabbath of Sabbaths, is Yom Kippur which is the Day of Atonement. (*Short pause*) There are seventy languages in the world, and the holiest among them is Hebrew. And the holiest work in the Hebrew language is the Torah, and its holiest part is the Ten Commandments, and the holiest word in the Ten Commandments is the name of God. (*Short pause*) Once a year, on Yom Kippur, the four holiest sanctities gather together precisely when the High Priest enters the Holy of Holies in order to pronounce the ineffable name of God. And at this immeasurably holy and awesome moment the High Priest and the people of Israel are in the utmost peril, for even a single sinful or wayward thought in the High Priest's mind at that instant might, God forbid, destroy the entire world. (*Pause*) Every piece of ground on which a person stands when he raises his eyes to Heaven is a Holy of Holies; everyone created in the image of God is a High Priest; every day in a person's life is Yom Kippur; and every word which a person speaks from his heart is God's name. Therefore, every sin and every wrong committed by man brings the world to destruction. (*In a trembling voice*)

After suffering great pain and enduring many incarnations, human souls, like infants hungering for the mother's breast, are drawn to their source, to the heavenly Throne of Glory. But sometimes, after a soul has finally achieved the highest level of purity, it is suddenly beset by evil forces, God forbid, and stumbles and falls. And the higher it has soared, the deeper it plunges. And when such a soul falls, a world is destroyed, and the spheres grow dark and all ten *sfires*, the emanations of God, mourn the loss. (*Pause; as if waking up*) My children, today we will cut short our farewell feast to the Sabbath. (*Everyone, except for Mikhoel, leaves in silence, under the spell of the story; short pause*)

MIKHOEL (*Goes to the table, uncertainly*)   Rebbe! (*Reb Azriel looks up at him wearily and sadly*) Sender of Brinitz is here.

REB AZRIEL (*Repeats*)   Sender of Brinitz . . . I know. . . .

MIKHOEL   A terrible misfortune has befallen him. His daughter has been possessed by a dybbuk, may Heaven preserve us.

REB AZRIEL   Possessed by a dybbuk . . . I know. . . .

MIKHOEL   He has brought her to you.

REB AZRIEL (*As if to himself*)   To me? To me? How could he have come to me when the "me" in me is no longer here?

MIKHOEL   Rebbe, everyone in the world comes to you.

REB AZRIEL   Everyone in the world . . . a blind world . . . blind sheep following a blind shepherd. It is only because they are blind that they come to me; if they weren't blind they would go to Him who alone can say "I," to the only "I" in the world.

MIKHOEL   Rebbe, you are His deputy.

REB AZRIEL   The world says I am, but I don't know for sure. For forty years I have occupied the position of rebbe, yet to this very day I am still not sure that I can speak for God, may His name be blessed. There are times when I feel the Almighty very close to me, and then I have no doubts; at such times I feel strong and I can influence the higher spheres. But there are times when I lose my confidence, when I am as small and as weak as an infant; then I need help myself.

MIKHOEL   Rebbe, I remember the time you came to me at midnight and asked me to recite psalms with you. We spent the night reading psalms, and weeping.

REB AZRIEL   That was in the past. Now it's even harder for me. (*With a trembling voice*) What do they want from me? I am old and weak; my body needs rest, my soul thirsts for solitude. Yet they come to me with all their pains and sorrows, they appeal to me for help, and every plea pierces my heart like a needle. I haven't the strength . . . I am no longer able to . . .

MIKHOEL (*Frightened*)   Rebbe! Rebbe!

REB AZRIEL (*Sobbing*)   I can't go on! I can't! (*Cries*)

MIKHOEL   Rebbe, you must not forget that you are the last in a long line of holy men and zaddikim. Your father, Reb Itshele of blessed memory, your grandfather the renowned scholar, the great Reb Velvele, a disciple of the Baal Shem Tov. . . .

REB AZRIEL (*Recovering, lifts his head*)   My ancestors . . . my saintly father, to whom the prophet Elijah appeared three times . . . my uncle, Reb Meyer Ber, who ascended to heaven during his prayers . . . my grandfather, the great Reb Velvele who could revive the dead. (*Turns to Mikhoel, his spirits restored*) Do you know, Mikhoel, that my grandfather, the great Reb Velvele, used to exorcise a dybbuk without using spells or incantations; he simply raised his voice and gave one piercing scream. In my hour of need I turn to him, and he supports me. He won't abandon me now. Call Sender. (*Mikhoel goes out and returns with Sender*)

SENDER (*Stretches out his arms and tearfully implores*)   Rebbe, have mercy! Help me! Save my only daughter!

REB AZRIEL   How did this calamity occur?

SENDER   When the veil was being placed over the bride's face, just as . . .

REB AZRIEL (*Interrupts*)   That's not what I'm asking. What I want to know is why this misfortune struck you? A worm can only bore its way into fruit that has already begun to rot.

SENDER   Rebbe, my only child is a good and God-fearing Jewish daughter. She is modest and obeys me in everything.

REB AZRIEL   Children are sometimes punished for the sins of their parents.

SENDER   If I knew of any sin I had committed I would do penance. . . .

REB AZRIEL   Has the dybbuk been asked who he is and why he has taken possession of your daughter?

SENDER   He doesn't answer, but we recognized the voice as that of a student from our yeshiva who died suddenly in the synagogue several months ago. He dabbled in Kabbalah and came to harm.

REB AZRIEL By what powers?

SENDER They claim it was evil spirits. A few hours before he died he confided to a fellow student that there is no need to fight sin and that there is a spark of holiness in Satan, may the merciful God preserve us. He even said that he would use sorcery to conjure up two barrels of gold.

REB AZRIEL Did you know him personally?

SENDER Yes, he ate at my house regularly.

REB AZRIEL (*Looks attentively at Sender*) Did you perhaps cause him grief in some way, did you insult him? Think, try to remember.

SENDER I don't know . . . I can't remember! (*In despair*) Rebbe, I'm only human. (*Pause*)

REB AZRIEL Bring the young woman in. (*Sender goes out and returns immediately with Frade who is pulling Leah with her; Leah stands at the doorway, refusing to come in*)

SENDER (*Sobbing*) My dearest daughter, have pity on me, don't shame me in front of the rebbe. Come in!

FRADE Go in Leah'le, go in my sweet dove!

LEAH I want to come in, but I can't.

REB AZRIEL Young woman, I order you to come in. (*Leah crosses the threshold and walks to the table*) Sit down.

LEAH (*Sits, obediently; suddenly she jumps up and screams, not with her own voice*) Let me be! I don't want to! (*She tries to run away; Sender and Frade hold her back*)

REB AZRIEL Dybbuk, I command you to tell who you are!

LEAH (DYBBUK) Rebbe of Miropolye, you know very well who I am, but I don't want to reveal my name in front of the others.

REB AZRIEL I'm not asking for your name. I'm asking who you are.

LEAH (DYBBUK [*Quietly*]) I am one of those who sought other ways.

REB AZRIEL Those who seek other ways have wandered from the straight path.

LEAH (DYBBUK) It is too narrow. . . .

REB AZRIEL The same thing was said by one who never returned. (*Pause*) Why did you possess this maiden?

LEAH (DYBBUK) Because I am her intended.

REB AZRIEL Our holy Torah teaches that the dead are forbidden to be in the vicinity of the living.

LEAH (DYBBUK) I am not dead.

REB AZRIEL You have departed this world not to return until the great ram's horn is sounded at the End of Days. Therefore, so that a living branch of the eternal tree of Israel will not wither and die, I command you to leave the body of this maiden.

LEAH (DYBBUK [*Screams*])   Rebbe of Miropolye, I know how strong and mighty you are. I know that you can order angels and seraphim to do your will. But you cannot impose your will on me. I have no place to go. All roads are closed to me and all paths are blocked; evil spirits lie in wait everywhere, ready to consume me. (*In a trembling voice*) There is a heaven and there is an earth and there are worlds upon worlds in the universe, but nowhere is there a place for me. And now that my anguished and harried soul has found a haven, you want to drive me away. Have pity on me, don't hound me, don't chase me out.

REB AZRIEL   Wandering soul! I cannot help but feel deep pity for you and will do everything in my power to release you from the angels of destruction. But you must leave the body of this maiden.

LEAH (DYBBUK [*Decisively*])   I will not leave.

REB AZRIEL   Mikhoel, summon ten men from the synagogue. (*Mikhoel goes out and returns quickly with ten men; they stand at the side*) Gentlemen, do you give me permission in your name and with your authority to exorcise an evil spirit who is unwilling to leave the body of a Jewish maiden?

ALL TEN MEN   Rebbe, we give you permission in our name and with our authority to exorcise an evil spirit who is unwilling to leave the body of a Jewish maiden.

REB AZRIEL (*Rises*)   Dybbuk, soul of one who has departed from our world! In the name and with the authority of this holy congregation of Jews, I, Azriel son of Hadas, command you to leave the body of the maiden Leah, the daughter of Hannah,[11] without harming her or any other living creature. If you do not obey my command I will cover you with curses and maledictions, with conjurations and oaths, with all the power of my outstretched arm. But if you obey my command I will use all my power to reclaim your soul and drive away the spirits of evil and destruction that surround you.

LEAH (DYBBUK [*Screams*])   I am not afraid of your curses and threats, and I don't believe in your assurances. No power in the world can help me! There is no more exalted realm than my present haven, and there is no deeper abyss than the one that awaits me. I will not leave!

REB AZRIEL   In the name of the Almighty God I make my final petition and command you to leave the maiden's body! If you do not leave, you will be excommunicated and given over to the angels of destruction. (*A fearful pause*)

LEAH (DYBBUK)   In the name of the Almighty God I am joined to my intended forever and will never leave her.

REB AZRIEL   Mikhoel, order white robes to be brought in for everyone. Bring seven rams' horns and seven black candles.[12] After that, take seven Torah scrolls out of the Holy Ark. (*Fearful pause while Mikhoel is out; he returns with rams' horns and black candles; the Messenger follows with white robes*)

THE MESSENGER (*Counts the robes*)   There is one robe too many. (*Looks around*) Is someone missing in the room?

REB AZRIEL (*Agitated, as if remembering something*)   To excommunicate a Jewish soul one must first obtain the permission of the chief rabbi.[13] Mikhoel, put away the rams' horns, the candles and the robes for the time being. Take my staff and go to Reb Shimshon; tell him in my name that he must come here immediately. (*Mikhoel gathers up the rams' horns and candles and goes out together with the Messenger, who is carrying the robes; Reb Azriel to the ten men*) You may leave for now. (*They leave; pause; Reb Azriel raises his head*) Sender, where are the groom and his parents?

SENDER   They remained in my house in Brinitz for the Sabbath.

REB AZRIEL   Send a rider to tell them in my name that they must remain there to await my orders.

SENDER   I will send a rider immediately.

REB AZRIEL   In the meanwhile you may leave; take the maiden into the other room.

LEAH (*Wakes up; in a trembling voice*)   Grandma, I am afraid. What will they do to him? What will they do to me?

FRADE   Don't be afraid, my child. The rebbe knows what he's doing. He won't harm you; he would never hurt anyone. (*She and Sender go out with Leah*)

REB AZRIEL (*Sits deep in thought; as if waking*)   Even if it has been otherwise decreed in the higher spheres, I will reverse the decree. (*Reb Shimshon enters*)

REB SHIMSHON   May you have a good week, Rebbe.

REB AZRIEL (*Rises to meet him*)   A good week, and a good year, Rabbi. Be seated. (*Reb Shimshon sits down*) I have put you to this trouble because of a very important matter. A dybbuk has possessed a Jewish maiden, Heaven preserve us, and he refuses to leave her body. Only one thing remains to be done and that is to drive him out through banishment and ostracism. I therefore ask your consent for this, and you will have earned the merit of saving a soul.

REB SHIMSHON (*Sighs*)   To pronounce a ban upon the living is difficult enough; how much more so on the dead. But because nothing else is left to be done, and because so godly a man as you finds this remedy necessary, I give my consent. But first, Rebbe, I must reveal a secret to you that has some bearing on this matter.

REB AZRIEL   Please do.

REB SHIMSHON   Rebbe, do you remember a young Hasid by the name of Nissen ben Rivke, a student of Kabbalah, who used to come from Brinitz to visit you regularly about twenty years ago?

REB AZRIEL   Yes, he left for distant parts and died there.

REB SHIMSHON   Well, the same Nissen ben Rivke appeared three times in my dreams last night and demanded that I summon Sender of Brinitz to a rabbinical court in his name.

REB AZRIEL   What is his claim against Sender?

REB SHIMSHON   He didn't tell me. He only said that Sender caused him the most grievous harm.

REB AZRIEL   You know that when a Jew has a claim against someone and demands a trial, the rabbi may not refuse. This is even more true in the case of a dead person who can petition the heavenly tribunal itself. But what has that to do with the dybbuk?

REB SHIMSHON   It has a very real connection. I have heard that the young man who died and entered the body of Sender's daughter was Nissen's son. They speak of a certain promise which Sender made to Nissen and never fulfilled.

REB AZRIEL (*Thinks a while*)   In that case I will postpone the exorcism of the dybbuk until tomorrow noon. Tomorrow right after the morning prayers, God willing, you will summon the deceased and we will cast your dream in a proper light.[14] After that, with your permission, I will drive out the dybbuk by excommunicating him.

REB SHIMSHON   Inasmuch as a trial between a living person and one who is deceased is very unusual and difficult I hope that you, Rebbe, will agree to be the presiding judge and conduct the trial.

REB AZRIEL   I agree. Mikhoel! (*Mikhoel enters*) Ask them to bring in the maiden. (*Sender and Frade bring in Leah, who sits down, her eyes shut*) Dybbuk! I am giving you exactly one day; if by tomorrow noon you haven't left of your own free will, I will, with the permission of the rabbi of this town, banish you by force through the agonizing means of the *herem.* (*Pause*) Now you can take the maiden out. (*Sender and Frade are about to take Leah out*) Sender, you remain here. (*Frade accompanies Leah out*) Sender, do you remember your old friend Nissen ben Rivke?

SENDER (*Frightened*)   Nissen, son of Rivke? But he died. . . .

REB AZRIEL   Do you know that last night he appeared three times in the chief rabbi's dreams? (*Points to Reb Shimshon*) He demanded that you be summoned to a trial to answer his charges against you.

SENDER (*Trembling*)   Me, summoned to a trial? Oh my God. What can he want from me? What shall I do, Rebbe?

REB AZRIEL   I don't know what the charge is, but you must accept the summons.

SENDER   I will do as you say.

REB AZRIEL (*In a different tone*)   Send the swiftest horse and rider to inform the bridegroom and his parents to be here by noon tomorrow. Let the wedding ceremony take place immediately after the dybbuk has been exorcised.

SENDER   Rebbe, what if they have had second thoughts about the marriage and refuse to come? (*The Messenger appears at the door*)

REB AZRIEL (*With authority*)   Tell them that the orders are from me. And make sure that the groom is here on time.

THE MESSENGER   The groom will be here on time. (*The clock strikes twelve*)

(*Curtain*)

ACT IV

▼

Reb Azrielke's home, half a day later

The same room as in act III, but replacing the long table at the left is a small table closer to the footlights; Reb Azriel, wearing a prayer shawl and phylacteries, sits at the head of the table in an armchair, and two rabbinical judges sit on either side; Reb Shimshon stands near the table, Mikhoel a little farther off; the three rabbis and Shimshon are participating in a ceremony whose purpose is to effect a favorable outcome of a dream which has troubled the dreamer.

REB SHIMSHON   I have seen a good dream, I have seen a good dream, I have seen a good dream.

REB AZRIEL AND THE TWO RABBINICAL JUDGES (*Together*)   You have seen a good dream; good it is and good may it be!

REB AZRIEL   Rebbe, now that you have been assured a positive outcome of your dream, come and sit with us as a rabbinical judge. (*Reb Shimshon sits at the table next to Reb Azriel*) We will send for the deceased to present himself at the trial. First, however, I will mark off an area beyond which he may not cross; Mikhoel, hand me my cane. (*Mikhoel gives him the cane; Reb Azriel rises and makes a circular motion with the stick, from left to right, in the left corner of the room; he returns to the table*)

Mikhoel, take my cane and go to the cemetery. Once you get there close your eyes and holding the cane before you, start walking. Stop at the first grave the cane touches. Knock on the grave three times, and say: "Righteous deceased! Azriel, the son of the renowned and saintly Reb Itshele of Miropolye, apologizes for disturbing your rest and enjoins you to inform the righteous deceased, Nissen the son of Rivke, through ways you know best, that the rabbinical court of Miropolye summons him to appear immediately, wearing the garments in which he was buried." Repeat this three times and then leave. And no matter how loud the shrieks, the wails, or the screams behind you, do not turn around, and never let my cane leave your hand for even one moment or you will be in mortal danger. Go! God will protect you for He watches over everyone who is sent on a mission of righteousness. Before you leave, send in two people to set up a partition for the deceased. (*Mikhoel leaves; two men enter carrying a sheet with which they partition off the entire left corner; they leave*) Ask Sender to come in. (*Sender enters*) Sender, did you carry out my orders? Have you sent for the bridegroom and his parents?

SENDER   I dispatched the fastest horses, but the groom's party has not yet arrived.

REB AZRIEL   Send another messenger to tell them to ride faster.

SENDER   I will do so. (*Pause*)

REB AZRIEL   Sender, we have sent a message to the righteous deceased, Nissen ben Rivke, informing him that he has been summoned to a trial by this court. Will you accept the verdict we reach?

SENDER   I will.

REB AZRIEL   Will you carry out all our directives?

SENDER   I will.

REB AZRIEL   Step back and stand to the right.

SENDER   Rebbe, now I remember! Nissen ben Rivke is probably bringing a suit against me in court because of a pledge which we made to each other. But I am not guilty in this matter.

REB AZRIEL   You will have a chance to explain everything after the deceased makes the nature of his claim known to us. (*Pause*) Soon a person from the true world will appear before us so that our tribunal can render a judgment in a claim he has against a person from our world of illusion. (*Pause*) This proves that the laws of the holy Torah rule all worlds and all persons and that they are obligatory for everyone, the dead as well as the living. (*Pause*) A trial such as this is difficult and awesome; and everyone is watching it. If, God forbid, the court deviates by even one hairsbreadth from the Law, protests will be heard from the heavenly tribunal itself. Therefore we must approach this trial with fear and trembling . . . fear . . . and trembling. (*Looks around anxiously; he stares at the curtain and becomes silent; a fearful silence*)

FIRST RABBINICAL JUDGE (*To the second judge, quietly, in a trembling voice*)   I think he has come.

SECOND RABBINICAL JUDGE (*Also quietly and fearfully*)   He has come, I believe.

REB SHIMSHON   He is here.

REB AZRIEL   Righteous deceased, Nissen ben Rivke! The court has decreed that you may not step out of the circle or beyond the partition which has been set up for you. (*Pause*) Nissen ben Rivke, the court invites you to tell what claims and grievances you have against Sender ben Henya. (*Fearful pause; all are frozen in their positions as they listen*)

FIRST RABBINICAL JUDGE (*As before*)   I think he is answering.

SECOND RABBINICAL JUDGE   I believe he is answering.

FIRST RABBINICAL JUDGE   I hear a voice, but I don't hear any words.

SECOND RABBINICAL JUDGE   I hear words, but I don't hear a voice.

REB SHIMSHON (*To Sender*)   Sender ben Henya! The righteous deceased Nissen ben Rivke states in his claim that in your youth you studied in the same yeshiva and that your souls were bound in loyal friendship. You both married in the same week. Not long after, when you saw each other at the rebbe's during the High

Holy Days, you pledged that if your wives became pregnant and one gave birth to a boy and the other to a girl, the two would marry when the time came.

SENDER (*In a trembling voice*)   Yes, that is true.

REB SHIMSHON   The righteous deceased, Nissen ben Rivke, further states that he later moved to a distant town where his wife gave birth to a son at the same time that your wife gave birth to a daughter. Not long after this he died. (*Short pause*) It became known to him in the true world that his son was blessed with an exalted soul and rose to ever more lofty heights, and his father's heart was filled with joy and pride. And when his son was grown he saw him wander throughout the world, going from place to place, from town to town, searching for the one to whom his soul was drawn, to his intended bride. And when he came to the town in which you live, Sender, he became one of your household and ate at your table. And his soul was drawn to the soul of your daughter. But you were rich, and Nissen's son was poor—so you turned from him and sought a match from among the richer families. (*Short pause*) And Nissen saw how his son grew despondent, and how he roamed the world over to seek new ways. And his father's heart was filled with worry and sorrow. And when the Powers of Darkness marked the young man's despair, they spread a net for him and caught him and removed him from the world before his time. And his homeless soul drifted from place to place until it entered the body of his intended bride as a dybbuk. (*Short pause*)

Nissen ben Rivke states that with his son's death he has been cut off from both worlds. Nothing remains of him, neither name nor memory; there is no one to succeed him and no one to recite the Kaddish on the anniversary of his death. His light has been extinguished forever, the crown of his head has plunged into an abyss. He therefore asks that the court sentence Sender, according to the laws of the holy Torah, for spilling the blood of Nissen's son and cutting off the family line forever. (*Fearful silence; Sender sobs*)

REB AZRIEL   Sender ben Henya, you have heard the claims brought against you by the righteous deceased, Nissen ben Rivke. What do you say in your defense?

SENDER   I cannot speak; I have nothing to say in my own defense. But I beg my old friend to forgive me, for it was not with evil intent that I sinned. Nissen left soon after we made our pledge and I never knew that his wife gave birth to a child and that he had a son. I found out that he died, but I never heard anything further about his family; with the passage of time I simply forgot.

REB AZRIEL Why did you not make inquiries and investigate the matter?

SENDER The usual way is for the groom's side to take the first step, so I thought that if a son had been born to Nissen he would have informed me. (*Pause*)

REB SHIMSHON Nissen ben Rivke asks why you never questioned his son about himself and his family during any of the many times he was at your house and ate at your table.

SENDER I don't know . . . I can't remember. But I swear that I was always drawn toward him as a son-in-law. This made me set such difficult terms whenever a match was proposed that the parents found it impossible to agree; three matches broke up this way. But the last time the family agreed to everything. (*Pause*)

REB SHIMSHON Nissen ben Rivke says that deep in your heart you recognized his son and were therefore afraid to ask about his family. You wanted someone who could give your daughter a rich and comfortable life and for this you were willing to discard his son. (*Sender covers his face and weeps quietly; long pause; Mikhoel comes in and gives Reb Azriel his staff*)

REB AZRIEL (*Speaks quietly to Reb Shimshon and the judges; stands up with the staff in his hand*) The court has heard both sides and has come to the following verdict: whereas it is not known for certain if their wives had already conceived at the time that Nissen ben Rivke and Sender ben Henya made their pledge, and whereas our holy Torah teaches that an agreement pertaining to something not yet created is not binding, we cannot conclude that Sender had an obligation to fulfill the pledge. However, since the pledge was accepted in the higher realms and the thought that Sender ben Henya's daughter was his intended bride had been planted into the heart of Nissen ben Rivke's son, and since Sender's consequent actions led to great tribulation for Nissen ben Rivke and his son, the court rules that Sender give half of his fortune to the poor and imposes upon him the lifelong duty of reciting the mourner's Kaddish for Nissen ben Rivke and his son, just as if they were his own relations. (*Pause*) The court appeals to the righteous deceased, Nissen ben Rivke, to forgive Sender fully; and it further bids him to order his son, with all the power of his parental authority, to leave the body of the maiden, Leah the daughter of Hannah, so that a branch of the fruitful tree of Israel will not wither. And may the Almighty shine His grace on Nissen ben Rivke and his wandering son as a reward.

ALL Amen! (*Pause*)

REB AZRIEL Righteous deceased, Nissen ben Rivke! Have you heard our judgment, and do you accept the verdict? (*Pause*) Sender ben Henya! Have you heard our judgment, and do you accept the verdict?

SENDER Yes, I accept.

REB AZRIEL Righteous deceased, Nissen ben Rivke! The trial between you and Sender ben Henya is over. Now you must return to your eternal resting place. We enjoin you not to harm any person or other living creature on your way. (*Pause*) Mikhoel! Order the curtain to be taken down and water to be brought in. (*Mikhoel calls in two men who remove the curtain; Reb Azriel draws a circle with his cane on the same spot as before, but from right to left; a basin and a dipper are brought in; all wash their hands*) Sender, have the groom and his parents arrived?

SENDER I haven't heard the sound of an approaching carriage.

REB AZRIEL Send another rider to intercept them and to tell them to drive the horses at full speed; order the wedding canopy to be set up and call the musicians; instruct the bride to put on her wedding gown so that the marriage ceremony can take place as soon as the dybbuk leaves her body. See that everything is ready. (*Sender goes out; Reb Azriel removes his phylacteries and folds his prayer shawl*)

REB SHIMSHON (*In a low voice to the judges*) Did you note that the deceased did not forgive Sender?

FIRST AND SECOND JUDGES (*In quiet, frightened voices*) We noted it.

REB SHIMSHON Did you note that the deceased did not accept the verdict?

FIRST AND SECOND JUDGES We noted it.

REB SHIMSHON Did you note that he did not respond "Amen" to Reb Azriel's words?

FIRST AND SECOND JUDGES We noted it.

REB SHIMSHON It's a very bad omen!

FIRST AND SECOND JUDGES It is indeed a bad omen!

REB SHIMSHON See how agitated Reb Azriel is? His hands are trembling. (*Pause*) We have finished our work here and can leave. (*The judges go out quietly and Reb Shimshon prepares to leave, too*)

REB AZRIEL Rabbi, stay here until the dybbuk is out. I would like you to perform the wedding ceremony. (*Reb Shimshon sighs and sits at the side with his head lowered; an ominous pause*) Master of the Universe, Thy ways are wondrous and beyond scrutiny! But I know that the path on which I tread is illuminated by the glowing flame of Thy holy will, and I will not turn aside from it, neither to the right nor to the left. (*Raises his head*) Mikhoel. Have you seen to all the preparations?

MIKHOEL   Yes, Rebbe.

REB AZRIEL   Call in the maiden. (*Sender and Frade usher in Leah, who is wearing a white wedding gown and a black shawl; they seat her on the sofa; Reb Shimshon sits next to Reb Azriel*) Dybbuk! In the name of the chief rabbi who is here beside me, in the name of the holy congregation of Jews, in the name of the great Sanhedrin of Jerusalem, I, Azriel the son of Hadas, order you for the last time to leave the body of the maiden, Leah the daughter of Hannah!

LEAH (DYBBUK [*Resolutely*])   I will not leave!

REB AZRIEL   Mikhoel, call in the men and bring the white robes, the rams' horns and the black candles. (*Mikhoel leaves and returns with fifteen men, among them the Messenger; they bring the robes, rams' horns and candles*) Take out the Torah scrolls! (*Mikhoel takes out seven Torah scrolls and hands them to seven men; he distributes seven rams' horns*) Unyielding spirit! Since you will not submit to our rule, I deliver you to the authority of the higher spirits who will expel you by force. Blow the rams' horns. (*They blow the sound of* tekiah)

LEAH (DYBBUK [*Leaves her seat, thrashes about, screams*])   Let me be! Don't force me out! I don't want to leave! I cannot give up my place!

REB AZRIEL   Since the higher spirits cannot control you, I now deliver you into the hands of the middle spirits who are neither good nor evil; they have harsher ways to force you out. Blow the rams' horns! (*They blow the sound of* shevarim)

LEAH (DYBBUK [*Weakens*])   What shall I do? All the powers in the world have risen up against me. I am torn by the most vicious and merciless spirits; the souls of the great and the righteous, my father's soul among them, have ordered me to leave the maiden's body. But as long as I have even an ounce of strength I will resist the forces that want to expel me.

REB AZRIEL (*To himself*)   A powerful force must be helping him! (*Pause*) Mikhoel, have the Torah scrolls returned to the Ark. (*They are replaced*) Hang a black curtain in front of the Ark! (*Mikhoel does so*) Light a black candle! (*The candle is lit*) Everyone, put on your white robes! (*Everyone, including Reb Azriel and Reb Shimshon put on white robes; Reb Azriel stands and raises his hand high; in a threatening voice*) Rise up, O Lord! Let your enemies fly from you and be dispersed; let them dissolve in the air like smoke. Sinful and rebellious spirit! With the power of Almighty God and with the authority of the holy Torah, I, Azriel the son of Hadas, sever all the threads that bind you to the world of the living and to the body and soul of the maiden Leah the daughter of Hannah!

LEAH (DYBBUK [*Screams*])   I'm lost!

REB AZRIEL   I banish and cut you off from the community of Israel! Blow the ram's horn!

THE MESSENGER   The final spark has dissolved in the flame.

LEAH (DYBBUK [*Feebly*])   I have no more strength to resist. (*The ram's horn blows again*)

REB AZRIEL (*Quickly silences the horns; speaks to Leah*)   Do you submit?

LEAH (DYBBUK [*In a dying voice*])   I submit.

REB AZRIEL   Do you swear to leave the body of the maiden Leah the daughter of Hannah, and promise never to return?

LEAH (DYBBUK [*As before*])   I promise.

REB AZRIEL   By the same authority that empowered me to excommunicate you, I hereby revoke your excommunication. (*To Mikhoel*) Put out the candles and take down the black curtain from the Holy Ark! (*Mikhoel does so*) Put away the rams' horns (*Mikhoel collects them*) Tell the men you assembled to remove their white robes, and send them home. (*The fourteen men take off their robes and leave together with the Messenger and Mikhoel; Reb Azriel raises his hand*) Lord of the Universe! Gracious and compassionate God! Behold the great misery of this homeless and tortured soul who has fallen because of the sins and misdeeds of others. Turn Thy gaze from his faults and permit his past good deeds and his deep affliction, together with the merits of his ancestors, to rise up to you like a vapor. Lord of the Universe! Remove every destructive spirit from his path and provide a place of eternal rest for him in your heavenly abode. Amen!

ALL   Amen!

LEAH (DYBBUK [*Trembles violently*])   Recite the mourner's Kaddish for me. My time has come!

REB AZRIEL   Sender! You say the Kaddish.

SENDER   *Yisgadal ve-yiskadash shmei raboh.* May His great name be magnified and sanctified throughout the world which He has created according to His will. (*The clock strikes twelve*)

LEAH (DYBBUK [*Jumps up in fright*])   Aah—aah! (*Falls on the sofa in a faint*)

REB AZRIEL   Lead the bride to the bridal canopy! (*Mikhoel runs in*)

MIKHOEL (*Very upset*) The second rider has just returned. He says that one of the carriage wheels broke and the groom and his family are continuing on foot. But they're very close. See, there on the hill; they're coming.

REB AZRIEL (*Very excited*) Let destiny take its course! (*To Sender*) Leave the old woman here with the bride and we will go out to greet the groom. (*Draws a circle around Leah from left to right with his staff; takes off his robe, hangs it near the door, and leaves with his staff in hand; Sender and Mikhoel follow him out; long pause*)

LEAH (*Wakes up; speaks in a very weak voice*) Who is here with me? Is that you, Grandma? Dearest Grandma, my heart is so heavy. Help me . . . rock me to sleep.

FRADE (*Strokes her face*) Don't be sad, child. Let the wicked despair, and the black cat weep with rue. But your sweet heart should be as light as a feather, as air, as breath, buoyant as a snowflake so that the holy cherubim can waft you on their wings. (*The band is heard playing a hasidic wedding tune*)

LEAH (*Trembles, seizes Frade's hand*) Do you hear? They are about to dance around the holy grave, to give the dead bride and groom a part in my wedding.

FRADE Don't tremble so, child. Don't be afraid. Strong and mighty guardians are watching over you. Sixty giants have their swords drawn to keep you from harm. And our holy patriarchs and matriarchs will protect you from the evil eye. (*Gradually moves to a rhythmic chant*)

> Soon you will enter the bridal bower
> We pray it will be in a favorable hour.
> Your pious mother in Paradise was told
> In Paradise was told
> And she has on her finest gown, her garment of pure gold.
> Two cherubim meet her on the way
> Meet her on the way.
> "Hannah'le our love," they say, "Oh, Hannah'le our dove,
> In your gown of golden cloth you look so very fine."
> "My joy is very great," she says, "that's why I want to shine.
> My only child, my jewel, my crown
> Is ready in her wedding gown
> To tie the nuptial knot."
> "But Hannah'le our love," they say, "Oh Hannah'le our dove,
> Why is your face so sad and wan. Is suffering your lot?"
> "My heart aches so, the pain is great

I grieve at my cruel fate
For I must stand far from her side,
When down the aisle they march the bride.
My precious pearl, my daughter dear
Nor will I be with her to hear
Elijah bless the wine and then
The congregation say Amen." (*Falls asleep; long pause*)

LEAH (*Eyes closed; sighs deeply; opens her eyes*)   Who is here sighing so sadly?

KHONON'S VOICE   It is I.

LEAH   I hear your voice, but I cannot see you.

KHONON'S VOICE   You are set apart from me by a spellbound circle.

LEAH   Your voice is as sweet to me as that of a violin on a silent night. Tell me who you are.

KHONON'S VOICE   I have forgotten. It is only through your thoughts that I can remember who I am.

LEAH   It's coming back to me now. My heart was drawn to a bright star. In the deep of night I shed sweet tears, and someone always appeared in my dreams. Was it you?

KHONON'S VOICE   Yes.

LEAH   I remember. Your hair was as soft as teardrops, and your eyes were mild and sad. You had long, slender fingers. Day and night I thought only of you. (*Pause; sadly*) But you left me and my light faded, my soul withered; I was like a lonely widow. Then you returned and my heart blossomed again; my death turned to life, my sorrow to joy. Why did you forsake me once again?

KHONON'S VOICE   I broke every barrier, surmounted death, reversed the law of the ages. I struggled with the strong and wrestled with the mighty and the pitiless. And when my strength finally failed me, I left your body in order to enter your soul.

LEAH (*Tenderly*)   Return to me, my bridegroom, my husband. I will carry you in my heart, and in the still of the night you will come to me in my dreams and together we will rock our unborn babies to sleep. (*Cries*) We'll sew little shirts for them, and sing them sweet songs. (*Sings, weeping*)

Hushaby, my babies,
Without clothes, without a bed.
Unborn children, never mine,
Lost forever, lost in time.

(*A wedding march is heard; Leah shudders*) They are about to lead me to the wedding canopy to marry a stranger. Come to me, my bridegroom!

KHONON'S VOICE   I have departed from your body. I am coming to your soul! (*He appears against the wall in white*)

LEAH (*Happy*)   The circle is broken. I see you, my bridegroom. Come to me!

KHONON (*Like an echo*)   Come to me!

LEAH (*Stands, joyfully*)   I am coming to you.

KHONON (*Like an echo*)   I am coming to you.

VOICES (*From offstage*)   Lead the bride to the wedding canopy! (*Wedding march; Leah leaves her black shawl on the sofa and now, all in white, walks to Khonon to the strains of the wedding music; she stands in his place, as if merging with him; Reb Azriel enters with his staff in hand; the Messenger follows; they wait near the door; Sender, Frade, and the others can be seen in the doorway*)

LEAH (*In a voice that sounds as if it's coming from a distance*)   I am enveloped in a blaze of light. My bridegroom, my destined one, I am united with you for all eternity. Together we will soar higher and higher, ever higher. (*Stage darkens*)

REB AZRIEL (*Head bowed*)   We are too late.

THE MESSENGER   Blessed is the true Judge. (*Total darkness; quietly, as if from a distance*)

> Why, oh why did the soul plunge
> From the upmost heights
> To the lowest depths?
> The seed of redemption
> Is contained within the fall.

(*Curtain*)

1912–17 (Translated by Golda Werman)

▲

Stories and Sketches

IN THE TAVERN

▼

1

The drunken gang spilled out of the tavern and dispersed in the alley, stomping in the soggy mud. Except for the women tavern-keepers, only two gentile "regulars" of the Whirlpool Inn remained inside, Axinya and Glashka. The first, a disheveled hag with a black eye, sat on the floor in a drunken fever. She kept shouting disconnected words and phrases. The younger woman, Glashka, was uncharacteristically sober. She busied herself scraping the floorboards with an iron shovel, removing whole clumps of dirt.

Malke squatted behind the bar lining up the empty bottles that her granddaughter, Khanke, handed to her over the counter. From the living quarters came the tavernkeeper, Malke's son and Khanke's father. He was stooped and had a matted, reddish beard. Throwing an anxious glance around the room, he too went behind the bar and began counting up the receipts.

"Leyb," said Malke, turning to him as she rose from the floor with difficulty. "Could you spend about an hour behind the bar? Khanke has to go to the liquor store, and I'd like to lie down for a while."

"Don't have the time." Leyb cut her short. "As if I had nothing better to do than sit behind the bar!" he added, putting on his coat.

Though he thought himself master of the tavern, Leyb rarely sat behind the counter; he had his own affairs, serious, important matters. He viewed the tavern with disdain, as a two-bit operation fit only for women.

"Pick up that towel—otherwise they'll steal it!" he muttered as he walked out.

Glashka had scraped all the mud off the floor, swept it into one pile, and taken it outside. With a cigarette for her labors, she lit up and sat down on the bench, calm and satisfied, like a person who had conscientiously fulfilled a given task. Then Khanke entrusted her with a more important one: to return the empty barrel to the liquor store. Deliberately but with a good deal of inner satisfaction, Glashka picked up the barrel. She was flattered by the trust shown in her; she also knew that she would be treated to a drink both in the liquor store and upon her successful return.

A Jew about thirty years of age, thin, phlegmatic, came into the tavern. He looked around, went up to the counter, put down a five-kopeck piece, silently pointed at the barrel with his chin. Khanke understood and poured him a glass.

"Reb Mikhel, you were two kopecks shy this morning," she reminded him.

He looked at her with disdain. "I'm not leaving town," he muttered through his teeth, spat to the side, picked up the glass with a shaking hand, and gulped his drink down in one swallow.

He was barely done when his wife rushed into the tavern; she was a short, sharp-nosed woman, with tiny wild eyes; she stopped in front of her husband and addressed him angrily: "Another little glass? Your throat all dry, is it? Gotta moisten it, do you? How many is that today? Eh?"

"The fif-tee-nth. . . ." Mikhel answered with imperturbable calm.

"Oh, you swine! You might at least be ashamed of yourself!"

"The fifteenth!" She mimicked him.

Mikhel looked at her with contempt and burst into quiet, monotonously steady laughter.

Malke and Khanke, talking in whispers, pretended not to notice the scene between husband and wife. But the wife's quick eye caught the fleeting smile on Khanke's lips.

"Oh, you drunk, you drunk!" she exclaimed in despair. "Even these people are laughing at you, laughing right in your face."

"It's you they're laughing at," Mikhel answered her, just as imperturbable as before. He sat down, took a cigarette holder out of his pocket, got a cigarette, knocked the holder against his thumbnail and lit up.

"Why are you sitting down? Isn't it time to eat?" the wife asked, somewhat restrained.

"I'm full just looking at you. . . ."

"Phew! You drunk, damn you, you atheist, you filthy swine!" she screamed, beside herself with anger, and ran out, slamming the door.

Malke and Khanke exchanged meaningful glances.

Mikhel calmly finished his cigarette and again went up to the bar. "Coun-tess!" he muttered contemptuously, and put a five-kopeck piece on the counter. Then he finished his second glass and left, unhurriedly.

The door had barely closed behind him when Axinya, striking the floor with the palm of her hand, broke into drunken laughter.

"Oy, Malkele! Oy, Khanele! Oy, I'm gonna die laughing!" she roared. "Oh, how she . . . and how he . . . Ha-ha-ha!"

"Axinya, dearest, sweetheart!" Khanke pleaded, "do me a big favor—go away, anywhere, at least for half an hour! You've been sitting since early morning doing nothing but talking! A person could go mad! . . . Give me half an hour's rest!"

"All right, Khanele, all right! I'll go!" Axinya answered good-naturedly, gathered up her bags from the floor, and rose with some difficulty. "I'll go and get some sleep in the barn, next to our darling little cow!"

"Go, go wherever you want—just go!"

After Axinya's departure, Khanke remembered Mikhel and remarked, "You know, he was almost telling the truth about having his fifteenth drink. How many did you serve him?"

"Two."

"This morning three and just now he had two—that makes seven. By tonight he'll make his fifteenth. . . ."

"Ugh! I can't stand a Jew who drinks!" the old woman exclaimed with disgust.

2

An old Russian beggar woman holding a tightly packed bag under her arm came into the tavern, limping. Looking around furtively and convinced that no one save the women were there, she approached the counter and stood waiting for something in silence.

"What do you want?" asked Khanke, looking at her inquiringly.

"No one here?" said the beggar woman in a rapid whisper as she glanced around the room.

"No one. . . ." Khanke answered her in the same tone of voice.

The beggar woman pointed to the fully packed bag. "Are you buying?"

"What have you got there?"

"Come on, let's take a look." And she headed off into the kitchen.

Feigning indifference, Malke's sharp eyes tracked the beggar woman while she murmured in Yiddish, "Watch her, she's a sharpie."

"I know," said Khanke, and went after the woman into the kitchen. The grandmother followed suit.

The beggar woman untied the tightly packed bag with a deft hand and shook out of it several pieces of delicate linen, still wet from the washing. She moved toward the stove, patiently and confidently awaiting the expert decision.

Khanke and Malke examined the linen closely, tried tearing it, examined it against the light.

"It's made in Holland," Malke whispered in Yiddish in a quavering voice.

"And it's brand-new," Khanke answered in kind.

"Look as much as you want—this is first-class linen!" The beggar woman reacted calmly.

"How much do you want for these rags?" the grandmother asked dismissively, with feigned irritation.

"Rags! Do you have anything better in your wardrobe?" The beggar woman got excited.

"Just hurry up and tell me: how much?"

"Give me two rubles!" the beggar pleaded. "Honest to God, this linen would go for ten!"

"Two rubles!" exclaimed old Malke, deeply hurt, almost horrified. And grabbing the linen in her hands, she began to shove it back at the beggar woman.

"Here are your rags, you swine, here, take them! Go to hell, go! 'Two rubles!' She's out of her mind!"

"Hold on, tell me how much you want to give me for it?" replied the beggar woman, dumbfounded, as she pushed the linens away from herself.

"Thirty kopecks!" Khanke replied decisively. "Not a penny more! And even that's too much! You can get caught red-handed with a bargain like this one," she added, looking around suspiciously.

"No, never! . . . don't be afraid, don't worry! . . ." the beggar muttered in a whisper, and added, pleading, "Give me fifty kopecks!"

"Stop driving me crazy!" Khanke shouted at her. "You should be grateful that I offered you thirty. . . . Someone might come in! Hurry!" And she looked at the front door.

"All right, take it. God be with you!" the beggar woman decided hastily.

"You're some buyer!" the grandmother responded in Yiddish reproachfully. "What was your rush? She would have given it to you for twenty kopecks. . . ."

"You're never satisfied." Khanke interrupted her, annoyed.

"It's like throwing money out the window."

Khanke, gathering up the merchandise, took it into the back room while Malke turned to the beggar woman in a reproachful tone. "You might at least drink up your thirty kopecks here, and not take it to another tavern."

"And I want to eat something too."

"Eat?" Malke was suddenly overjoyed. "Oh! I have fish today—it melts in your mouth! It's delicious! Take two pieces, and I'll add some sauce too. And take a roll. . . ."

"Right, let's have it. . . . And let's have a pint. . . . And the rest I'll drink up later."

The vodka and fish before her, the beggar woman sat herself down at the table and began to eat voraciously.

3

A piercing scream was heard from behind the front door, and following the noise, Glashka rushed in, pale and out of breath, and ran to the far corner of the room. Akulina tore in after her panting, enraged. "Oh, no, little daughter of mine, just hang on! Oh, no!" she screamed, trying to grab Glashka.

"What do you want from me, damn you! Bitch! What do you want!" Glashka shouted, rushing from one corner of the room to another.

"Oh, no, little daughter of mine, you're not going to get away from me!" Akulina repeated, choking in her anger.

Grabbing Glashka by the collar of her jacket, she pulled her toward her in a fury.

"Give me the eight kopecks, you bitch you! Do you hear me? Or bring me back my jacket!"

"Why should I give you eight kopecks?!" Glashka screamed, trying to free herself. "And what about you, didn't you sell my skirt, didn't you drink it away? Damned bitch! You're out of control today, completely out of it, damn you! Didn't you have enough to drink today? And no one else is allowed, eh! You bitch, let me go!"

Infuriated to the last degree, Akulina released the collar of Glashka's jacket and with her fat hand grabbed at Glashka's face. The latter screeched and grabbed Akulina's hair. For several minutes mother and daughter tore at each other in a frenzy. Foam appeared on Akulina's lips, and Glashka's entire face was bloodied. For a moment they let go of each other but only to catch their breath, and with renewed strength, they took hold of each other and silently, with concentrated bitterness, began to tear at each other's rags.

"Oh! is that the way you treat a mother! . . . Some little daughter I brought up! Look at her!" Akulina kept shouting.

They went at each other for a long time; they fell, got up, and finally, completely exhausted, let go of each other and stood in the middle of the tavern, bloodied and gasping.

"You filthy bitch! . . . give me six kopecks at least!" Akulina muttered, somewhat calmer now, convinced that she would get nothing by force.

Glashka's bluish colored face became distorted. With feverish speed she took out of her blouse a kerchief tied in a knot; using her fingernails and her teeth, she quickly untied it and flung several coins in her mother's face.

"Here, you scum!" she raged. "Here, take the whole twelve kopecks! I hope you choke on them! Drown in your goddamned booze! . . . You sucked it out of me, you bloodsucker! You really sobered me up today! Your hysterics sobered me up!"

And she wept bitterly.

Akulina, struck by her daughter's unexpected action, was at first confused, but then she quickly regained her composure and began to pick up the coins from the floor.

She went up to the bar where Malke was sitting and began to speak in a hurt tone. "Well, Malke, you see the kind of nice little daughter I've brought up? I fed her on my own blood? Eh? . . . Let's have a pint!" She immediately interrupted her complaints and gave Malke the money.

Her vodka in hand, she began to drink it slowly, with pleasure. Finishing half of it, she put the container on the counter, took a deep breath, looked around, and after some hesitation said calmly, without looking at Glashka, "Here, bitch, finish it up!" And she went over to the sleeping cot.

Glashka, following all her mother's movements with a feverish glance, was not in the least touched by her mother's magnanimity. Looking at her with hatred, she muttered, "Damn your eyes," walked up to the counter, looked into the glass, and making sure there was still some vodka there, she finished it off. She asked Malke for a cigarette, lit up, and calmly sat herself down on the other end of the cot, where Akulina was sitting.

Axinya returned, filthy, disheveled, sleepy.

The beggar woman, who had sold Malke the linen, had not paid any attention to the fight between Akulina and Glashka; she finished eating her fish, polished off her vodka, and was getting ready to leave.

Looking at Axinya, she asked indifferently, "Where have you been lying?" And without waiting for an answer, she left.

"In the barn, I slept next to our dear little cow," answered Axinya, yawning sweetly and rubbing her sleepy eyes. Axinya finished her drink, sat down on the floor, and began to go through her bags.

4

The door was kicked open from the outside. A man came in, bent over by a fully packed sack of yellow sand; he was a man of middle age, wearing an old, patched coat covered with sand through and through, old worn-out boots, and a new hat only slightly covered with sand dust.

Going up to one of the tables, he stood with his back to it, lowered his load of sand, removed the rope which held the sandbag, and straightened up.

His thin, yellow, sickly face showed extreme exhaustion; his forehead was covered with perspiration; the eyes gave off a consumptive sheen.

The appearance of the sand carrier for some reason alarmed the beggars. Akulina, who was sitting on the bench, her eyes closed, with an expression of dull apathy, quickly rose and, grabbing a stick that was standing near the wall, took a defensive posture. Her eyes flashed an angry challenge. Glashka, remaining in her place, straightened up and directed a look of deep hatred at the newcomer. But the appearance of the new visitor made an especially strong impression on Axinya. She jumped to her feet, then quickly bent over, struck her palm against the floor, straightened up and exclaimed: "Stanislav the bum is here!!"

Stanislav was not in the least taken with this greeting, even pretended that he had not noticed. Glancing at the beggar women with a calm derisive look, he mumbled under his breath: "Aha, I see all the bitches are here; has none of them dropped dead?"

And without waiting for an answer, he went up to the bar. "Hello, Malkele. Are you going to buy the sand?" he asked in a low, tired voice, and wiped the perspiration from his brow with his sleeve.

"I'll buy it," Malke answered. "Not at five kopecks but four. Mikhailo is selling at four."

"Malkele," Stanislav began plaintively and drawn out, "you know it's dirty work there; the sand is hard to get at, and it's hard to drag it so far. . . . and it's great sand! Just look!" Taking a handful of the sand, he let it flow in a stream to the floor.

"I don't care if it's made out of gold! I won't give you more than four kopecks."

"Well, all right, God be with you!" Stanislav agreed, sighing; he threw the handful of sand in a corner and, returning, put three kopecks on the counter. "Give me a drink."

Finishing it off, he once again looked at the beggars with an indignant glance. The women were cursing him roundly. Turning to Malke, he said, "Malkele! Why do you let these bitches into the tavern? Why don't you throw them out?"

"You're a bum! Stanislav the bum!! Re-mem-ber!!" Axinya screamed in a frenzy.

"General! . . . You piece of shit! . . . You dumb Polack!" Glashka taunted him.

"Just wait, you jailbird. I've got a good strong stick for you here!" Akulina hissed.

Stanislav, not deigning to answer them or look at them, calmly went up to the sleeping cot, sat himself down, and directed his remarks to Malke once more. "Malkele, why are these bitches screaming like they were deaf?"

"Antichrist! He even hocked his own cross with Khaim," Akulina exclaimed.

"Aha, you bum! hocked your own cross! hocked your cross!" Axinya picked up the refrain triumphantly.

Stanislav finally looked at her and said, smiling, "Hey, who gave you that nice black eye? Was it Mikhalik?"

"None of your business!!" Axinya screamed, as though someone had struck her with a whip.

"Oh, you bitches, you bitches!" Stanislav began again with deep contempt, shaking his head reproachfully, still in the same calm, soft voice. "Just look at yourselves, what sense is there in your living? You're just living off someone else! What are you, too sick to work, like other people? You're debauched, like swine. The only thing you know is getting drunk and hanging around in the streets, under the bridge there. You stinking pieces of meat! You ought to be hanged, all from the same tree!"

He fell silent and, moving forward, directed a look of tremulous expectation at the beggar women. He knew what sort of effect his words would have and was already reveling in passionate satisfaction.

And he was not wrong. Those same reproaches, had they come from a person of a different class, would have met with complete indifference; but they worked like hot pitch when thrown in their faces by someone just like them: fallen, drunk, and homeless, one whom they did not want to see as being above them, although he himself was not a beggar. Perhaps their lack of deference toward him was just what fueled Stanislav's own cruel persecution of them.

The beggar women were infuriated and they all began to scream.

"I have rich family in Warsaw!" Glashka exclaimed in a hoarse patter, trying to imitate Stanislav's voice. "He himself has rich relatives, but here he is quarreling with old beggar women! What do you want to bother them for?"

"I do have rich relatives!" she went on. "And when no one is looking, *he* asks for handouts! You're a beggar yourself, and then you go around blaming us!"

"Beggar's sack! That's what you are, a beggar's sack! Bah-a-a!" Axinya worked herself into a frenzy.

Glashka's words finally had some effect on Stanislav, and he lost his composure. Red, consumptive spots appeared on his yellow face; evil little fires appeared in his eyes. Jumping off the cot, he shouted in a quaking voice, "Glashka! . . . Watch out! When did you see me begging for handouts?! I'll show you a handout, all right; you'll remember it for three years, and in the fourth you'll drop dead. . . ."

But at this point Akulina rushed up to him with her stick raised high. "Just you dare touch her, you jailbird! I dare you! I'll smash your head!"

Faced with a common enemy, mother and daughter had made a silent truce.

"Oh, you good for nothing! You had to come here today, didn't you!" Axinya screamed, rushing about the tavern. "Akulina! Belt him one with the stick! Go ahead, do it! Oh, you bastard! You're a beggar too! A beggar."

"A beggar! Bah-a-a!"

Stanislav stood there, surrounded by the women, shaking with anger. Then he turned suddenly and shouted at them: "Bitch! Bitch! Bitch! Phew!"

Jumping back onto the sleeping cot, he wanted to shout something else, but he began to cough. He coughed for a long time, a hollow kind of cough. It seemed that everything in his chest was going to burst forth because of this tormenting cough. Large drops of perspiration appeared on his brow, his face turned crimson, his eyes became dull. Finally, something seemed to bubble up in his chest; he sucked in his breath as though he were choking and he spat a viscous clot of blood onto the floor. Grabbing at his side, he leaned against the wall, exhausted and barely breathing. His face grew waxen, the little feverish flame reappeared in his eyes. Stanislav now looked at the beggar women with sickly indignation, as though they were the ones at fault for this attack.

When he began to cough, the beggars at first felt triumphant.

"He's a dead man! A dead man! A dead man!" Axinya rejoiced.

"This consumption will kill you! It'll kill you!" Akulina prophesied.

"He's dying, the dog, but he's still itching for a fight," Glashka uttered indignantly.

But the sight of fresh blood forced the beggar women to fall silent in fear and disbelief. It was Stanislav who shook them out of this mood. Recovering somewhat, he began to speak in a weak, lowered voice. "Malkele . . . Tell the bitches to leave me alone . . . Because of them no decent man can come into your establishment. That's what everybody says, the Whirlpool stinks of beggars. . . ."

Stanislav had touched a sore spot in Malke. She came out from behind the bar and turned to the beggar women. "Maybe it is time for you to go? You've driven me crazy long enough. You sit over one pint all day, driving me nuts . . ."

"Go ahead and parrot him, Malke, take his side, the bastard! And he'll probably break your neck as a reward!" Akulina shouted.

"No decent man can come in here," Glashka aped him. "So don't come in! We'll send a carriage for you! Careful, children, the governor is coming!" she added in Yiddish.

"Malke, throw him out! Throw him out!" Axinya screamed excitedly. "Throw him out, Malke! . . . I'll take a pint! . . . I'll redeem all the junk I pawned with you. Honest to God, I'll do it! Just throw the bum out!"

"Nice guy!" Glashka continued spitefully. "A bum! A jailbird is what he is! . . . Khaim says that you stole a towel from him! You're a thief!"

"A thief?" Stanislav screamed furiously and, jumping off the cot, threw himself at Glashka and struck her in the face with all his might. Akulina ran to join Glashka and, together with her, attacked Stanislav. A fierce battle ensued. All three fell to the floor, tearing one another and filling the tavern with a deafening howl.

Axinya, caught unawares by the battle, was at first confused but soon enough was seized by a kind of frenzy and ran around the tavern screeching. Picking up a stray stick, she rushed at the combatants and began to strike at them, not bothering to make distinctions between friend and foe. Then she threw the stick away, rushed up to the counter and shouted, quite out of breath: "Malke! Give me a drink!" And pulling her last five-kopeck piece out of her pocket, almost tearing the pocket in the process, she flung the coin onto the counter.

"You've had enough to drink" Malke tried to stop her. But Axinya began to stomp her feet with such vehemence, screaming "Maalke!" that the latter shrugged her shoulders and gave her the drink. She finished her drink in one gulp; blinded by the alcohol Axinya once again rushed at the combatants, whom Khanke had now managed to separate. She rushed about the tavern, howling "Bum!" at Stanislav.

Stanislav, having just gotten off the floor, bloodied, out of breath, shoved Axinya with all his might; she seemed to fly away from him and struck her head against the table and remained lying there motionless. At this point the beggar women and the tavernkeepers rushed to Axinya's side with shouts of horror and began to pull at her, trying to revive her. But she gave no sign of life. Khanke ran to the kitchen, brought a pail of water, spilled it on Axinya's head and brought her to. She opened her eyes, looked around her, rose, all covered with blood and wet, and suddenly recollecting what had happened, began to swear. But she did not continue the fight. Akulina and Glashka also calmed down. The latter, putting her clothes right, turned to her mother. "Let's go, Mama. This jailbird bastard is going to drop dead on his own! The consumption will get him!" she added as consolation.

Akulina, gathering up her bags, still threatened Stanislav with the stick. "Just you wait, jailbird!"

And she went out together with Glashka.

5

Having flung Axinya aside, Stanislav climbed back onto the cot and, grabbing at his chest with both hands, sat for a short time in a kind of unconscious state, pale, breathing with great difficulty. Recovering, he muttered in a quavering voice: "Jesus, Mary, and Joseph!" and rubbed his hand across his bloodied face. Seeing the blood on his hand, he came down from the cot, went into the kitchen, washed himself thoroughly, and returned yet again to the bench.

He sat motionless, a pensive look directed somewhere in space. His entire figure became pinched; the stamp of breakdown and defeat seemed to permeate his very being.

Contact with the beggar women had brought him so low that he had rolled around the floor with them. It was that awareness that tormented him now. How many times had he sworn not to get involved, to avoid them, not even to look their way! But crossing their path made him forget his vows. Just looking at them filled him with hatred. They made him sick and awakened an irrepressible need to mock them, to torture and insult them, to bring them to a state of fury.

He sat motionless on the bench for some time. Then, as though awakening, he looked around, sighed deeply, climbed down and went up to the bar. "Give me ten kopecks' worth," he muttered in a defeated voice, and gave Khanke the money.

She wanted to talk about the fight. Guessing her intention, he gave an irritated look, and she handed him the vodka in silence. He drank it down slowly, sighed deeply, and left the tavern, head bowed.

Axinya, now recovered, cursed Stanislav for a long time. Then she sat down on the floor and began to weep, punctuating her weeping with an occasional cry—"Why did he beat me?"

The more she shouted, the more she felt sorry for herself. "Why did he beat me?" She wept, flooded with tears. "My beloved father was an officer!! My dear mother was from Kursk! . . . I went to school! . . . Why did he beat me!"

And striking her palm against the floor, she continued to shout hysterically, "I went to school! I know everything, everything! everything! . . . Grammar! Listen, I eat, you eat, she eats, he eats, we eat . . . I know everything! . . . Why did he beat me?"

Khanke went to her, took her by the hand to help her get up.

"All right, enough screaming! Enough! Get up! Go wash up—you're as bloody as a slaughtered pig!"

"I will not wash! Why did he beat me?"

"All right, so take him to court!" Khanke laughed. "Why did you provoke him?"

Seeing that Axinya was not going to be mollified, the young tavernkeeper pulled out the trick she had used with Axinya more than once. Directing a concentrated, steady gaze at her, she said quietly, "Ax-in-ya, listen! Listen: 'Oh . . . I came across a . . .' Well?" And bending over her, she continued to look at her expectantly.

Axinya immediately dropped her complaints and began to declaim, plaintively, striking her palm against the floor each time:

> "Oh! I came across! A little bird! Stop!
> And, you'll escape! The Net!
> And I'll remain, like you!"

"Axinya! Listen! 'May my cart! . . .' Well?" Khanke interrupted her in the same manner and tone.

Axinya immediately cut short her "song" and began to sing again:

> "May my cart get all destroyed!
> All her four wheels!"

"Axinya! 'Oh, my cigarette, my friend' . . . Well?"

> "Oh my cigarette, my secret friend!
> I love you with all my heart!"

Axinya sang, although still in a weepy voice but much calmer than before. She sang two or three more songs under the compelling look and gesture of Khanke, until she calmed down completely. Then Khanke helped her get up and took her to the kitchen. Axinya washed, went up to the bar, and shouted, quite irritated, "Give me a drink, for my skirt!"

Khanke understood that now Axinya absolutely had to have a drink and gave her the vodka without protest. "Remember, Axinya, now you owe me fifty-one kopecks: twenty-eight for the kerchief and twenty-three for the skirt."

Axinya finished her drink, seemed to come alive, and said happily: "I remember, Khanke, I remember! Twenty-eight for the kerchief and twenty-three for the skirt."

Catching the rhythm of the phrase, she joyously burst into song:

> "Twenty-eight for the kerchief!
> Twenty-three for the skirt!
> Twenty-eight for the kerchief!
> Twenty-three for the skirt!"

The repetition almost roused her to dance, but she fell down instead. Lying there, she continued to drag out her ditty until she lulled herself to sleep.

6

Two peasants came in and sat down to drink away their profits. Then, one after another, groups of government clerks came in and headed for the back rooms. A workman came in with his elderly mother whose eyes were red from tears. They ordered a pint, sat down at the little table, and in a half-whisper, the son began to console his mother, who had been beaten by the father.

Slowly, the tavern became lively. Some "ordinary folks" crowded around the buffet. Now and then one could hear exclamations emanating from the back rooms. "Let's have a bottle here!" "Beer!" Remaining behind the counter, Malke nimbly measured out the vodka, served it, carefully keeping a sharp eye lest some careless visitor "accidentally" walk off with the goods. Khanke rushed around the tavern, delivering the vodka and the food, exchanging laconic expressions with her mother. Amid the continuous hubbub, quiet conversations, laughter, and swearing all merged together. The air, thick with tobacco smoke and the odor of raw vodka, had become yellowish and heavy.

Awakened by the noise, Axinya crawled off to a corner and for some time sat silently, examining everyone with her dazed eyes. Recognizing one of the women visitors, she began to speak, not so much to her as about her. Then she turned her attention to someone else, and then to a third person, and said something about each one of them. One she blessed, another one she cursed, and yet another she insulted mercilessly. The appearance of a new visitor broke the weak thread of her thoughts—and indignant reproaches turned to tender blessings. But her speech got lost in the general noise, and only Khanke, rushing about, once or twice on the run swore at her, especially when she happened to be in the way.

An old man in dark glasses and a reddish brown coat, wearing the official government workers' hat and a soiled dicky, all askew, came into the tavern. He marched in with mannered, mechanical steps, and drew himself up to his full height. His face was haggard from drink, tortured but intelligent; it had the expression of a man coming out on stage and feeling that all attention was focused on him. A big, shaggy dog followed him into the tavern.

"Fedosya's Bigshot!" Axinya greeted him with a bitter shout, striking her palm against the floor. "Go ahead, walk around with your nose in the air, go ahead and swagger around her! She'll throw you out just like she did Makarov. She'll throw you out!"

"Fedosya's Bigshot," Abramov, that is, not suspecting that in this general cacophony one scale related specifically to him, stopped in the middle of the tavern in a theatrical pose, lifting his head high and sticking out his chest. Proudly taking in everyone at a glance with a challenging look, he walked up to the counter, directed a grandiloquently indignant glance at Malke through his glasses, put thirty kopecks on the counter, and with a commanding gesture demanded a bottle of vodka. Vodka in hand, he took a roll and went up to the little table. Still standing, he poured himself a glass of vodka and drank it slowly in one swallow. He threw the roll of bread to the dog, sat down, rested his elbows on his knees, and sat motionlessly for a long time, staring ahead blankly. He poured himself a second glass and took up the same pose as before. Abramov's eyes became turbid, his gaze intensified with the vanishing vodka. His face grew yellowish and pinched. Now he stared at the dog, who had finished the roll and was lying at his feet, waiting patiently. The dog became agitated, got up, and began wagging its tail.

"Hamlet!" its master called quietly but precisely, and continuing to gaze at it, he asked intently: "To drink—or not to drink?"

He asked this so seriously, with a strain of such serious doubt in his voice, that one might have thought that he had before him his closest friend.

The dog began to move, looked longingly at the door, barked abruptly, and raised its eyes. For about a minute the two looked into each other's eyes with a wise, questioning gaze. Man and beast— each tried to read what the other was thinking.

Abramov bent over, took the dog's head in his hands, drew his own face nearer and began to speak to it intimately in a whisper: "Hamlet, my friend! Don't look at me so reproachfully. Don't judge me—lest you be judged! Surely you must know one thing: I am better off than all the other two-legged creatures whom you see here!"

He kissed the dog on the muzzle, patted its back, drew himself up once more and disdainfully began to examine the crowd. By accident his gaze happened to stop on Axinya, who had at that moment been screaming curses at an incoming coachman. Abramov became interested in her, and moving closer, he began to listen to her disjointed exclamations; he would look at her, then at the other customers at whom her words were directed. His face again took on a soft friendly expression, as it had during his conversation with his dog.

He made little balls out of soft bread and began to throw them at Axinya with a playful expression. One of the balls hit Axinya on the forehead. She interrupted her words, roused herself, looked around, and screeched at random, "You bum!"—and once more took up the discussion of someone's family life. The second ball of bread made her look more attentively.

Seeing that Abramov was aiming at her again, she shouted out in indignation, "Fe-do-sya's Bigshot!" She was about to start swearing, but observing a well-intentional, sadly tender smile on Abramov's lips and hearing his laughter, she momentarily forgot her anger. Squinting, she cried, "Go ahead and throw it! Throw it!"

But Abramov stopped and just said in a friendly tone, "You are a wise creature . . . You are—'The Critic-at-Large!' "

And with a burst of laughter, he added, "Come here, Critic-at-Large. Let's have a drink!"

Axinya began to work her arms and legs, rose, ran up to Abramov on her unsteady legs and exclaimed in rapture, "Fedosya's Bigshot! . . . I'm sloshed!"

And she began to laugh.

Abramov took her by the hand, sat her down near him, and said: "Let's drink; then we'll talk business! . . ."

"We'll talk business!" Axinya repeated ecstatically.

Abramov rose to his full stature, looked around, and yelled at Khanke, "Hey! Mathematical Genius! Come here!"

Khanke, scurrying around the room, turned around to the call and from a distance asked impatiently, "What do you want?"

Abramov raised an arm and declaimed with pathos, "We need bread! We need money!"

And once again he yelled, "Mathematical Genius! Get over here!"

"I have no time to waste on you," Khanke answered. "Tell me what you want."

"I want you to convert to Christianity, you accursed Jewess!"

Khanke shrugged her shoulders contemptuously and ran off to the other room.

Abramov followed her with an intense look, and bending over to Axinya, he said quietly but with conviction, "She is smarter than Aristotle, smarter than Newton, smarter even than Voltaire, I assure you!"

"Smarter!" Axinya repeated joyfully.

"She has come to understand what life is. Life—is mathematics!"

He rose and, staggering, went up to the bar. Directing a fixed gaze at Malke, he stood silently for about a minute.

Knowing his crankish ways, Malke burst out at him indignantly, "Well, what do you want? Don't drive me crazy! I have no time for this nonsense!"

"You are going to die without repentance and without communion!" Abramov said gravely, and throwing a silver coin into the plate of fish, he added nastily: "Damn you to hell!"

"May you be damned yourself!" Malke answered angrily, and fishing the silver coin out of the fish sauce, she added, with more restraint now, "What can I serve you?"

"A pint and a roll," Abramov answered in his usual tone. Picking up his order, he returned to the table.

During all this, Axinya's mood changed radically. Remembering Abramov's landlady, she remembered at the same time that the woman had once called her a thief.

"That bitch, she dared call me a thief!" she shouted in a flood of tears. "I never stole anything in my life! Oh, Lord!" And tearing at the collar of her blouse, she continued, "Chaim had trusted me with three rubles! To get change! I got the change from Zissel. I brought back every kopeck! Everything! And she dares to suggest that I stole."

Returning to the table, Abramov listened attentively to her complaints, and putting his arm around the beggar woman's shoulder, he asked: "Who insulted you, Martha?"

"I'm not Martha! I'm Axinya!"

Abramov laughed and looked around with some surprise. "Are you offended? . . . I guess everyone values their name . . . even she."

Taking Axinya by the hand, he began to speak to her softly, "All right, sit down, Axinya. Sit down and tell me who offended you."

"Your landlady! Fedosya!"

"The Bourgeoisie of Life? Ha-ha-ha!" He burst into a dry feigned laugh. "That's why I love you. The Bourgeoisie of Life offends me too!"

He poured out two glasses of vodka and gave one to Axinya. "Drink up, you'll forget all the insults!"

Drinking it down, he picked up the roll and wanted to throw it to the dog but changed his mind.

"Hamlet!" he called in a whisper. The dog rose lazily and approached him. "Hamlet, drink up . . ." Abramov ordered. He poured out a little bit of vodka, and brought the glass to the dog's lips. The dog remained motionless, shuddering once or twice.

Abramov bent over and whispered something in the dog's ear. "I'm asking you!" He opened the mutt's jaw and poured down some vodka. The dog quickly swallowed it, began to whirl around the room, sneezed and barked once or twice, piteously jerking.

Abramov followed the dog's actions with an expression of deep sadness. Then he gave the dog the roll and whispered, "Here, take a bite and . . . forgive me. . . ."

Axinya was enthralled with this scene. Forgetting her tears and her insults, she began to shout rapturously, "It's drinking! The dog is drinking vodka! Oh, Lord!"

And sitting down on the floor, she began to call to the dog, "Here, doggy, here, here!"

Abramov put his arm around Axinya's shoulder and said with a bitter sigh, "Leave it alone! . . . It's a poor animal. Miserable—and noble! . . . Drink your vodka!"

Bending over Axinya, he embraced her. "Good-bye, my joy, my happiness!" he said tenderly. "You, too, are a noble creature! . . . Someday you will die, drunk, beside some fence. . . ." Straightening up, he glanced around the tavern once more with that stately gaze and shouted loudly, "Good-bye, Princess Whirlpool! Good-bye, Mathematical Genius!"

And holding his head high, he slowly walked out with that mechanical strut of his, followed by Hamlet.

1883–86 (Translated by Robert Szulkin)

THE SINS OF YOUTH

▼

At the beginning of 1881 I left Vitebsk, my birthplace, to become a tutor in the town of Liozno. Seventeen years old, this was the first independent act in my life, but I abounded in dashing self-reliance and was greatly inspired by the high ideals which lit up my vision. About a year earlier, I had left the straight and narrow; I became engrossed in worldly books and turned into an ardent maskil. I was then most influenced by Lilienblum's *Hattot Ne'urim* (*The Sins of Youth*).[1]

I did not go to Liozno so much to teach as to spread Haskalah among the young people, to open their eyes. I took a bundle of Haskalah books along: I. B. Levinsohn's *Zerubavel*, Mapu's *The Love of Zion*, Smolenskin's *A Donkey's Burial*, and, of course, *Hattot Ne'urim*.[2]

At that time, the Jewish towns of Lithuania were congealed in the old Orthodox ways and absolutely refused to face up to new trends and movements. Liozno, once the residence of the old Lubavitcher rebbe, Schneur Zalman, was in this respect even more backward than the other towns. Until my arrival, the town had had only one teacher, a former yeshiva student, whom the rabbi and the melamdim persecuted at first and then persuaded to repent. They cut his hair, took him to the ritual bath, burned the hair with the short coat, dressed him in a long garment and a skullcap, and sat him down in the synagogue to study the holy books. But their joy was short-lived: a few months later the penitent ran away and became converted.[3]

It was not easy for me to find jobs tutoring. To avoid provoking malicious acts against me from the start, I put on a mask of piety and showed that my only purpose was to earn my keep. I played my role well, I obtained lessons, and soon I was in touch with several boys. Despite its isolation from the great world, the town nevertheless had a few "infected" young people, who reached out for light and knowledge and thirsted for a word of Haskalah. They understood immediately I was not as pious as I made out, and wordlessly, but with expressive glances, they hinted they wanted to establish contact with me. They soon succeeded. Once, late at night, I heard a cautious quiet tap on my window. Opening it, I saw before me two boys who, quietly but joyously and spiritedly, told me they came to discuss an important, a most important matter. Not waiting for an invitation, they entered my room through the window.

A conversation began which lasted till dawn. It would be hard to define what we talked about. The conversation consisted almost entirely of passionate exclamations (whispered, of course, so the landlady would not overhear) extolling the radiant and sacred Haskalah. I do not remember what I told my new comrade-pupils, but the substance was not in my words but in the exalted mood of the listeners, who saw some sort of prophecy in my words. They left, joyous, as if newborn, with a firm decision to throw off their yoke, run away from home, and begin a new life, bright and promising.

The nightly visits repeated themselves. After the first two boys, others also so idealistically inclined came. Soon they formed a peculiar club of six or seven. They usually assembled at my place Fridays late at night when the town slept soundly: the visits were so furtive and conspiratorial, the discussions conducted so quietly, that for the several months I was in the town no one learned of these meetings. When I became better acquainted with my comrades and became convinced that they could be trusted, I began to lend them my secret books, even the most precious and most "dangerous," *Hattot Ne'urim.*

But over my head, clouds began to gather little by little. It began with a ludicrous incident. I had told one of my pupils to order from Vitebsk a chrestomathy, or foreign-language reader. The melamed whose classroom I had used surmised this must be a book about Christ's mother and made a commotion in town. It took considerable effort to convince the parents that the reader had no connection with Christ or Christianity.

A few weeks later, an even funnier incident happened. I kept a diary in which I used to write down my impressions, describe all sorts of scenes and types, my pupils, their parents, and others. I wrote the diary in the form of letters to my childhood friend Chaim Zhitlowsky. Once, when I forgot to lock the box where I kept my manuscripts, the landlady's daughter, a grown girl and apparently a literary connoisseur, came in during my absence. She fished out the diary and began reading. Interested in its subject matter, she assembled a few of her friends for a literary soiree. The next day, the contents of my diary were known all over town.

Unaware of all this, I went as usual to give my lessons. When I arrived for the first lesson, the lady of the house, a well-to-do shopkeeper, greeted me at the door with this welcome: "Listen here, you writer! I hired you to teach my children to read and write, but not for you to write down that my Abie's nose is dirty, and that my Frieda has big teeth and that I go about in a bedraggled dress. I can assure you that even if I wear a bedraggled dress, whatever I put in the garbage is worth more than you and your fine learning. And you can go back where you came from. Writers like you I don't need."

I got the same turning out at the next lesson. I was beside myself with despair, not knowing what had caused this misfortune. I expected that I would find the same reception at my other lessons, but apparently my dear first reader had no time to read the whole diary or forgot to tell everything. At the other homes, I was received not only without anger and abuse, but even with more friendliness than usual. These women, splitting with laughter, begged me to come read for them how I described their neighbors and acquaintances.

The episode concluded in my losing only the two lessons. But it also hurt my reputation with the solid householders. Besides, no matter how carefully I conducted myself, people began to suspect I was masquerading, and talk that I was a nonbeliever spread in town.

Just at that time, the pogroms took place in southern Russia, calling forth the deepest despair and bitterness among the Lithuanian Jews.[4] At the same time, the religious mood became stronger. Reports about the pogroms reached our town not from the newspapers, which no one received, but from unclear rumors. One day the rabbi received a letter from, I think, the Vitebsk rabbi, describing the horrible events and proposing that a communal fast be decreed. The letter was read in the synagogue and had a powerful impact. A fast day was decided on. Then the rabbi chastised the people, calling them to repent and pointing out that there were those in town who had forgotten God and allowed their children to study forbidden subjects.

Precisely then, the mishap with my clandestine maskilim had to occur.

A few days before the fast, one of the maskilim, a sixteen-year-old boy, came to me about midnight. From the nervous tapping on the window, I realized that something unusual had happened. When my nocturnal visitor entered through the window, he was white as chalk, depressed, and upset. In answer to my question about what happened, he shot out despairingly, "Oh, what a misfortune happened! We are lost!" With much effort on my part, I managed to find out what had happened.

About a week earlier, I had lent the boy *Hattot Ne'urim*. He read it several times and memorized several passages. Since he had a fourteen-year-old brother whom he had already led astray, he let him enjoy the book too, warning him to be careful. The boy sat up all night in a tiny room and read. In the morning, after prayers, he went to the study house where, under the cover of a Gemara, he continued to read. But the sleepless night and the excitement had their effect, and he fell asleep, leaving the book on the lectern. A yeshiva student entered, approached the lectern, and immediately recognized one of those secular books. He began leafing through it till he came upon the sentence: "Who can prove there is a God?" He became so terrified that he began screaming. The boy awoke and, seeing the book in a stranger's hand, leaped to retrieve it. He managed to tear the book out of the yeshiva student's hands and run away. The yeshiva student went immediately to the rabbi, telling him of the horrible occurrence. A couple of hours later, the father of both my maskilim was furiously beating the younger one, demanding he confess where he got the forbidden book. But the boy did not talk. Then the father locked him in a dark room, threatening to starve him until he would talk. The older boy got a beating, too. In short, the town was in a real uproar, and all as one claimed that only the "writer" could have lent the boy such a book; they were convinced that the "writer" had been sent from Vilna by those nonbelievers to demolish the town.

Relating this story, the boy shed bitter tears. He brought me the salvaged *Hattot Ne'urim*. But in what a condition—all tattered! He insisted that I must burn it immediately, because the townspeople would surely come to search me here.

Calming him, I proved to him that his and his brother's sufferings were a sort of self-sacrifice for the Sanctification of the Name—on behalf of the Haskalah. This reasoning encouraged him. He even exclaimed spiritedly: "Very good, this will bring things to an end sooner and we will both run away from home!"

Early the next morning, I found out that there had been a meeting the night before at the rabbi's house in which the affair was discussed. They spoke a great deal about me, and the rabbi even proposed excommunicating me.

I went to the synagogue for services. My arrival at this time agitated the congregation. The rabbi, a little old thin Jew, stood at the eastern wall, his head enveloped in a prayer shawl, and he prayed. I walked boldly toward him and called, "Rabbi!"

He looked up. Seeing me, he turned his frightened pleading glance to the people nearby; someone whispered to him, "The writer." Hearing who I was, the rabbi lowered his head, turned, and began to move farther away from me.

I took several steps toward him, and I spoke out, purposely loud and bold, "Rabbi, I came to ask what you have against me that you consider excommunicating me. I want you to tell me here, in the synagogue, in front of everyone!"

The rabbi began to wring his hands and without looking at me, backed still farther away, stammering in fear, "Go, go, go. I don't know you; I don't know you."

I stepped right up to him. Then someone grabbed me by the hand and shouted in anger, "Unbeliever, where are you crawling? Can't you see the rabbi does not wish to look at you and does not wish you to remain in his presence?"

"Out of the synagogue, unbeliever," came the shouts.

I had no choice but to leave. But now I was relieved. What did I care if they excommunicated me? I had long excommunicated them. But I worried about the boy caught with the book. His father had beaten him with such violence that he had fainted.

I had an idea. I noticed that in speaking about the heretical book which the yeshiva student found on the lectern no one called it *Hattot Ne'urim*, but "Two Days and a Night in the Inn," the title of a story by J. L. Gordon, bound with *Hattot Ne'urim*.[5] The yeshiva student had apparently just glimpsed at the title page and remembered the name of Gordon's story. I tore the story out of the book, took it to a young, somewhat worldly, lumber merchant. I asked him to read it and testify before the rabbi that there was no disbelief in it and that it did not contain the incriminating sentence "Who can prove there is a God?" The young man read the story and found only flowery rhetoric, not a word of heresy. He went to the rabbi, explained to him that I and the boy were less guilty than he had thought, and warned him not to think of excommunicating me because the government could punish him severely for this.

That worked. The father released the boy from his cell, extracting a holy vow from him never to read such books or associate with me. All talk about excommunicating me ceased. But on the fast day, the rabbi in his sermon showed that I, and such as I, were the only ones to blame for the pogroms. He demanded that I be discharged as tutor. Besides, he issued rulings which were posted that same day in all the prayer houses. Of these rulings, I remember only four:

1. All males, from thirteen years up, must wear skullcaps and not remove them at night;
2. Girls and, especially, married women must not sing in the presence of a man, or even when alone;
3. At weddings, women and girls must not appear immodestly exposed;
4. A search should be made in all homes and in all attics; all books, except religious books, that might be found were to be brought the next day to the synagogue courtyard for burning so that evil should be purged from the town.

About six or seven Hebrew books, quite innocent ones, were turned up, including also Gordon's story, which the young man had not returned to me. To this, they added about a dozen Yiddish novels, mostly by Shomer.[6] They made a pyre in the synagogue courtyard and set it afire. From the distance I could see only the smoke of the auto-da-fé. It reeked of the Middle Ages.

The next day, Saturday, after havdalah a townsman came and in a calm businesslike tone ordered me to leave town—unless I wanted to be marched out by the police. Besides, why did I have to stay? I would not have any more lessons anyway. In answer to my question as to how someone as innocent as I could be sent out with a convoy of prisoners, he said quietly, with a smile, "Can't you understand? You're not a child. Two pounds of tea to the police commissioner, and tomorrow you march out with the prisoners."

I do not know if they would really have carried out the threat. But since there was no longer any point in my staying in Liozno, I left.

For a long time I kept the tattered *Hattot Ne'urim* as a memento.

1910 (Translated by Lucy S. Dawidowicz)

HUNGER

▼

1

When I was twenty and studying for my entrance examinations to the university I lived for a while in a town in White Russia, far from home. I had long been estranged from my fanatically religious parents and had nothing to do with the local Jewish community, so I was on my own, as free as a bird. I supported myself by giving private lessons.

All in all, I enjoyed my life. I had an intimate circle of friends with whom I spent endless hours in discussions and debates. My head was full of ideas for solving the problems of the world, and my soul overflowed with hope in a bright future. If I occasionally went hungry, I didn't really mind.

One fine morning in May I woke up with a throbbing headache. The bright sunlight streamed through the window of my small room and played on my face, but I decided to stay in bed for a while. For some minutes I lay quite motionless with my eyes shut against the glare. But I made no attempt to fall asleep again.

At eight A.M., when I got up, I heard shouting coming from the next room, and without even listening to the words I knew what it was about. The landlady was heaping abuse on her son Grishka, a coach driver, for staying out all night and returning home drunk and without money. The same old story.

By the time I washed and dressed I felt better. The pain in my head had eased somewhat, but in its place there was a gnawing sensation at the pit of my stomach. Then I remembered: I hadn't eaten a thing since the previous morning's bread and tea. The bread had cost me three kopecks—all the money I had left in the world. I spent most of the day in the library and when I returned in the evening to study at my desk I discovered that there was no kerosene for the lamp. So I went to bed.

Things were bad. I didn't have a single private student and was often hungry during the last month. But until today I was able to buy enough food to keep body and soul together. Now, there was nothing left—no bread at all and only enough tea and sugar for one cup at the most. Something had to be done! Should I go to the grocery store and ask for bread and sugar on credit? Oh, but I can't abide the old Jewish lady who owns the shop. She always looks at me with such sad, accusing eyes. And she knows perfectly well that I'm Jewish but insists on calling me "My lord" anyway, probably cursing me under her breath while she says it. No—there's no point in asking her for credit; she's sure to refuse me and might even insult me into the bargain.

I'd be better off borrowing some bread and a few cubes of sugar from the landlady. But how can I ask her for bread? It's undignified. So I worked out a little stratagem: I would pretend that I had been to the grocery shop and, finding it closed, had decided to return home rather than go to the store farther down the road. Then, in the most offhand manner, I would say to her, "Cut a few slices from your bread for me, Vlasievna. I'll return it when I go shopping. And while you're at it, add a few cubes of sugar, too."

The old landlady was working in the kitchen when I came in. Her ten-year-old daughter, Peklusha, was sitting on a bench under the pictures of the holy family, quietly munching on a slice of bread. On the bed, drunk and disheveled and muttering something in his sleep, lay her eighteen-year-old son, Grishka.

"Did we wake you?" asked the landlady. "That cursed fool could wake the dead."

"What's wrong?"

"He's what's wrong. Just look at him," she said, pointing toward the bed. "He drove around the whole night, wore out the horses till they were nearly dead, and all he brought home was a measly twenty kopecks."

"M . . . m . . . Manka," stammered Grishka.

"I'll split his head open," screamed Vlasievna, grabbing the oven poker. But she put it back, crying out in a voice wracked with suffering, "Oh, what troubles I have! A grown-up son, and drunk. I'm lost, and so are my poor orphans." Then, calming down a bit, she said, "I'm going to the bazaar"—she sold pots—"so when you leave the house, let Peklusha out and lock up. Put the key near the doorpost. He can stay alone," she added, throwing Grishka a look of contempt.

"All right. But do you know if the grocery store is open," I asked.

"Why shouldn't it be? The old Jew lady's never sick, curse her blood. She opens the shop at five in the morning and stays there all day. I'd like to see her in her grave!"

I knew that the landlady had a long-lasting grudge against the Jewish grocery woman, so I made believe I didn't hear her abusive answer. As I turned to leave, I said, "I'll have to go for bread and sugar."

"Go! Go! The samovar is boiling."

I left the house and walked slowly down the street, turned at the corner and passed the grocery. It was open, of course. The old lady sat on a case near the door and looked at me with her usual pathetic expression. I walked past her up to the corner and then turned to go home.

"The samovar is boiling and Mamma has gone to the bazaar," said Peklusha in a frightened voice as soon as I entered the house."

"My little battle plan didn't work," I thought, smiling bitterly. I went into my room and began rummaging through the table drawer, hoping to find a hidden treasure. God be praised! I found a sugar cube.

"It hardly pays to drag the samovar in here," I thought. "I might as well save myself the trouble and just eat the sugar cube." But in the end I brought the big-bellied samovar into my room and steeped all the tea leaves I found. Then I started to read.

"I'll drink my tea, finish with Peklusha, and try to raise money somewhere—at least thirty kopeks," I thought. This was the amount I needed for bread, tea, sugar, and kerosene. If I could raise that sum, all my problems would be over.

I had the first glass of tea with sugar and then drank several glasses without. The hot tea dulled my hunger pangs and I started to read an interesting article in the journal that I had brought home from the library the evening before. In the next room the clock struck eleven.

It was time to give Peklusha her lesson. She was my only pupil—nonpaying, of course, but I was very pleased with her. I enjoyed her quick intelligence; she always solved the problems I set for her most cleverly, answering in her high-pitched voice while her little birdlike face shone with excitement and her fingers tapped rapidly on the table.

This time I cut the lesson short. The hunger pangs were torturing me; not only my stomach but my whole body ached—my head felt heavy, my heartbeat was weak, my mouth dry. I must get some money, but where? There was no point in asking my friends; I had made a mental list of them all, and most of them were just as hungry as I.

"Maybe I should go to Aunt Basha," I thought. I had a number of relatives in the city, all religious, fanatically religious, and I had nothing in common with them. But Aunt Basha was different; she even had a son who studied at the Gymnasium. Still, I only visited her once during the entire two years that I'd been in the city, even though she was very warm and hospitable to me when I went to see her that first time. Somehow, I didn't want to be part of that scene, to return to the old memories. So how can I go to her now and ask for help? It's impossible.

"I'll go to Alyusha," I decided.

2

Alyusha Rogov, a member of our circle, was a student at the Gymnasium. Everyone liked the quiet and shy young man, though no one was especially close to him. Living at home and supported by his parents, he never suffered the deprivations we had to endure—but he was too tactful to offer us help.

I arrived at the Rogovs' house at an awkward time, just as they were about to sit down to dinner. They were obviously going to invite me to join them and the thought of eating at the table of strangers in my state, with everyone's eyes fixed on me, made me very uncomfortable; they would see in a moment that I was pinched with hunger. I wanted to get away from there as soon as possible, so I told Alyusha that I needed a German dictionary and that I was in a hurry.

"Wait a while, until I finish dinner," he said in his soft, feminine voice. "The dictionary is somewhere in the room among my books."

So I had to wait. Alyusha's father, Andrei Stepanovitch, a gray-haired, well-built elderly man, came into the dining room. He was a medical doctor, but being independently wealthy he spent very little time at his practice. Most people considered him somewhat idiosyncratic: he would sometimes sit with his patients for three or four hours, chatting with them about all kinds of things; he walked everywhere, using a coach only for special occasions; and he avoided rich patients on principle, while he was very popular among the poor. With Alyusha's friends he was friendly and congenial, though somewhat ironical. He shook my hand silently and, as he walked to the table, said, "Will you join us for dinner?"

"Thank you, but I'm not hungry," I quickly replied, feeling my face turn red.

"But have you had dinner? Sit down with us," he continued, casting a penetrating look at me.

If he hadn't looked at me in that way, I might have come to the table, but now I simply couldn't; I was sure that the old man could tell that I was starving just by observing my face and dry lips.

"No, I've just had dinner," I lied again.

He glanced at me a second time and said nothing more.

Dinner was served. I hadn't eaten a proper meal for weeks, and the odor of the hot cooked food hit me in the face like a blow; I was actually in pain. My head reeled, and it took all my self-control to keep my eyes off the table. I was really annoyed with myself for being too stubborn to accept his invitation. Why? I could just as easily have said, "Oh, thank you, with pleasure," and enjoyed a good meal.

"Why haven't we seen Melchin for such a long while? He hasn't been here for two weeks. Do you know how he is?" Rogov asked, wiping his mouth with a napkin.

This question put an end to my bad spirits. I even forgot about my hunger pangs, and deep in my heart I was pleased that I hadn't joined them for dinner.

"Melchin? I don't know. I haven't seen him for quite a while either." I replied impatiently.

Melchin, a mutual friend, had been expelled from the Gymnasium for a minor infraction of the rules. He had a good income from his private lessons and was no fool, but none of us could stand him because he was extremely tactless. Propriety meant nothing to him. He had no compunction whatsoever about encroaching on someone's privacy—if it suited him he would go into a friend's room uninvited and in his absence eat his last piece of bread, borrow a book that he needed, or help himself to some clothes. And afterward, when the owner asked him why he took his things without permission, the answer was always the same—"Bourgeois"—the worst stigma for someone in our circle. It didn't matter how many times we told him straight out that we didn't want to be his friend or how often we refused to shake hands with him—none of it seemed to penetrate. After a day or two he would return as if nothing happened. Some time ago he started visiting the Rogovs once a week, always during their dinner hour; and, of course, he always remained to eat. This bothered me more than anything else. I considered it degrading, a form of begging.

And now, from his place at the table, the elder Rogov was talking to me about Melchin. Why was he reminded of him just now? If I had joined them for dinner, Rogov would have thought, "From now on, he will come for dinner every week, too."

I went into Alyusha's room, and he followed soon after. He found his dictionary and handed it to me.

"Would you happen to have thirty kopecks on you?" I asked casually as I was leaving.

"No, I have only twenty. But I can get another ten kopecks from my father."

"It doesn't matter," I said at once. "I'll take the twenty."

3

I was in rare good spirits as I walked home; in my mind I pictured myself sitting at the table, a boiling samovar nearby, eating fresh bread and herring and drinking tea contentedly while I read a book.

Suddenly Isakov rushed past me. I called to him, and he turned around, delighted to see me.

"I was just looking for you," he said. "I thought you were in the library."

"What is it?"

"Do you have any money on you?"

I started to laugh out loud.

"Tell me quickly, without the frills. I have no time," he shouted, impatiently. "It's terrible. I can't raise a groschen anywhere."

"How much do you need?" I asked weakly.

"Give whatever you have."

"I don't have a single groschen," I told him firmly.

"It's tragic," he shouted, beside himself. "Let's both go and try to borrow money somewhere."

I began to feel uncomfortable about lying. If Isakov was so persistent, there must be a very good reason for it. And how can I go with him to raise money when I have twenty kopecks in my own pocket?

"Actually I have twenty kopecks on me," I said despite myself. "But I need the money badly."

He looked at me in amazement and said, "Don't be a fool."

"What do you need the money for?"

"An entire family is starving—they are, quite plainly, dying. Two of them are sick," he added, almost in tears.

"I'm dying of hunger, too," I said, smiling foolishly, and realized at once that both my smile and my answer were inappropriate. I blushed in confusion, but Isakov didn't notice. He was engrossed in his own thoughts.

"Don't make such a tragedy of it—you won't die," he said, but his mind was clearly elsewhere. Then he continued, "The dramas one sees! Today, while giving my lessons, I was startled by the most terrible shouting and screaming coming from the adjoining room. The mistress of the house was in a rage and cursing her servant. Seeing me, she pointed at the maid and shouted, 'Look at her, the slut! We have a house full of small children, and she allows a little girl whose entire family is sick with typhus to come to see her here! How can I stand it—it's past endurance!'

"I heard her out, went in to finish my lesson, and left. Looking back, I saw a little girl of about eight coming through the gateway. She was a thin child with her hair pulled back in a single braid; she kept her head down and she was barefoot. It was hard for her to walk. 'That must be the girl whom the mistress drove out,' I thought, and followed her. When I got close enough to see her pale, bloodless little face and her eyes, dulled with suffering, I felt that my heart would break.

" 'Where are you going, little girl?' I asked.

" 'Home,' she answered me quietly.

" 'Who is sick in your house?' I asked, curious to know who was in her family.

" 'My mother and my brother.'

" 'And your father, where is he?'

" 'He's dead,' she answered, surprised that I didn't know.

"Then I asked her what she was doing in the big house.

" 'Our aunt works there, and she always gives me bread. But the mistress threw me out,' she said, trying to hold back her tears.

" 'And don't you have bread at home?'

" 'No, none. My mother doesn't eat at all—she can only drink. Sienka, too. And Kalka and Dunka are always crying for bread. The nights are the worst because then Mama's fever goes up and she screams.'

"I walked with her to the other side of town, behind the Church of St. Nicholas, until we came to an old, battered, rotting ruin. As I entered the house, I almost choked from the sour stench. The ceiling, at the point of collapse, was propped up by two posts in the middle of the room; the floor was made of dirt. Two long benches and an overturned barrel, which served as a table, were the only furnishings. There wasn't a single chair in the hovel. The beds were wooden planks that leaned against the wall, which also supported a decrepit kitchen. Aside from an icon on a black board in the corner of the room, there was nothing else.

"An elderly woman with a flushed, feverish face and shriveled skin lay on the bed. Not a sound came from her blackened lips; she only raised and lowered her arm in what appeared to be unconscious movements. Near her lay a boy of about fifteen, writhing fitfully and pleading for water. Two younger children rolled on the dirt under the plank beds. Oh my God, what a sight!"

Isakov was moved to tears, and his deep sympathy affected me, too.

"Where shall we go to buy bread, tea, sugar, and milk with the twenty kopecks?" asked Isakov. "I've brought them my samovar and the little bread I had, but I've been out of tea and sugar myself for a couple of days; my cupboard is empty. I have only one lesson to give today, and I was paid for it two months ago."

Isakov hadn't exaggerated. The picture before my eyes left me in a state of shock.

"Wait here while I run to Rogov's house and bring him back with me," I said.

4

Rogov was in his office leafing through the latest issue of a medical journal. I must have run very fast because when I entered the house, my head began to reel and I saw black spots in front of my eyes; if I hadn't held on to the wall for support, I would have fallen. Alarmed, Rogov quickly came over to me.

"What's wrong with you?" he asked.

I sat down, and when I had recovered a little, I answered, "Nothing is wrong. I'm just tired because I ran too fast, and I have a headache; it's not serious. I'm here for something else."

Then I told him about the unfortunate family. He sat with one arm resting on the table and his head turned in my direction, never removing his intelligent, penetrating gaze from me.

"All right, I'll go with you," he said to me calmly when I finished. And still looking at me intently, he added, "This is probably the first time you've been exposed to a situation like this."

"Yes," I answered.

"I've been practicing medicine for thirty years and see these things every single day," he said sadly. "And do you know where the majority of such cases are? In the poor, crowded Jewish neighborhoods. Have you ever been there?"

"No."

He looked at me, amazed. "Why not? Aren't you interested in them? You're a Jew, aren't you?"

It's very strange. I never concealed my Jewishness, yet whenever someone reminded me of it, I would blush nervously, as if I were embarrassed. Not that I was in any way ashamed of my Jewish roots; I was simply uncomfortable when I was reminded about them. Rogov's question seemed to me a bit irregular, even somewhat tactless, and I answered him coolly. "My being a Jew has nothing to do with it. I make no distinction between Russians and Jews, and I feel no obligation to live among Jews just because I was born one. Everyone has the right . . ."

Suddenly, before I could finish the sentence, I doubled over with a terrible pain in my stomach.

"What is it?" Rogov asked, concerned. He took my pulse and examined my eyes while I kept apologizing, like a guilty schoolboy. It was a difficult and unpleasant situation for me.

Shrugging his shoulders, he said earnestly, "The devil only knows what it is. You're sick, too; you can't continue to live the way you do."

I became more and more anxious; any minute now Rogov would bring up the embarrassing subject of my not eating. I felt like burying myself alive.

"Andrei Stepanovitch," I said, heavy-hearted, "let's leave the subject. I assure you that I'm perfectly fine. But we'll talk about that another time. Now, come with me to the sick family."

Without saying another word, he put on his hat, took his thick walking stick, and we went out. Contrary to his usual custom, and for my sake no doubt, he hailed a coach. To my relief he was silent during the entire ride. The relentless pounding of the coach over the pavement jogged my stomach and made the pain even worse; it would have been difficult for me to talk.

We arrived at the hovel. Rogov went in, greeted Isakov, and silently examined the sick members of the family; then he interrogated the little girl. We learned from her that her mother used to wash laundry in people's homes, that this was the fifth day that she was unconscious, that she had been sick for a long time but continued to work, that her brother had been lying ill for three days, and that no one came to see them because everyone had moved out of this area; not long ago the entire street was burned to the ground.

"Well, we must take the sick ones to the hospital. I'll take care of that immediately. But what about the little ones," he said, pointing to the children who were huddled together in the corner and looking at us transfixed, with a fear that was almost palpable.

"Don't be concerned about the children. We'll arrange for them to be cared for," said Isakov at once.

"Will you find a place for them?" asked Rogov, curious.

"Don't worry, we'll take care of everything," answered Isakov, even more quickly than before.

When Rogov left, we began to think about what to do with the children.

"One of us will have to stay with them," I proposed.

"No, we can't leave them here," Isakov protested. "We have to get them out of here. I would take them to my house, but I can't possibly take care of them."

A happy thought crossed my mind. "Let's take them to Anushka."

"You're right—the best thing will be to give them to Anushka," said Isakov, also pleased. "But we must ask her first; she lives with her parents. You go to her house and I'll wait here."

5

Anushka Pavlov, the daughter of a retired functionary, a drunkard, was a former student of Isakov's and now belonged to our circle. A thin, wide-eyed, nervous girl with a limitless capacity for sympathy and goodness, she was studying to become a village teacher.

I found Anushka alone in the house, busy sewing. She greeted me with a childishly beaming smile.

"I was just at your house looking for you. I wanted to borrow the newest journal. They told me at the library that you borrowed it."

"Yes, I have it at home. I'll bring it to you tomorrow," I told her. "But now I have important business to discuss with you."

I told her about the sick family. Anushka listened attentively, and her face reflected both fear and pain.

"And the children? How can they remain there?" she cried out, looking at me with tear-filled eyes. "Why didn't you bring them to me?" she added reprovingly.

"We felt we had to ask you first because you live with your parents," I answered.

"You're right, I didn't think," said Anushka sadly, with an expression of suffering on her face. "You know what? We'll take them to Isakov, and I'll take care of them there. I'll bring them everything they need from here."

And she quickly went to the cupboard and took out rolls, tea, sugar, and preserves. "Tie everything up in this cloth," said Anushka hurriedly and went into another room.

I felt so hungry while tying up the provisions that without even being aware of it, I broke off a piece of the roll. But just as I was about to take a bite, the thought hit me that the bread would be stolen from hungry children, and I quickly put it back. Meanwhile Anushka came back with a pillow, linens, and clothes.

"You're bringing all of this to Isakov?" I asked, amazed.

"Quiet!" she whispered nervously. "My mother is at home, and if she hears us, there'll be no end of questions."

In the past if I happened to be hungry while visiting Anushka I never found it embarrassing to ask her for something to eat. But this time I simply couldn't bring myself to tell her that I was hungry. Several times I almost said to her, "Give me some food, too, while you're at it," but the words always got stuck in my throat. It would have looked as if I had come to her for my own needs, too, and not only to help the hungry children. No, I couldn't ask that of her, not even Anushka. And, as luck would have it, she never offered me anything to eat.

We went out. Anushka walked quickly and I, carrying the packages, could hardly keep up with her. When we got to the end of the street, I was so out of breath that I had to stop; I felt dizzy and my heart was racing.

"What's wrong with you?" asked Anushka.

"Nothing. I have a headache," I answered and started walking again.

"Poor thing," said Anushka, almost casually, adding, "will we be taking the children to Isakov right away?"

"No," I answered weakly, "I have to go home. I can hardly stand on my feet."

"What is it?" Anushka asked with real concern this time, as she looked at my face. "Are you sick?"

"Nonsense! I'm perfectly all right. Come, let's walk faster," I shot back, not wanting to frighten her.

By the time we got there, the sick people had already been taken to the hospital. Anushka and Isakov took care of the children and I went home.

6

It was about nine in the evening. I walked slowly, feeling completely exhausted. All I could think of was getting home and lying down.

"Wait!" someone called and I felt a tap on my shoulder from behind.

I looked around and saw Melchin, dressed in new clothes and looking quite dazzling.

"Good evening," he shouted, grabbing my hand. "I haven't seen you for ages, you devil."

"You're quite the dandy! What happened? Did you strike it rich?" I asked, amazed.

"I have *indeed* become rich, my brother," he said, delighted. "I earn forty rubles by teaching students privately and I'm provided with my dinners, too. And what meals! Each one three courses."

I began to smolder with indignation and said dryly, "Good."

"How about coming to my place tomorrow, pal?"

"The devil will come to you," I answered angrily, and turned to go.

"Wait!" he said, pulling on my sleeve. "I want to get the newest issue of the journal from you. They told me that you have it."

"I do, but I won't give it to you."

"Don't be ridiculous!" he said calmly. "I'll come to your house tomorrow for the journal."

I was getting more and more angry.

"I seem to remember that before you got rich, Isakov fed you for a month or two, isn't that right?" I asked him, controlling my anger.

"And so?"

"It would only be fair if you would share two or three of your private lessons with him."

"I had no idea that he has no pupils. If he had come and told me, I would probably have given him some."

"Probably?" I repeated and wanted to say other insulting things, but I couldn't get the words out. Something made me choke up. I turned to leave.

"Moralist!" Melchin shouted at me. "Let's shake hands before we part. Why don't you give some of your pupils to Isakov? Well, aren't you going to give me your hand—the deuce take it. I don't even want to know you. But for all that I'll take the journal from you."

The conversation with Melchin made me feel even worse, and I could barely drag myself home. It was an effort to undress, and I fell into bed. But I couldn't sleep; I just lay motionless, without thinking, feeling the pain in my chest and listening to the blood coursing through my veins and the roaring in my head. Suddenly I thought I saw a huge spider coming from the balcony straight toward me; trembling, I covered my face with my hands. With my eyes still covered I thought I detected someone standing next to the window, but when I looked, I saw nothing at all. But to put my mind to rest I had to pull myself out of bed and light a match to make sure no one was there. When I lay down again, something made me think about my dead mother; this filled me with grief and I began to cry. I let the tears stream down my cheeks freely until I felt a gentle weakness overcome my body and the heaviness flow out of my heart. Soon I was sobbing out loud and, worried that the landlady would hear me and come in and make a fuss, I limped out of bed weakly, drank some water, and rinsed my neck and forehead. Once in bed again I was able to rest more quietly, thinking of nothing and feeling nothing; I even fell asleep briefly. But I soon woke up.

As I lay awake, the most extraordinarily vivid scenes of my childhood passed before my eyes. There was so much warmth and love in those scenes of the family circle, the heder, and the synagogue that all my present acquaintances and friends—Isakov, Anushka, and Rogov—seemed strangers in comparison; they were as remote and superfluous to me as I was to them. The painful realization that I was alone and homeless deadened my moral sensibility, and pity for the sick washerwoman and her hungry children soon turned to self-pity. I suffered from hunger pangs in my stomach, but my soul was starved, too, and aching for love and affection, for the tenderness of home. I wept, not knowing whether the physical or the spiritual hunger was causing me more pain. Finally, at dawn, I fell into a deep sleep.

7

I woke up late. My head and all my limbs felt very heavy, and I lay for a while without moving, waiting for the clock to strike. It struck eleven.

I knew that I was in a critical state, but somehow it didn't matter. I didn't even think about trying to raise money; it seemed petty and insignificant to me.

I got washed and dressed and then went into the landlady's apartment. Only Peklusha was there.

"The samovar is boiling," she said as soon as she saw me.

"I won't drink any tea, darling," I said to her quietly and weakly. "And we won't have a lesson today either."

She looked at me bewildered. She wanted to ask me something, but I quickly returned to my room. I took a book and began to leaf through it; soon, however, I put it down.

"I have to go somewhere, to visit the sick washerwoman, to Isakov, yes, it's very important."

I left my room but didn't go to the sick woman. I was exhausted and had to rest. I'll go to the sick woman later; now I'll stop off at the library.

The library reading room was a welcoming home for our circle, and we went there not so much to read as to rest. The silence of the large, high-ceilinged, book-lined room, and the friendly smile of the old librarian had an extraordinarily soothing effect on us.

There was no one in the reading room. I sat down near the window and took a newspaper, read the headlines mechanically, put the paper down, picked up another one and then another one but it was no use—I couldn't concentrate. I tried reading a journal, but nothing registered; when I tried again, the letters jumped around in front of my eyes and my heart pounded against my breastbone. I put the journal on the table and stared out the window aimlessly, overcome by a terrible sadness; I wanted to cry.

I sat like that for a long time; the gnawing pains in my stomach were getting worse, and I could feel spasms coming up and constricting my throat. I was restless; I couldn't find a comfortable position. All I could think of was that I had to eat, to eat, to eat—if only to chew on a piece of moldy bread, just to have something in my mouth.

I tore off some leaves from the flowers that were standing on the windowsill and began to chew them; but they were bitter and I quickly spat them out. I tried to drink a glass of water, but it made me feel nauseated. I sat down, bent over double, bit my lips until they bled, and closed my eyes. The pain subsided a bit.

The clock struck.

"I'll eat dinner with Rogov," I decided without thinking, and got up. But at that moment Isakov came in.

"I'm coming from the hospital. The woman is better, thank God," he informed me. "Anushka is with the children. She wanted to bring them to her house, but her mother wouldn't permit it."

"I'm starving," I whispered.

"So am I," he retorted, laughing. "I didn't even have tea today. But it's not important. We really have to talk about Laskin."

Laskin was our joint pupil, an unfortunate creature with a great thirst for knowledge and very limited ability. It was torture for us to teach him.

"Let him become a bookbinder, a locksmith, a tailor—anything, as long as it doesn't involve higher education. It makes me miserable just to look at his unhappy and dejected face," I told him.

"He'll never consent to learning a trade."

"Then you prepare him for the Gymnasium," I replied impatiently.

Isakov laughed. "It's impossible to prepare him for the Gymnasium. Algebra will kill him one day—it will break his heart. Oh, by the way," he said, suddenly remembering, "you have a seven-ruble lesson, provided by—would you believe it—Melchin himself. He came over especially to tell me about it. He was dressed like a fop and told me that he earns a million rubles from his lessons and that he is provided with lunches that are worth ten thousand rubles."

"He's out of his mind," I said, and told Isakov about my experience with Melchin yesterday.

"Nevertheless," he said, smiling amiably, "you should take the lesson."

"Why are you giving it away? He proposed the lesson to you."

"I already have one, and you have none. Besides, I have no time. I'd love to parcel out my market women's children to someone, too. I've been paid two months in advance in any case," he added, laughing.

"I won't accept any private lessons from Melchin; I'd be in his debt forever," I answered irritably and began to cry. I was so weak that the slightest annoyance brought tears to my eyes.

Isakov started to tell me something about Anushka, and sensing my preoccupation, he said in a puzzled tone, "You're not listening to what I'm saying."

"I'm starving," I told him, barely able to pronounce the words.

"You don't look good," he concurred without visible emotion. And to comfort me, he added, "Just wait until I get some money—then we'll really celebrate."

Strange—Isakov was a sensitive person, always responsive to the problems of others. Yet he didn't even notice that I, his most intimate friend, was dying of hunger. I don't think I remained in the library much longer, though I have no idea when I left or what I did afterward—it's all tangled and confused in my mind. All I know was that I felt my strength ebbing.

8

I woke up to the most wonderful singing, feeling well and at peace once again. It seemed perfectly natural for me to be lying with my eyes closed and my head resting on a soft cushion, though I hadn't slept on a pillow for months. When I finally opened my eyes, everything was unfamiliar. It was nighttime and a light glimmered through the half-open door. At first I didn't recognize the lovely song that had awakened me—I only knew that I was unusually moved by the soft feminine voice which came from the other side of the wall, so sad yet so gentle and caressing. Then I remembered: it was the prayer beginning, "God of Abraham, Isaac and Jacob" which women sang at the close of the Sabbath. And the voice was that of my aunt Basha. The tenderness and warmth of her voice comforted me and made me feel content, so much so that I never even thought of asking how I got there.

"Aunt."

"I'm coming," she quickly replied and entered the room holding a lamp.

"Oh, Yossele—you gave us such a scare," said the elderly woman gently, her eyes sparkling with goodness and her face glowing with a loving smile.

"What happened? I don't know anything," I said, laughing as if it were a joke.

"What happened was that you came into my house, muttering something I couldn't understand. I thought that you stopped by because you happened to be in the neighborhood; but all at once you turned white and fainted. It took the doctor a full hour to revive you. Then you fell asleep."

"I don't remember a thing."

Shouts of "He's alive! He's come out of it!" could be heard from the next room, and then Anushka, Alyusha, Rogov, and another one of our group, a student at the seminar, appeared at the door. I was not prepared for these unexpected guests, and seeing them upset me and spoiled the peaceful and quiet mood I had enjoyed. A sense of anxiety overcame me and I felt upset and uncomfortable at my friends' seeing me here. I thought of my aunt's chanting and understood why she sang so quietly; the idea that my friends heard her embarrassed me. I wanted to leave, and the sooner the better. Sitting up in bed, I asked, "How is it you're here?"

"His father took care of you," said my aunt, pointing to Rogov. Her intonation and bad Russian accent humiliated me.

"You can't imagine what went on here, God help us," said Alyusha. "My father was called in and told us the whole story. We've been sitting here all day. Your aunt served us tea and all kinds of delicious Jewish dishes."

"I served them! They wouldn't even eat a small piece of fish!" complained my aunt and left the room.

"What a darling your aunt is! She's a jewel!" Anushka spoke up, enchanted. "I've simply fallen in love with her during the past few hours."

"My father knows her well," said Alyusha. "He told me that she is an interesting and intelligent woman. Every once in a while he spends an entire evening with her; he calls her 'sweetheart.' "

All my anger and vexation melted away and I felt unusually exhilarated. Turning to the door, I called out cheerfully and without any embarrassment, "Aunt, why do you let me starve? Won't you give me some of your gefilte fish?"

"I'm coming with some for you right now," she replied at once.

1892 (Translated by Golda Werman)

MENDL TURK

▼

1

In the summer and fall of 1877, at the height of the Russo-Turkish War, I was tutoring in one of the outlying Lithuanian towns where I lived a very lonely existence. One day, on my way home for lunch, I saw a sight that made me stop in my tracks. A young man whom I didn't know, wearing a skullcap but no jacket, had pushed his head through the open window of my room and, with both hands on my table for support, was reading the Russian newspaper that I had left there. When I approached him, he raised his head in alarm, quickly pulled his trembling upper body out of the window, and remained standing, confused and very embarrassed.

"Oh, please don't get the wrong idea," he stammered with a guilty half-smile on his lips. "I didn't touch a thing in your house, God forbid. I was just passing by when I noticed the newspaper on your table and a headline caught my eye. . . . I couldn't restrain myself from reading it."

I calmed him down and handed him the paper.

"Thank you! Thank you very much!" he said to me, warmly but

still not entirely at ease. "Something caught my interest, something important."

"What was it that was so important?"

"What do you think? What is it that newspapers write about these days? Only war and politics."

"You're interested in politics?"

He gave me a penetrating look and then lowered his eyes; a little incoherent at first, he soon spoke up clearly, "What do you mean am I interested in politics? And who isn't interested in politics? In normal times, I agree, it's not worth spending time on. But it's different in wartime. Now politics is all-important!"

The young man roused my curiosity, so I invited him into my room.

"I would come with the greatest pleasure, but I have no time now," he answered me. "The boys are about to return from supper."

Now I realized who he was. My window overlooked a courtyard that resounded all day with the clamor of children's voices from the heder, which was located in an old house. I often saw emaciated little boys, dressed in rags, scampering across the yard like frightened mice—but I had never seen their teacher. I don't know why, but I imagined him to be an old man with an angry face. The teacher who stood in front of me was a young man of twenty-eight with delicate features and a short black beard. The deep, thoughtful look of his large, black eyes gave his face an unusually serious expression. His velvet skullcap, the long, curled earlocks, and his short beard framed his face beautifully.

He thought for a while, and then he said, "But if you're not busy in the evening I'd be happy to come then. It's been a long time since I've had the chance to speak to someone like you. Tell me, do you read the newspaper each day?"

"Yes, every day."

The teacher looked at me enviously.

"Oh, I can understand that," he said with a sigh. "That kind of reading makes sense; it has meaning."

"And you, what do you read?"

"What do I read? I catch things in the wind; I don't read. I get the newspaper *Halevanon* maybe twice a month[1]; the rest of the time I have to depend on the 'Telegrams' which are pasted on the walls in the market—and on what people tell me, always complete with their own opinions, of course, which are never based on facts."

I invited him to come that evening.

2

The teacher came as soon as heder was over. This time he wore a long frock coat and a velvet cap.

"Good evening," he said, remaining standing in the middle of the room without attempting to shake my hand. I motioned to him to sit down and as he did he carefully surveyed the room and saw at a glance that none of the books were traditional Jewish sacred texts.

"Are they all goyish books?" he asked, amazed.

"Most of them are Russian or German."

"Really?" he began hesitatingly. "What are they about? Law and grammar?"

The question didn't surprise me at all; I explained to my guest that grammars and legal texts were not the only books written in Russian; there were all kinds—stories, poems, science, and philosophy—in Russian and in other languages, too."

"You don't say! Philosophy? Are there really Russian books on philosophy?" he asked, astounded, and looked at the bookcase more attentively this time.

But a moment later he had regained his composure and turned to me with a deprecating smile. "Well, any passages of deep wisdom or of penetrating philosophic inquiry in these volumes must come from the Talmud or from Rambam. Politics is different," he continued, changing his tone of voice. "Politics is a special science, dealing with all the countries in the world; it has its own rules. Take Bismarck, for example. What a mind! A brilliant mind! Bikensfeld[2] is an even greater genius—his thinking is deeper, more penetrating. But that's to be expected—he's a Jew."

For a while he sat in silence, looking thoughtfully at the glass of tea which I had placed before him without his noticing.

"Listen," he said suddenly and emphatically, moving the glass of tea away as if he needed a clear space in front of him. "I want to discuss the war with you, to discuss it properly."

He pushed himself farther back in his chair, leaned over the table and began slowly and deliberately, "Everything in the world has its foundation, its substance and its essence. In order to understand anything properly one must uncover its essence. Obviously, this war has its essence, too, its crux, around which everything revolves. Now please tell me what the war is all about, what is its substance, its essence—I'm listening with rapt attention."

But seeing that I was about to answer, he quickly raised both hands in my direction, gesturing me not to talk yet.

"Wait, just wait a minute, please!" he begged. "I said the 'essence,' but we must define our terms. We must be clear about what that essence is. What is the basic cause of the present war? How did it start and what propels it on? What are the assumptions of those who are responsible for seeing it continue? And now we come to the real point: pick up a newspaper, any paper at all, and read it. You'll soon discover that the same word—'Slav'—is repeated over and over again. This view claims that the Russians are the righteous redeemers who are sacrificing their lives and shedding their blood to free their brothers, the Slavs, from the Turkish yoke. This is all very good, very fine! You couldn't ask for better? But then there is also the other side, presenting the more daring point of view: the Russians, say the proponents of this side, care as much for the Slavs as they do for yesterday's snow. So what is the fighting all about? It's very simple; the Russians want to capture Turkey's two seas, the Bosphorus and the Dardanelles. The Slavs only serve as their excuse. And that's not all; there's a third side which states that the war has nothing to do with either Russia *or* Turkey. England is the culprit. According to this view, she leads them both by the nose, inciting one side against the other, urging them to tear each other apart like fighting cocks. And then, when both sides are exhausted, England will step in and finish them off. Now I ask you, which view is correct? Obviously, each person must keep a clear head on his shoulders and decide for himself. But in order to find the correct path it is essential to look at the world objectively and to try to understand it. And this brings me to my request."

"Which is?"

"Very simple: give me the whole political story of everything that took place between the Russians and the Turks from the very beginning."

"From the beginning" was no simple matter, especially since my guest didn't even know that Russia and Turkey had been at war before. Nonetheless, I gave him a brief survey of the history and politics of the region, trying to draw a clear picture of the kind of country Turkey was and how her interests clashed with those of Russia. My guest was fascinated, leaning forward as he listened and looking up at me from time to time with a serious expression. When I finished, he remained in the same position, apparently still deeply absorbed in what I had told him.

"I must tell you that you've made me see things I never knew

existed before," he stated in a quiet voice, but with genuine enthusiasm. "Now the world is open before me and I can see a road, a
path—new ideas come to me, new hypotheses."

And then he lapsed into complete silence. He dipped a cube of
sugar into his cooled tea, recited a blessing and began to drink.
When he finished, he thanked me and picked up the discussion
from where he had left off.

"I gather from your analysis that you also tend toward the view
that the Russians care about the Slavs, the Bulgarians and the
Serbians. To tell the truth, I can't see it that way. To me it's sheer
madness to think of Mother Russia as being altruistic."

Seeing that I was about to answer him, he quickly added, "But
let's assume for argument's sake that you're right—it isn't the essence
of the matter. I gather from your discussion that you believe that
Russia is unconquerable. This is precisely the point that I don't
understand. Do you really think that Russia will be victorious?"

"I am certain of it."

"Now hear me out," said the teacher with self-assurance. "It goes
without saying that you know much, much more about the facts of
the war and its politics than I do. And you may call me a fool and
say that I'm arrogant, but I assure you that the Turks will win! To
me it's as clear as day. Wait a week, just one week, and you'll see for
yourself that I'm right."

And as if he were afraid that I might try to prove him wrong, he
quickly buttoned his coat, said good-bye, and left. At the door, he
kept droning under his breath, scornfully, "Beh! Mother Russia will
overcome! And whom? The Turks!"

3

In the morning as I was drinking my tea, the landlord, an elderly
Jew, stopped by. He was one of those unfortunate men who were
completely under their wives' thumbs. Very quiet and depressed, he
was like a stranger in his own home, where his much younger,
energetic third wife ruled the roost. There were no children.
Whenever his wife left the house, she locked up all the cupboards
and took the keys with her, afraid that the maid would steal; often
she would forget to leave her husband the few cubes of sugar he
needed for his tea, or the two kopecks for his snuff, without which
he felt like a "goose going to the slaughter." She was barely civil to

him and would sometimes scold him, as if he were one of the servants. The only time she showed him any respect was on the Sabbath and on the holidays when she needed him to recite the blessing over the wine or to usher out the Sabbath for her.

All day long the old man either wandered around the house or "sat" in the study house. At first he was afraid to look at me and would quickly get out of my way whenever we happened to meet. But he gradually got used to seeing me around and even began to visit me in my room to drink an occasional glass of tea or borrow a few kopecks for snuff. He was always diplomatic about hiding the purpose of these visits; before asking for the loan he would invent some question or other regarding the rent, a matter of only theoretical interest to him, since his wife handled all the money matters.

This time, too, he came under a pretext: he said he was looking for the copper ladle. I knew very well that the ladle was lying in its accustomed place near the well and that he had come only so that I would offer him a glass of tea. However, since a face-saving measure of this sort was essential, I shrugged my shoulders and told him that I had no idea where the ladle was, but would he do me the honor of joining me in a glass of tea?

"Eh? What?" the old man asked, as if he hadn't heard what I said.

"I asked if you wouldn't, just this once, have a glass of tea with me in my room?"

"Tea?" The old man looked at me as if this invitation came as a great surprise to him, even though I was sitting right next to the samovar. "No, thank you, not for me. I just had some," he declared emphatically.

That was the first part of the ritual. Now it was my task to urge him, to plead with him.

"I can never get you to drink a glass of tea," I said in a tone of annoyance. "What's wrong? Are you afraid that my house isn't kosher?"

"How can you say such a thing? Of course, you're a God-fearing man," he shot back, flushed. "What do you mean not kosher? How can you even think such a thing? I simply don't want tea because I've just had some. But if it's so important to you, pour me a glass; I'll force myself to drink."

And, just as prescribed by the ritual, the old man was soon sitting at the table.

"Tell me, Reb Ber," I asked him, "what kind of person is the young man who teaches in the courtyard?"

"Who? Mendl Turk?" My guest put down his glass. "What do you mean by 'what kind of person'? A human being, a young man, a religious person, a Hasid, a scholar, a very learned and promising scholar, if you must know."

"What was that you called him—Turk? What kind of a family name is that?"

"It's not a family name at all," said the old man, smiling. "They nicknamed him Turk in the synagogue, for some reason, so that's what I call him."

"Why did they give him that nickname?"

"Why? That's a good question. They gave it to him, that's all. You read the paper, so you know that we're at war with the Turks. And since Mendl sides with the Turks, they call him Turk. If he'd sided with the Russians, they would have called him Russky. It's as simple as that."

The old man looked at me with a satisfied expression and returned to his tea. When I poured him a second glass, he pushed it a bit to the side and continued the conversation. "Don't talk to me about Mendl! He's lost his head, along with everyone else in town! All they do is talk and talk. Actually, they don't talk—they scream, they argue, they fight, they pull down the walls. It's a regular war. And what is the fight about? About the Turks and the Russians."

"Tell me—where do these heated discussions and arguments take place?" I asked.

The old man looked at me, unbelieving. "What do you mean, where? Where do you think they argue? In the synagogue, of course. Where else? Oh, I forgot. You're a modern person and don't go to the synagogue on Sabbath. If you did, you'd see for yourself what amazing things go on there! Everyone, and I mean each and every one, young and old alike, is so hot under the collar about this that as soon as the 'Turks' and the 'Russians' get together they begin to fight; it's a real war, it's Gog and Magog."[3]

The old man spoke with such passion about the battle between the Jewish Turks and the Jewish Russians that I was curious to know which side he was on.

"And you, Reb Ber, where do you stand—with the Turks or with the Russians?"

"I?" he asked in a startled voice. "Ha, ha! Do you really think that I'd let myself get involved in all this? Do I look like a fool to you? No, I only listen while they talk—it goes in one ear and out the other."

"But, Reb Ber, you haven't told me everything. Tell the truth," I insisted, knowing that he really wanted to express his opinion but was too timid.

The old man suddenly became very serious, very grave indeed, and leaning toward me, he began to whisper, as if he were sharing a secret with me, "Ishmael is a cutthroat, but he's better than Esau! Listen to me! If Ishmael should win, then the Messiah will have to come."

"Good God, Reb Ber," I interrupted. "What does Ishmael's victory have to do with the Messiah?"

"Don't press me," he blurted out. "I've heard them talking—Jews talk. Do I know what they're saying? People talk, that's all. I don't mean you or me."

Then he began to babble something incomprehensible. I didn't interrupt him, and little by little he calmed down.

"Last evening Mendl Turk visited me," I told the old man.

"Mendl? At your house?"—as if asking what a hasidic teacher could possibly want with me. But then he had a sudden insight.

"I've got it! I understand," he said resuming his secretive tone and twisting his long, dry, outstretched finger in the air. "You know what I think? It wasn't you he wanted; he wanted your newspaper. Yes, of course! Believe me, I know him well," he shouted, with rising excitement. "Isn't he a clever one! He doesn't miss a trick, our Mendl Turk!"

"You're right, that's exactly why he came," I said, confirming his hypothesis.

"You see, I'm no fool! It's obvious. Why else would Mendl visit you? To find out what's in the papers! So he must gather his politics the same way, in bits and pieces—like a chicken, peck, peck, peck, grain by grain until the crop is full and the egg is ready to be laid," he said, sharing a bit of incorrect embryological know-how with me.

"I shouldn't be telling you this," he continued confidentially, "but I have the feeling that since he became interested in politics he doesn't study Torah as fervently as before. He used to spend his nights in the study house and now—now he spends his time looking for newspapers to read. Yes, yes, that's how it is," he said, all excited, even giving me a little push as if to say that he wasn't about to accept any excuses for him. Since I had no intention of defending Mendl against his terrible suspicion, the old man calmed down and took a third glass of tea.

When he finished drinking, he thanked me and rose to go. Suddenly, a big, twinkling smile spread over his face, and with childish innocence and a pitiful look in his eyes, he blurted out, "Eh, eh, I have something to confess: I really wanted a glass of tea. My wife went shopping and forgot to leave me the sugar. . . ."

What a diplomat my old friend is! He's almost a Bismarck, even a Bikensfeld.

4

On the next Sabbath I went to the big synagogue in time for afternoon prayers so that I could see for myself the war of Gog and Magog as played out by the Jewish "Turks" and "Russians." It was dusk. All the contours were blurred, and the shadows of evening playing on the high walls of the synagogue created an eerie picture. The sight of several hundred men waving back and forth as they silently recited the eighteen benedictions made me think of a forest of trees stirring in the wind. And the spell of their muted, mystical chanting brought back memories from my own distant childhood.

I recalled the old synagogue of my youth in the shtetl where I was born and that special time on Sabbath between the afternoon and evening prayers. The old men would walk slowly back and forth in the little synagogue, their hands behind their backs, dreamily humming a tune while they waited for darkness so they could recite the evening prayers. When they got tired of walking, they sat on the benches and, still in a state of reverie, would tell each other stories. Someone would begin with a hasidic legend, another would relate some interesting event in his life—and everything became bewitched and full of mystery in that shadowy twilight hour of early evening. The men listened, spellbound, and remained in their seats long after the stories were finished, so as not to interrupt the magical stillness.

At that hour the world of everyday cares was forgotten—everyone was pensive, lost in his own musing. Someone invariably began to sing a well-known melody, "Bim, bam, bom," and soon everyone would chime in, each adding his own dreamy tune. Then someone would suddenly jump up, as if awakened from a sleep and say pleadingly, "Zerach, begin!"

And Zerach always complied. From his seat, he would quietly begin to hum the traditional Rosh Hashanah and Yom Kippur melodies, and as one congregant after another joined in, the singing became louder and louder. The echoes of the infinitely sad High

Holiday melodies would ring through the little old synagogue for a long time.

The singing continued even after the sky was filled with stars and the synagogue was dark. No one wanted to begin the evening prayers which usher out the Sabbath; no one was in a hurry to go back to the prosaic cares of the everyday world.

It was a golden hour for the children, too, for they were touched by the same special mood that overtook the grown-ups. Some youngsters would stay close to their fathers to listen to the tales the men told. Others formed little circles at various points in the synagogue and told each other ghost stories. The livelier ones found the darkness a good cover for their pranks and games of hide-and-seek; some even threw "bombs" made of twisted towels at the beadle or the congregants. No matter! At this magical hour childish tricks like these went unpunished. "They're only children; let them have fun" was the sentiment. The kind-hearted congregant would further express his warm feelings toward the youngsters by taking a mischievous little boy on his knees, stroking his head as tenderly as if he were his own son and singing all the while. He didn't even look to see who his captive was. The startled child would be silenced by this unexpected benevolence from a stranger. His heart would beat with joy, and he would smile contentedly, grateful for the gentle hand on his head.

I have never forgotten these hours of amity and love.

But in the large synagogue it was not like that. The storms of war had penetrated here and had displaced the dreamy quiet of the Sabbath dusk.

5

When the afternoon prayers were over, the members of the congregation left their seats and began a lively discussion. Everyone talked at once until a loud "Sha! Be quiet!" gradually calmed them down. In the middle of the synagogue a large circle formed around two or three men who were arguing; the others, curious to hear what was being discussed, cupped their hands over their ears while they shoved one another to get closer.

An elderly man of medium height with a broad build, intelligent gray eyes, and a tobacco-stained mustache stood in the center of the circle and spoke with quiet confidence. He gestured with his hand while holding a package of snuff between two fingers.

"Well, well, well—why are you so excited? So we didn't capture Plevne. So what? Show me a war in which there are only victories, where one victory follows on the heels of the other! If we didn't take Plevne this week, we'll get it next week."

"You, Mikhoel, say that the Russians will take Plevne" came the excited shout of a tall man with a blond beard and a red neck. "Are you mad enough to give us a guarantee? How do you figure the Russians will capture Plevne? Did you forget that they've already put half the army behind Plevne? . . ."

"Hold on there," interrupted a thin young man, who stretched his long neck out in the direction of the circle. "Why not put the question another way? You ask how the Russians will capture Plevne. What I ask is, how will the Turks restrain them? You're not taking into consideration what it costs the Turks every time the Russians attack them."

"Tha-at is the poi-oint," responded a young man with a goatee, in a talmudic singsong. "No bullets will reach Plevne. You can shoot where you want, even to the sky, it's all the same. And from Plevne . . ."

"You with the beard, shut up! You've got a lot of chutzpah to enter this argument, you dimwit! I'll give you such a beating that you'll forget you ever heard of Plevne," screamed an older Jew in anger. (He was the young man's father.)

The goateed fellow quickly disappeared.

"Can you beat that? Even he has something to say about Plevne! Another expert heard from," the father exclaimed, unable to calm himself down.

"And you, wise guy, what do you know about Plevne?" burst out the man with the blond beard. "Plevne is impenetrable. It is located in the hollow space inside a huge cliff; this cliff is three versts tall and has straight walls. How do you think it can be breached? How can such a fortress be captured?"

"Of course it will be taken," retorted a fat man with a wide satin sash around his protruding stomach and a face that had wealth written all over it. He pushed his way into the circle and thundered, "You fool! You're talking nonsense—all these stories about cliffs and fortresses. I wouldn't give three kopecks for your Plevne. More people, more talk. Plevne, Shmevne!"

"The kugel at Chaim Isser's must have been really special today to make him so aggressive," chimed in an old Jew with a long gray beard, bright eyes, and an ironic smile. "What does he need politics for? With a shout, and a kick of his boot, he topples nine in one blow."

"And you, where do you stand? Do you also believe that Plevne won't be captured?" asked Chaim Isser in a loud but less belligerent voice.

"My opinion is that to talk about the war you have to know what it says in the paper. Take a lesson from Mendl. Who is better informed about politics than Mendl? And what's he doing? Sitting on the side and reciting Psalms," he ended in a mildly ironic tone.

Mendl! I remembered him now and looked for him. He was sitting in the back of the synagogue huddled over a Book of Psalms, which he was reading with amazing speed. At first I thought that he was indifferent to what was going on in the synagogue. But on closer view, I realized that from his quiet corner he could hear and see everything, like a hunter.

Mikhoel, the man with the mustache who had spoken up at the beginning, was standing in the middle of the circle and talking loudly in a tone of bitter reproof.

"It's just as the Bible says: 'Eyes they have, but they cannot see; ears they have, but they cannot hear.'[4] So why won't you see? Why won't you realize that the Turks are finished? You're always arguing 'Plevne.' Don't you understand that Plevne will be captured in the end, if not by arms then by starvation? Just open your eyes—in the four or five months since the Russians crossed the Don they've captured several fortresses, taken tens of thousands of Turks captive, and crossed halfway into Turkey. Doesn't that impress you? What kind of signs and wonders do you need? A month ago you were screaming 'Suleiman Pasha, the great hero Suleiman Pasha'! Then it turned out that the hero was not Suleiman Pasha at all—it was Hurko.[5] And now you shout 'Plevne,' 'Osman Pasha.' Tell me, what will you shout about when the Russians take Plevne?"

"Then there'll be no need to shout. Now I'm screaming so that everyone will know what a liar you are!" thundered the man with the blond beard. Then he quickly went over to where Mendl was sitting and said to him reprovingly, "Mendl, honestly, it's not right! You're making a fool of yourself sitting on the side and reciting Psalms like an old lady! Just listen to him. He has the nerve to peddle lies in a holy place!"

"Mendl, Mendl, enough of your Psalms. Come, join us," came the cries from all sides.

It was obvious that Mendl had no great desire to get involved in the debate, but he put away his Psalms nonetheless and got up to join them, first motioning to a boy to come over to him.

"Velvl, run to the marketplace and see if a new notice has been posted."

The boy ran out and Mendl walked slowly over to the circle, turned to Mikhoel and said, smiling, "I hear that you turn the world around, that you uproot mountains and demolish countries. You ground the poor Turks to dust in no time and spread their ashes over all the seven seas."

"And you, Miracle Worker, have you come to gather the dust and to mold a golem out of it?" Mikhoel retorted.

Then, in a more serious tone, he asked, "Do you honestly believe that the Turks aren't finished?"

"For heaven's sake, where did you get that idea?" interrupted Mendl, angry. "You argue that Plevne is besieged. But a person has to be blind not to see that it's not Plevne but the Russian army that's under siege. Do you all hear that?" He was shouting at the crowd which had formed a circle around them both and was listening to every word. "Do you want to hear how the war is really going? If you do, I'll make it all as clear as day. The whole Russian army and all its generals are now in Turkey between the Don and Plevne. Osman Pasha is waiting in Plevne with a division of one hundred thousand soldiers and is making it impossible for the Russians to advance. At the left is Suleiman Pasha . . ."

"Who was beaten by Hurko," said someone.

"Shsh, be quiet!" said Mikhoel.

"As I was saying, Suleiman Pasha has a strong army. To the right is Mohammed Ali with an even larger army. Now listen—and use your brains. The Russian army is besieged on three sides; they can't go forward and they don't want to retreat. The summer is over and the rains will soon begin. They're tired, hungry, and far from home. How do you think it will end?"

He looked at the audience thoughtfully and soon continued confidently, "One of two things will happen. Either a fresh Turkish division will encircle the Russians, capture the Don, and take the entire army and its generals captive, or Osman Pasha will join Suleiman Pasha and Mohammed Ali and strike the Russian army from all three sides and drive it out of Turkey."

Mendl's convincing argument and the clear picture he drew of the possibilities greatly impressed the audience, which now had some sarcastic comments to make against Mikhoel. He listened calmly and attentively, never taking his eyes off Mendl.

"Have you finished?" he asked.

"Finished," the other answered curtly.

"It's a pity, a real pity, that you're done so soon," said Mikhoel, with a look of disappointment on his face.

He took the snuffbox from the pulpit, tapped it with two fingers, opened it and took a large whiff. Then he closed the case and put it back, slowly and deliberately.

"Yes, it really is a pity that you finished so quickly. You could have gone much further. You drove the Russians out of Turkey— that alone is worth something. But why did you stop there? Why didn't you also bring the Turks into Russia and have them capture a few cities such as St. Petersburg or Moscow? It wouldn't have been difficult to do that—here in the synagogue," he ended, laughing.

"The Turks took a vow never to tread on Russian soil," one of the synagogue wits called out.

"My friend," replied Mendl calmly, but looking at Mikhoel sternly, "you know very well that the Turks are primitive and cruel. If they were merciful people, they would be freeing nations from the yokes of their oppressors. Don't worry, there'd be plenty of candidates— Poland, would be one, for example. You think the Poles suffer less from their oppressors than the Bulgarians? But what's to be done with Ishmael, the wild man, who feels no mercy for anyone?"

"Do you mean to say you don't believe the Russians will free the Bulgarians from the Turks?" asked Chaim Isser.

"What do you mean, I don't believe?" asked Mendl, with a look of surprise on his face. "What do you think I am—an apostate, God forbid? How can you even suggest that I don't believe that the Russians only mean to free the nation? Who in the entire world is better cast in the role of a liberator than Russia-the-thief?"

The last was met with a resounding laughter.

"Well said!"

"On the mark!"

"Russia the Messiah!"

"Sha, I've heard these wisecracks," Mikhoel called out irritably. "Then tell me one thing—why did Russia start the war?"

"If you're really interested, I'll tell you," answered Mendl. The Russians have always been enemies of the Turks. This is not the first war they've fought, and in the course of many battles through the years the Russians have captured a lot of Turkish territory. Russia's ultimate aim is Constantinople. In short, Russia wants to free Turkey and annex the greater part to herself."

Mendl was repeating everything almost word for word from my lesson on the military history of Russia and Turkey.

Mikhoel listened impatiently to what Mendl had to say. Finally, unable to restrain himself any longer, he screamed out, "Fool! Ass! You talk such nonsense that I get sick listening to it."

Then he turned to the audience and said, "Listen, Jews! Russia covers an area of ten thousand versts, which is one-sixth of the world's surface; its riches are greater than those of any other nation. Now, do you think that the Russians would spill rivers of blood just for a little corner of the Turkish desert?"

"Reb Gershon," said Mendl, turning suddenly to an obviously wealthy, older member of the congregation, "they say that you're worth thirty thousand rubles. Is that correct?"

Reb Gershon was a bit confused by this unexpected question about such a delicate issue, but at the same time he was pleased to have his reputation as a rich man made public. It goes without saying that Mendl didn't ask the question simply to satisfy his curiosity; he was leading up to something in his argument with Mikhoel. He slowly stroked his beard and continued with a coy smile on his face, "Thirty thousand rubles of your own, you say? Now let's figure that I have—it doesn't matter what I have. You don't stop doing business, do you? You continue going to your store every day, and you do other business, too. I hear that you're involved in a big venture to build meat markets right now. So, clearly, you don't think you have enough money—you want more."

"Oh, and do I ever want more!" chuckled Gershon, good-naturedly.

"Do you hear what he said, Mikhoel? He said, 'I don't have enough; I want more.' Do you know the meaning of 'more'? 'More' means 'everything.' You talk about a sixth of the world, but why not the whole world? Haven't there been seven kingdoms in the world since the time of Nimrod? And not one of them—not Nimrod, not Sennacherib, not Nebuchadnezzar, not Alexander of Macedon were satisfied with their share. Believe me, the Russians aren't satisfied with their sixth of the world either. And it's not the Turkish deserts they're after; they want the Turkish seas—the Bosphorus and the Dardanelles."

"What you're saying is that the entire war is being fought only for plunder and that the Turks are pure and innocent," shouted a tall, thin man with an ascetic face and eyes alive with anger. "What's the real story? Are you fooling yourself, or do you take us all for idiots?

Don't we know what those cruel Turks, the murderers—may their names be blotted out—are doing to the Bulgarians? They destroy whole cities, burn villages, murder people by the thousands—it makes your hair stand on end and your blood turn to ice to hear about their brutality. And you take their side and turn them all into innocent sheep. You deserve to be torn limb from limb!"

"Only a thief and a murderer could take the side of the Turks," repeated an intense young man. And jumping on a bench he began an emotional speech, which could be heard throughout the synagogue. "Listen, friends! As you see me stand here, as it is Sabbath today throughout the world, I swear to you that when the call is made for new recruits I'll be the first to enlist! I'll leave my wife and children and go to war. And if I'm killed, it will be a martyr's death; I will die for God's honor."

The overwrought speech aroused everyone. It was as if a dam had burst. There was a loud outcry in the synagogue. Everyone was screaming. The "Russians" attacked the "Turks" with the worst kinds of recriminations and invectives. The "Turks" came back at the Russians with accusations of their own. Mendl tried to take the floor, but they wouldn't let him.

Night had fallen; the synagogue was dark. The pale moonlight, which shone through the dusty windows, lent a melancholy glow to the strange scene of all these people arguing in the synagogue. The beadle, a small dark Jew, went from one congregant to the other, pleading with them over and over again to go to their seats. "It's time for evening prayers!"

But no one paid any attention to him. Who could think of the evening service at a time like this? And then, suddenly, the door flew open and in flew Velvl from the marketplace, where he had been reading the new notices for Mendl.

"There's a notice, a notice," he screamed breathlessly.

In an instant the synagogue was totally silent; everyone turned to the boy.

"Oh . . . a slaughter . . . it lasted three whole days . . . oh, Hurka!" was all Velvl could get out.

"Come, come—tell us. Did they capture Plevne?" asked Mikhoel impatiently.

"No . . . oh . . . they didn't take Plevne. They captured Hubniak and some other city. Two thousand Russian soldiers were killed . . . that's what was written, two thousand. And the Turks lost about ten times that number. They didn't say how many."

Everyone was shaken by the news. Mendl grew pale and nervous as he listened wide-eyed to Velvl's news. And then, suddenly, he stood up, looked at the congregation with intense loathing, and shouted: "Murderers! Innocent blood is on your heads!" Then he quickly ran out of the synagogue.

A tense silence reigned for several minutes. Then, as if they were personally to blame, the "Russians" and the "Turks" separated, their heads lowered in shame. One person mumbled to himself, "I can't understand why he's the only one who's right. Who knows who's to blame?"

As if in response, the restrained melody of the weekday evening service was heard from the pulpit, with the words: "And He, merciful one, will forgive our sins and keep us from destruction. . . ."

The "three-day battle," which Velvl reported on from the notice on the marketplace wall, ended with the Russians occupying Gorni-Dubniak and Telish. This meant that there was a total blockade around Plevne and that it was cut off from the rest of the Turkish army. Now no one but the "Jewish Turks" doubted that Osman Pasha would surrender. The newspapers assured us that Plevne had no provisions and that the beleaguered army would soon capitulate. Everyone was impatient for Plevne to fall; the long-awaited peace, or at least the cease-fire, depended on it.

Only it didn't happen quite so fast. Days, weeks, the entire month of October passed, and Plevne still did not surrender. Osman Pasha repulsed the mightiest units of the Russian army, and it became clear that the outcome for which we all waited was not as sure as we originally had thought. Pessimistic voices were beginning to be heard; Plevne, they said, was an unconquerable fortress and Osman Pasha was a mighty leader in war.

6

After that first encounter Mendl continued to drop by in my room from time to time. However, his visits were always brief and to the point. I didn't side with the Turks and I had no great passion for politics, so he never engaged me in political discussions. He came either to see if the paper reported on some new and important development or to ask me to explain a political issue.

A few days after the Russians had captured the fortress of Kars (November 6) Mendl dropped in and wished me a lukewarm "good evening." With an almost unfriendly expression, he walked over to the table where I was sitting and said with strained politeness, "They tell me that you're in thick with the local nobility. Could you possibly get me a Turkish newspaper?"

"A Turkish newspaper?" I asked, surprised. "What for? Why would you need a Turkish paper?"

"I need . . ."

"Take off your coat and sit down."

"Thanks, but I have no time," he replied, barely concealing his impatience. "What about a Turkish newspaper?"

"I don't know what to tell you. I can't think of anyone around here who would get a Turkish paper."

"What do you mean? Aren't there people among the local nobility who are interested in politics?"

"And if there are, why would they read the Turkish papers?" I asked, still puzzled.

"To find out what's happening on the other side," he shouted excitedly.

"Can't you see how impossible it is to get a Turkish newspaper around here? Just for argument's sake, let's say that we did manage to find one—who would be able to read it? Who knows Turkish?"

"What do you mean 'who knows Turkish?'" he asked, quite nonplussed. "I thought that all aristocrats know Turkish. I was sure that you knew Turkish, too. When they told me that you know both German and French, I took it for granted that you knew Turkish as well. No!"—he suddenly shouted with a new wave of energy— "say what you will, without a Turkish newspaper we can never know the truth."

"The truth about what?"

"About Kars! 'Kars is captured.' Do you think that the Russians took Kars so easily? There was probably some kind of double cross. Someone who shouldn't have been involved is responsible for this. The English? But what I don't understand is how Osman Pasha could have permitted it to happen!"

"For God's sake, Reb Mendl, what are you saying? Where is Kars and where is Plevne? They are at either end of Turkey. And besides, how could Osman Pasha have helped when he himself is beleaguered in Plevne?"

"Beleaguered—bah!" Mendl repeated angrily. "What kind of stories are you telling me? How do we know that Osman Pasha isn't holding the Russian army beleaguered and won't let them move?"

I didn't answer him on this point. A few minutes later, however,

I asked him a question of my own, "Tell me, Reb Mendl, why do you hate Russia so much?"

My question didn't surprise Mendl, but he didn't answer immediately. He sat a while and answered calmly, "The truth is, I see no reason why I should love Russia. I would give away the favors I have gotten from Mother Russia in a moment. But if you must know, I don't hate Russia."

"How can you say that you don't hate Russia when you want the Turks to be victorious?"

"That's a different matter and has nothing to do with love or hatred. If I believed that the Russians were in the right in this war, I would defend them with all my might, just as I defend Turkey. This is a question of honesty and justice. Blood is being spilled—can you think of love and hatred in these circumstances?"

"But don't you feel some sort of sympathy, a bond with the people with whom you have lived since you were born?"

"How can you say that I live with them? With whom do I live? With the Russians? When do I have any contact with them? And when you get down to it, with whom could I have a bond? With the peasant who begins his day in the pigsty and ends it in the tavern? With the nobleman who thinks about nothing but a good dinner, stylish clothes, and—please don't be offended—a beautiful woman? How can we be friends with them? And on the other hand," he added with a smile, "I understand very well that they can't take me seriously either. What sort of a person do they see?—someone who doesn't eat pork, who is called Mendl instead of Ivan, who wears earlocks and a long frock coat. To them I must look like a wild man or some sort of fool."

He smiled bitterly and ended the conversation with a wave of his hand.

7

Plevne finally fell on November 28 and Osman Pasha and his entire army of forty thousand men surrendered. I learned these facts from the posters that were pasted on the buildings on the same morning and ran home immediately, anxious to see how Mendl would take the news. For some reason I felt sure that he had already seen the news.

But I was mistaken. Mendl knew nothing about it. I caught him in the middle of a lesson with two of his six pupils. They studied with their bodies as well as their minds, shaking to and fro and gesturing with their hands, while they discussed an important and puzzling talmudic problem in the customary singsong. The other four pupils, swaying over their open Gemara texts, were listening quietly. It seems that they were studying a difficult and complicated subject that the students couldn't grasp. They were tired and frightened and their eyes looked defeated. Mendl was even more exhausted than they. His yellow, waxen face was covered with perspiration as he worked with all his might—with his hands, his voice, his eyes—to make the boys understand the difficult subject. But in vain. The boys were giddy from their efforts and their chanting, and simply weren't in a condition to study seriously. They repeated Mendl's words mechanically, shouting them in confused and pained voices.

I had visited Mendl several times before, so he wasn't taken aback at my presence. He stopped shouting immediately, breathed deeply, wiped the sweat from his face with his sleeve (he didn't wear his coat, as usual), and in a weak voice asked, "Is there any news?"

I didn't have the heart to shock the exhausted teacher, so I only nodded my head uncertainly. He took a deep breath and said bitterly, "They've taken my last bit of strength and they just don't understand; even if I killed myself they wouldn't understand!"

He quickly returned to the pupils and swaying back and forth, he called out in the Gemara chant, "Now, once again. Our rabbis teach . . ."

I wasn't there ten minutes when Mikhoel, the "Russian" who had stalked out of the synagogue, also appeared. He was Mendl's fiercest political opponent, but he was also his closest friend. Both were teachers, both were Hasidim who followed the same rebbe, and politics aside, they were bound by common interests and spent a lot of time together. Mendl didn't see anything unusual in Mikhoel's visit, but I understood immediately why he was there. He winked at me, as if to tell me not to say anything.

He had a sad expression on his face and entered the room slowly and quietly; then he mumbled "good morning," sat down on one of the benches, got up quickly, walked to the table, and looked into an open Gemara.

"Aha, this is what you're up to," he said in a tone of sympathy, "a familiar piece of ground. It's a mire that I don't wish on anyone.

Last year I spent a whole week slogging through this passage with my dumb charges before they got anything out of it!"

"It's not such a difficult subject, really," Mendl replied. "If they would only give themselves to the subject, they would surely understand. But what can I do? They don't want to. I'm so frustrated with these blockheads."

"Now you exaggerate. It is a difficult item. I've seen many older, learned Jews sweat over this passage. It's a kind of Plevne—it's hard to take hold of," Mikhoel finished with a good-natured laugh.

Mendl also smiled. "Still, we'll conquer it in less time than it will take the Russians to conquer Plevne," he said confidently.

"Oh, my friend—there you're making a big mistake. Plevne has been captured."

"Oh sure—it goes without saying," quipped Mendl ironically.

"No, it's true—Plevne was captured yesterday," repeated Mikhoel, looking at Mendl very seriously now.

Mendl shivered, but he still couldn't believe what he heard.

"What do you mean? What are you babbling," he shouted, in a state of agitation.

Mikhoel took out the snuffbox, opened it slowly, took a long whiff, wiped his nose with his handkerchief, and turned to Mendl. "My good friend, I'm not babbling at all. I came purposely to give you the good news. Plevne has been captured, and, what's more, Osman Pasha and his entire army have surrendered. That's it in a nutshell."

Mendl was astounded by the news. He turned to me, looking for help.

"What . . . what is he saying?" he asked me.

I could only confirm what Mikhoel said.

"What can it mean?" said Mendl, even more astounded. "You know about it, too? Why didn't you say anything? How do you know? Did you read about it in the newspaper?"

"No, a notice was posted."

"Where? In the market?"

And Mendl jumped up from his seat, ready to run to the market to read the notice.

"Sh, sh. Don't fly," said Mikhoel, stopping him, "I spent a few kopecks to bring the good news straight to you, all for your pleasure." And handing Mendl a folded gray paper with the printed news, he walked over to a small shelf on the other side of the room where some old, torn books were kept and searched among them for a thin notebook. It was a densely filled manuscript, written by his rebbe in a narrow, curved script. He sat near the window and concentrated on the text, as if he had forgotten all about Mendl and Plevne.

"Study the passage on your own for a while and see if you can understand it," said Mendl to his pupils.

The pupils, who were delighted to have their lesson interrupted even for a little while, were very interested in the news which Mikhoel brought. While pretending to be looking into their Gemaras, they were actually straining to hear every word of our conversation and kept up a constant whispering among themselves. From the few words that I overheard and from the expressions on their faces I understood that the boys were also divided into "Russians" and "Turks," and now under the cover of their texts the "Russians" were celebrating their victory over the "Turks."

Mendl nervously unfolded the paper and was entirely engrossed in it. He read Russian slowly and with difficulty and had to concentrate on every phrase, not satisfied to understand the content alone but anxious to get to the deepest meaning of every word. Several times he gestured, as if he wanted to say something, but he always restrained himself and returned to the paper.

When he finished reading, he sat deep in thought, his head lowered and his brow wrinkled, as if he were trying to remember something. With every passing minute, his face became calmer. Suddenly he raised his head, looked at Mikhoel, at me, at the telegraphic notice with a bright, wide-eyed look and gave a shudder, as if someone had just woken him from sleep. Then an entirely different expression appeared in his eyes—more earnest, sterner, almost ascetic. It was as if he had experienced a complete change in personality in the last few minutes, as if he had found the answer to a difficult problem and had been released from a nightmare.

Mikhoel sat engrossed in the kabbalistic manuscript for about half an hour. Figuring that enough time had passed for Mendl to read through the notice and think about it, he slowly closed the notebook and put it back in place, took a stool and sat next to him. Staring at him apprehensively, he spoke quietly but with a certain hardness, "Well, Mendl, what do you have to say about this?"

Mendl didn't answer immediately. He looked back at Mikhoel with an equally unshaken expression, and with just as much control in his voice, he answered, "And you, Mikhoel, what do you think about it?"

Mikhoel was not prepared for such a cool reply. He was amazed at Mendl's stubborn control and cried out indignantly, "*Meshugener!*

You have to be crazy to talk the way you do! Isn't it enough for you that Plevne was captured and that Osman Pasha has surrendered? What kind of signs and wonders do you need? Do you expect the heavens to come down to earth?"

Mendl wasn't upset by Mikhoel's shouting.

"Don't raise the roof," he answered, calmly. "One might think that it was you, in your wisdom and strength, and not Skobelev who has taken Plevne. What would you like me to say? Do you want me to admit that you were right and that I was wrong?"

"Yes, yes, that's what I want," answered Mikhoel.

"Then I'll tell you straight off that I will not admit it."

"You're crazy, a complete *meshugener*," shouted Mikhoel again.

"If you'll just listen calmly, you'll see for yourself that I'm not crazy. Think back—what argument did I use all the time?"

"You claimed that . . ."

"Just a minute. I'll review my arguments myself," Mendl interrupted. "My first premise was that the Turks were in the right, not the Russians. So, does the Russian victory prove that they were right? Is the victor always right? Don't we know that just the opposite is often the case: 'The evil man flourishes while the just man begs for bread.' "

"But you were always shouting . . ." Mikhoel began.

Mendl cut him short again. "Let me talk. I know what I said. I always pointed out that the Turks were stronger than the Russians, and I still believe that. The fact that the Russians were victorious proves nothing. The strong side doesn't always triumph; often the weaker party wins. A gnat, the tiniest of flies, vanquished the great Titus. Delilah outmaneuvered the mighty Samson . . ."

"David and Goliath!" cried out one of the pupils—and then hid his face in shame. The other children laughed.

"Children, don't mix into matters that don't concern you! Do what I told you to do," Mendl said to them mildly, and turned back to Mikhoel:

"My only error was to state that the Turks were certain to win. There, I agree, I was mistaken."

"Aha, so you do admit . . ."

"Now just hold on; you made the same miscalculation," declared Mendl.

"I? Where did I miscalculate?" asked Mikhoel, taken by surprise.

"My mistake wasn't in predicting that the Turks would be victorious, but in trusting the news in the papers and in the notices. And there you were just as mistaken as I was. We both ran around in search of the latest news as if we were drugged. But the newspapers and notices could tell us only what had already taken place, not what was about to happen. The true cause and significance of events could not possibly be discovered in the papers. Because neither the newspapers, nor Bismarck nor Bikensfeld, with all their political theories, have the slightest idea of the causes from which events stem!"

And he glared at me with a challenging expression, as if I were a journalist or commentator who reported on political issues.

Mikhoel listened attentively, but when he wanted to offer his own point of view, Mendl just continued, "If we really wanted to penetrate into the essence of the war, into all the events and victories, we should have searched sources besides the newspapers and the notices—we should have looked into the Zohar and other sacred texts."

Suddenly he became quiet and lost in thought; his expression took on a lofty air.

This made Mikhoel uneasy, and he didn't know what to answer. He pulled the snuffbox out of his pocket, opened it quickly, and took a good long whiff of snuff; it calmed him somewhat and cleared his mind.

"Perhaps . . . you are right. But that's a different matter altogether," he stated, as if to himself. He sat quietly for a while, and then added: "Just recently a young man showed me an allusion in the form of a notarikon[6] based on the first verse of the Bible, 'In the beginning God made.' It's a very deep matter."

"What is it?" asked Mendl, suddenly interested.

"If interpreted according to the method of notarikon, the verse 'In the beginning God made' reads *in the days of the Romanov, Alexander the second, the Turks will be caught in great Russia's net.*"

"What was that? Say it again," demanded Mendl, curious.

Mikhoel repeated the statement, and Mendl wrote it down.

Both teachers were quiet for a time; then Mikhoel got up wearily and asked, "Are you coming to the 'early risers' meeting this evening?"

"Of course," Mendl answered. "We have to discuss raising money for the delegate here to collect money for the holy land. It would really be a disgrace if we couldn't raise a few rubles for him."

"An absolute disgrace," agreed Mikhoel, sighing, and with a nod to Mendl and me, he left the room.

Mendl's eyes followed him up to the door; then Mendl returned to the table and said almost cheerfully, "Well, dear children! Now we have to get back to our text. If you give it everything you have, I'm sure you will understand it." He brushed both hands softly, almost caressingly, over the old, crumpled pages of the Gemara, sighed deeply, and began to intone in his singsong: "Our rabbis teach . . ."

When I came home, I found my old landlord in a state of nerves. He was walking restlessly from one side of the room to the other, and when he saw me, he rushed over and said excitedly, "Is it really true?"

"What are you talking about?"

"That the Russians captured—the city of—what is it called again? I forgot."

"Plevne?"

"That's it, Plevne. Did they really take it?"

"Yes, they captured it."

"*Ai, ai, ai,*" he cried in despair. "And what will happen now?"

"Now they'll sign a peace treaty."

"Peace treaty," he blurted out, shaking, "and that's it?"

"That's it."

The old man stared at me for a while with a frightened expression on his face. When he had calmed down somewhat, he turned to the door but added sadly, "What do you think of my good wife? She went off to the store without leaving me money for snuff. I've been walking around all morning like a slaughtered goose."

I gave him two kopecks, and this soon made him forget all about the historic events which had so disturbed him.

My acquaintance with Mendl came to an abrupt end. He stopped visiting me, and when we met by chance, he avoided talking to me. Soon after that I moved to another room, and some months later I left town for good.

1892 (Translated by Golda Werman)

BEHIND A MASK

▼

1

Anton Kovadle's ramshackle house in the gentile section of V——
was considered the center of the town's heretical activity. Known to
the pious as "The Nest of Abomination," it had achieved almost
legendary fame. Whenever elderly Jews had to walk past the house,
they hitched up their coats, turned aside, and quickened their pace,
sometimes even spitting as they went by. The women walked past
slowly, shaking their heads mournfully and muttering softly. But if
a high-pitched argument was heard from inside, or a chorus of male
voices harmonizing a sad, sentimental ballad, the frightened women
scurried across the street.

Kovadle's house first acquired its notorious reputation when a
certain young extern, a fiery exponent of the radical ideas of the
Haskalah, became a lodger in one of its modest rooms, attracting
soon after his arrival a small circle of young maskilim like himself,
most of them ex-yeshiva students. The student was not there for
very long, but the room passed to a like-minded young man, and
then to another, so that little by little it became the headquarters of
all the local maskilim. Lodgers changed frequently; sometimes there
were several, at other times none, but the room was kept in the
group's domain. As for Kovadle, the landlord, he was a Russified
Lett, a childless widower who loved his bottle and loved to philoso-
phize as he drank. Once he got used to the boys, he accepted as a
matter of course the constant noise they made and the transitory
nature of their stay. He never quite knew which of the young men
was his lodger. Only one name, Borukh, remained fixed in his mind,
and by that name he addressed whoever happened to be living in
the house, or all of them together. He kept no record of the rent,
but when short of money he would enter the room, stand at the
door with a stern expression on his face, and call out in a terrifying
voice to no one of them in particular: "Borukh! Who d'you think

you are, not paying me my rent?! Let's have a ruble right this minute, or I'll take your whole gang and . . ."

He would conclude with an expressive gesture or an even more expressive threat. The "gang," unintimidated, usually tried to patch things over with promises. If he was adamant, the bargaining began, and if they finally agreed on half a ruble the money was collected on the spot. Kovadle would then leave contentedly.

Kovadle enjoyed frightening his tenants, especially when he was drunk. He would stop at their door and twirl his mustache with a murderous look in his eye. "Just you wait, Borukh!" he would threaten in his most menacing voice, "I'm going to tell your rabbi that you eat pork! That'll be the end of you!"

He was sure he had them all frightened to death.

At his work in the foundry he discussed "his boys" with great affection. "What a jolly bunch! They never stop talking and shouting; they sing as if they'd just downed a pailful. But the truth is, they don't drink anything except tea. Maybe their liver is made different and they can get drunk on a glass of tea!"

2

When Joseph Krantz became Kovadle's lodger, the room already had one permanent occupant, a young man named Braines, about twenty-four years old, very skinny, with a blond goatee and weak, myopic eyes. His shoulders were hunched, and he spoke little, but his face sometimes registered a slow, world-weary smile. Ill-suited by temperament to the frivolous merrymaking of the group, he nonetheless tried to show an interest in all that interested them, taking active part in their pranks and disputes. His smile was clouded by the sadness in his eyes, and his forced laughter was frequently interrupted by a hacking cough. Actually, Braines was interested only in his textbooks. He was preparing to take examinations at the local college and was completely engrossed in his studies. Twice before, in different cities, he had taken the same exams and failed. His self-confidence had been badly shaken, and he was on the lookout for an "easy school."

As soon as Krantz moved in, Braines immediately deferred to him, letting the newcomer take over the iron cot, the most respectable bed in the room, though it lacked a mattress and had only a sofa cushion for a pillow. It turned out that Braines had never used the bed in the first place, but slept on the settee, knees curled up under his chin.

Braines's voluntary surrender of seniority was due primarily to his deep respect for his new roommate. Krantz was three years younger than he, but could already boast a "heroic past." His father was a distinguished rabbi and he had been raised in strictly orthodox surroundings. Yet somehow, by the age of fifteen, Krantz had already become a fiery heretic, seized with the passion of the Enlightenment. One day in the synagogue, in the presence of his father and other worthies, he publicly referred to the prophet Moses in a derogatory manner. The congregants were outraged. His father fainted on the spot. People hurled themselves at the "heretic," and he barely managed to escape the synagogue alive. He never returned home again. About two weeks later, several students were caught reading forbidden books and driven out of the yeshiva. Krantz tore into the place and slapped the rabbi, an old and revered teacher. He broke off all relations with his parents, apprenticed himself to a Russian locksmith, donned a red shirt, and in his new garb strolled through the streets in the company of his Christian fellow workers. He used every conceivable means to outrage the older generation, and exhibited a fanatical, passionate hatred for everything that smacked of religion and orthodoxy. The older generation he held responsible for all the evil and ignorance in the world. Small wonder he soon became popular among the maskilim not only of his own town but of the entire region.

3

Soon afterward the room acquired its third occupant. His name was Shekhtl, he was only seventeen, and he came from Mohilev where he had studied in the yeshiva until expelled on suspicion of heresy. A slight, friendly boy with lively eyes and curly hair, he was not studying with any particular goal in mind and gave no thought to his future, but just gobbled up as many of the new Hebrew books as he could lay his hands on. Each new volume made him wildly enthusiastic: new vistas had opened before him, the deepest chasms of thought had been plumbed. Besides reading, he was always bursting with fantastic plans for the improvement of mankind. Once he came up with a foolproof way for turning all Jews into free-thinkers: the police need only decree that every Sabbath, before the reading of the Torah, a representative of the "new ideas" give a lecture in each synagogue. What good Jew would leave before the reading of the Law or the conclusion of services? The congregation would be compelled to hear out the maskil's lecture, and having heard, would be converted. Another plan was for ridding the world of poverty: the poor, he said, should be treated as yeshiva students; if every wealthy or comfortable Jew agreed to support one or more of the indigent, no paupers would remain. Once Shekhtl even proposed that the mountains be leveled and the valleys filled in— then all the world would be flat and beautiful. These fantasies annoyed his friends, but they were so naïve and childlike that no one could stay angry with him. Once in a while Krantz even took sufficient interest to engage Shekhtl in a discussion of his ideas; in order not to insult his roommates, Braines would toss in an occasional remark, but he kept one eye on his textbook, and the smile on his lips remained ironic and pitying.

It goes without saying that Kovadle's tenants lived in a commune; that is, they shared in the common hunger. None of them had a steady means of support. Once in a while a low-paying tutoring job came along, or an odd bit of work. A few rubles a month came in from the collection taken up by students of the local college, but it simply wasn't enough. For a long period their diet was limited to bread and tea, and there were times when they even did without that. Their clothes were threadbare, their shoes were in tatters, and their underwear hadn't been changed in months. But they handled their poverty like true philosophers, always with a merry quip, making light of their hunger and laughing at the way their toes had begun to protrude from their torn shoes. They even flaunted their poverty, as though it were a sign of high idealism.

Eventually, however, the steady hunger began to make itself felt, and their personalities underwent a change. Frustration and bitterness overcame them, and they grew steadily more depressed. They scarcely did any work, but wasted their days in an endless search for a few pennies to buy some bread. Stretched out across the cot or settee, they traded stale jokes and dull witticisms, livening up only briefly when one of their more prosperous comrades brought a little money or some food. At such moments a meal was served up "with tea and cigarettes," and the requisite songs and disputes. Debating or singing, they preferred to lie stretched out at full length. According to them, this was the more aristocratic pose, but in fact they lacked the strength to sit upright.

The most successful at coping with poverty was Braines, who had gone hungry as a child. His mother was a cook, and his sister worked in a hat factory. He worried more for them than for himself. Krantz, on the other hand, with his carefree frivolity, could not endure the destitute life they were leading, especially since it promised to drag on for years. Shekhtl too was beginning to tire. As long as he had remained in the Mohilev yeshiva he had received a few rubles every month from his parents, and he had been well provided with eating days at the homes of several local families. Since his arrival in V——, his parents had stopped sending him money. Vague rumors had reached them about the goings-on in the Mohilev yeshiva, and they had insisted that their son come home. Shekhtl wrote his parents that he had been accepted into the yeshiva at V——, thereby hoping to allay their fears and to win their renewed support; but in the meantime he went hungry. During his five or six months in Kovadle's room, he grew gaunt and lost his former cheerfulness. Sprawled across the cot, he sometimes chanted biblical passages in a tearful strain: "Ai, who shall give us flesh to eat, ai, ai, ai . . . in vain do we remember the fish that we ate in the land of Egypt, and the cucumbers and melons, and the radishes and onions, and the garlic . . . and now is our spirit faint, for we have nothing. . . ."

His fantasies now began to take a new turn. Instead of broad plans for religious and social reform or geological transformation, his mind turned to the simple dream of finding a wallet stuffed with money or an easy way of making a bar of silver: if you took ten thousand silver coins and filed a little off each of them. . . . The only trouble was, he didn't know where to find the ten thousand silver coins.

4

Late one night, when everyone was asleep, Shekhtl suddenly woke Krantz with a shout: "Get up! I have a brand-new idea!"

Krantz started, and opened his eyes; when he discovered the cause, he flew into a rage: "Go to hell! Leave me alone with your ideas! I want to sleep!"

"You'll have plenty of time to sleep. Just listen to this inspiration I've had. You'll hit the roof when you hear. It's a gem! If it works, we're all saved!"

Accustomed though he was to Shekhtl's harebrained schemes, Krantz was intrigued in spite of himself. Maybe this inspiration was

the very same day. Then there was the costume: like an actor preparing to step onstage, Krantz studied every detail of his wardrobe. The jacket should be long, but not too long; a kerchief at the neck, but only in black; the cap neither velvet nor satin, but of plain cloth; the trousers, worn over the boots. And of course the phylacteries and prayerbook.

At the same time, Shekhtl briefed Krantz on the town. He described its leading citizens, especially those who might be dangerous; he explained how each one of them ought to be handled, and from whom he could expect to get work. The most fascinating information concerned the secret cell of enlightened radicals, a well-organized group of some eight or ten youths who met under the leadership of Khayim-Wolf, the butcher's son, a young man who was already married. Khayim-Wolf was considered one of the most pious young men in town. Shekhtl spoke of him with great admiration, and kept repeating: "When he puts on a mask, it's a real mask all right!" He made Krantz swear at least ten times to keep the name of Khayim-Wolf a secret. The cell had its own library, but no one except Khayim-Wolf knew where the books were kept. Potential members were admitted only after a difficult series of tests. The cell even had its own password. For four or five years it had been doing its work slowly and methodically; thanks to the strong leadership of Khayim-Wolf, it was still intact, and not one of the local worthies even suspected its existence. Shekhtl gave Krantz the password and the name of a contact with whom he could set up a meeting.

Together they also worked out a detailed plan for deceiving Shekhtl's parents. Krantz was to meet them accidentally; they were to learn only by coincidence that Krantz was acquainted with their son. After that he was to fill them with stories of Shekhtl's prodigious scholarship, his dedication to learning, and so on.

Listening to Shekhtl's descriptions and careful advice, Krantz was struck by his practical bent, and his keen insights into human psychology. How did this jibe with those wild fantasies and outlandish projects? When Krantz asked him about it, Shekhtl burst out laughing: "Silly fool! You can't confuse the two. When you're flying, you're up in the clouds, and when you're walking, you keep both feet on the ground. As it says in the good book, 'The heavens are the heavens of the Lord, and the earth was given to the sons of man.' "

6

Krantz's trip to Bobiltseve took five days. As might be expected, he traveled without a ticket, by hopping a freight. Part of the distance he covered on foot, and the final stretch in the back of a wagon, where he made the acquaintance of a young man from Bobiltseve, a storekeeper, who began to ask about the purpose of his trip but then immediately supplied his own answer: "Why are you going to Bobiltseve? If you like, I'll tell you why. I can tell just by looking at your nose. You're going to try to get a job with Riebelman."

From Shekhtl's briefing, Krantz knew that there was a wealthy man in Bobiltseve named Riebelman who owned a sawmill. He decided to use his fellow-passenger's shrewd insight as the ostensible reason for his journey, although he knew as well as the storekeeper that no jobs at the mill were available; this way, though, it would appear that he was being forced to take up teaching as a substitute livelihood.

"Perhaps you're right, and perhaps you're wrong," Krantz replied coolly. "I've heard that it's very hard to get a job there."

"It's not just hard, it's impossible! You've come here for nothing!"

"What are you saying!" Krantz cried fearfully, "then what will I do?"

"What will you do? You won't do anything. You'll go back to where you came from."

"But I can't go back, I can't," said Krantz with mounting anxiety, "I must find some job or other. Do you understand? I have to!"

"No one can help you," droned his companion, rubbing salt into Krantz's wounds. "Now if you had some coin of the realm, say a few hundred rubles, I could send a nice little bit of business your way, the chance of a lifetime. There's a landowner who's getting rid of a load of oats for next to nothing."

"If I had the money, I wouldn't need your advice," Krantz interrupted. "Let's see if you're really so smart. Tell me what I can do without money. . . ."

"Without money you're in trouble," he answered firmly. "Do you know how to make punch? Lemonade?"

"No, I don't."

"Ink?"

"No. But I can write in ink."

"Can you draw up petitions to the authorities?"

"No. . . ."

"Ha! So what are you good for?" But then relenting somewhat he added, "Is your handwriting good?"

"Beautiful. Like a painting."

"Well then, you could become a teacher."

Krantz, who had been waiting for this suggestion, hesitated a moment, and sighed. "It's a bitter way to earn a living. . . ."

"And where will you find a sweeter?"

"It's so common. . . ."

"And where will you find something more refined?"

"Well then, tell me, are there at least pupils, I mean ones who will pay?"

"And how! As many as you want! The teachers in this town were rolling in money."

"So where are they now?"

"The devil take them! Who knows? One led a respectable girl down the primrose path and then took off. Another was a heretic of the new kind who smoked on Sabbath, and spoke against God and religion, so he was sent packing. A third got married and gave up teaching. . . ."

"No! That's no job for me." Krantz was indignant. "My family would be humiliated if I stooped so low."

"Don't worry," the young man consoled him, "If you're from a good family, and if you're good with a pen, you won't have any trouble finding a match in Bobiltseve, with a dowry of several hundred rubles. That's the best business of all nowadays. . . ."

7

In a while Krantz turned the conversation to lodgings, and asked where he might find a room. His companion reeled off about a dozen unfamiliar names; he also mentioned Krayne, Ephraim's wife, who had a small room to rent. Krayne was the name of Shekhtl's mother, but in order to make perfectly certain of her identity Krantz asked, "What does Ephraim do?"

"He's a heder-teacher."

"What kind of a man is he?"

"He's just an ordinary man, that's all, neither too smart nor too stupid. A simple, honest man. But his wife, Krayne, is a real Cossack! She runs a little shop and at home she runs the show."

"So you'd advise me to stay at their place? Maybe you could point out where she lives."

"Any child in town could tell you that. When we pass it, the driver will stop and you can get off."

The wagon drove into town, and after passing several narrow streets, stopped in front of a small, run-down cottage. This, said Krantz's traveling companion, was Ephraim's house.

Krantz climbed down, paid the driver, and took up his parcel. In the doorway stood an elderly woman, rather stout, with an energetic face and calm, clever eyes. She had come out to see why the wagon had stopped.

"Krayne! This young man needs a room. Do you have one to rent him?" inquired his companion on Krantz's behalf.

Krayne studied the newcomer slowly, from head to toe.

"I'll see. . . ." Still looking him over, she invited him into the house.

The room they entered was dim and low-ceilinged, with signs of poverty and disorder everywhere. There were books, however, in plenty, all over the cupboards, dressers, tables, and windowsills.

"Sit down. Where are you from?" asked Krayne.

"I'm from V——."

"From V——?" she repeated in surprise. "Is that your home?"

"Yes."

Krayne lapsed into silence, but without once taking her eyes off the newcomer. Krantz understood that she was probably eager to ask about her son, but for the moment she restrained herself.

"Why have you come to Bobiltseve? On business?"

"Yes . . . I was hoping to find a job. At Riebelman's sawmill if I'm lucky."

Krayne opened the door into the other room:

"Have a look. That's the room. A whole family used to live here."

The room was tiny, almost without light. It was separated from the main room of the house by a thin partition that did not even extend all the way to the ceiling. Nevertheless, Krantz immediately decided to take it so as to establish close contact with Shekhtl's parents. Once he had settled the financial arrangements for his friend, he would move on to other quarters. He and Krayne agreed on six rubles a month for room and board. Krantz was a little surprised that Krayne was prepared to rent the room without even consulting her husband; apparently he had no say whatever in household matters.

"You'd probably like something to eat," Krayne ventured, "we've already had our lunch, but I'll prepare something for you."

She placed some bread and butter, a couple of eggs, and a glass of buttermilk on the table. Krantz washed up in the traditional manner. She sat down opposite him at the table, but for a long time remained silent. Then abruptly she asked, "Tell me, is there a big yeshiva in V——?"

"And how! One of the biggest in Lithuania!" Krantz spoke without taking his lips from the glass of buttermilk.

"Are there many students?"

"About a hundred, I think . . . maybe more."

She paused for a few more seconds, and then said offhandedly, "I have a son there, in that yeshiva."

"In V——?" asked Krantz in surprise.

"Why are you so amazed?"

"It's very far from here. Aren't there any yeshivas closer by?"

Krayne dropped her head and said in a pained voice, "It just happened that way . . . you've just come here from V—— yourself, in spite of its being so far away. . . ." She smiled weakly with this last comment, and then probed further: "Do you know any of the yeshiva students there?"

"I know almost all their faces, and I'm friendly with a few. I used to attend the daily lecture there myself."

"My son went to V—— only recently, about half a year ago."

"What's his name?"

"Hillel . . . probably 'the Bobiltsever,' after this town."

"Hillel? 'The Bobiltsever'?" repeated Krantz, as if trying vainly to recall, and then firmly deciding that he could not: "No. There's no one at the yeshiva by that name."

Krayne blanched, and her face took on a very anxious expression; the bitter truth was about to emerge—her son was not at the yeshiva. Watching the woman, Krantz felt the elation of an actor who knows that his performance has captivated his audience.

"Maybe you haven't noticed him," Krayne tried to calm herself. "He's not a very tall boy . . . dark, nice-looking, and very gentle. . . ."

"Not very tall? . . . dark and nice-looking . . ." Krantz rehearsed the description as if racking his memory. "Who could that be, now? The Yonevitser . . . the Lyozner . . . the Mohilever . . ."

"Yes! Perhaps the Mohilever!" Krayne grasped at this straw. "He used to be at the yeshiva in Mohilev."

"Does he have curly hair?"

"Yes! Yes!"

"When he speaks, does he sometimes blink his eyes very quickly?"

"Well! That's him!" Krayne determined. She was completely reassured, and even rose from the table as though to show the matter was settled. "In other words, he's at the yeshiva and you know him."

"Of course! The Mohilever! I know him very well. I used to see him at the synagogue almost every day. . . . What a shame I didn't know he was from here. I would have brought you a letter from him."

"Well, how is he doing there? How is he managing at the yeshiva?" Krayne began to probe, finding it difficult to phrase the questions properly.

"I don't know exactly how he's doing. . . . He eats days like most of the boys, but I don't know if he has a house for every day of the week. Actually, his clothes are not in very good condition, but of course that's nothing unusual. As far as his studies go, it's hard for me to say because he's way ahead of me. He's considered one of the star pupils at the yeshiva. . . . The rabbi thinks the world of him."

Krantz, speaking with deep humility, seemed to be carrying off his role successfully. Krayne's eyes shone with joy. She walked over to the open window and called to a little girl who was playing near the house, "Hannah! Run over to the heder and tell Ephraim to come home for a while. Tell him we have news of Hillel."

8

The man who came in was a thin, little old Jew with a sparse gray beard and round bulging eyes. His mustache was stained yellow from snuff and his whole face was the color of earth. Beard and earlocks were disheveled, as though the hairs were about to run off in different directions. His coat fell to his heels, and the fringes of his soiled undergarment hung below his knees. His expression was absent-minded, as if he were still engrossed in whatever he had just been doing in the heder.

"Well? Regards from Hillel?" he muttered dreamily, looking all around him. When he caught sight of Krantz, he shook his hand quickly and sped through all the formalities. "*Sholem aleichem!* Where are you from? How is Hillel doing over there?"

"Why do you pounce on him, before you even know anything?"

interrupted Krayne with ill-concealed annoyance. "Sit down and talk to him like a human being. . . ."

At her reproach Ephraim came to. He tucked his coat up and seated himself at the table. Krayne briefly explained who their visitor was, the purpose of his coming, and the news he had brought of their son. As an aside, she mentioned having rented him the room.

Too impatient to wait until she had finished, Ephraim suddenly asked, "What's he studying now? Which section of Talmud?"

Krantz casually replied with the first chapter that came to mind: "*Erubin.*"

"What do you mean, *Erubin?* Didn't he write that he was studying *Zeraim?*" cried Ephraim almost fearfully.

"The head of the yeshiva lectures on *Zeraim* at a separate class for some of the better students. Your son is considered one of the brightest lights of the yeshiva. He has an exceptional mind. . . ."

"Are you telling me? Don't I know it, eh? If that boy weren't so lazy, he would have been ordained long ago."

"I think that he's working seriously toward it now."

"Is that right? Working seriously?" repeated Ephraim, his eyes boring into Krantz. All at once he turned on his wife with a bitter outcry: "And she tries to drag him home! Drag him home by the hair! Once a tyrant, always a tyrant!"

To Krantz's amazement, Krayne did not try to stop her husband. Instead, she faltered, and found little to say in her own defense. "You don't know what you're talking about. . . ." Then, as if gathering strength for a confession, she began to speak in a much softer, intimate tone: "I'll tell you how things stand. I didn't believe that my son was really at the V—— yeshiva."

Krantz showed surprise but said nothing.

"Have you ever heard anything like it?" Ephraim laughed. "She didn't believe it! Go talk to a woman! A woman is afraid of everything and believes no one."

"Let me finish!" his wife interrupted. "You must understand what happened. In the yeshiva at Mohilev there was a whole . . . I don't know what you'd call it. . . . Students were caught with 'books' and expelled on the spot. And at the very same time my boy suddenly moved to V——. So you see, I was sure that . . . I'm only a mother, after all. . . ."

"Why didn't you write to the director of the yeshiva at V——?" Krantz was so certain of his success that he took the most direct and perilous course of action.

"That's true. . . . Somehow it never occurred to me."

"Now have you finally stopped worrying?" challenged Ephraim, pointing toward her with his beard.

"Yes. I've stopped worrying. You can go back to heder!"

"But that still isn't enough. You have to do something about it . . . you know what I mean!" he persisted.

"I know, I know! Go on!" Krayne shooed him away. When he had gone, Krayne explained that it was a long time since she had sent her son any money. The very next day, God willing, she would send him a few rubles.

In the evening, when Ephraim returned from heder, they resumed their conversation about Hillel, the yeshiva, and the details of life in V——. Having exhausted these subjects, his hosts began to show an interest in Krantz, who spoke freely of himself and his past. His father had been a very wealthy man and Krantz had been tutored in everything there was to know. But without warning, his father went bankrupt one day and then suddenly died. Krantz was left with a widowed mother and two grown sisters to support. Somehow, it didn't really matter how, he had to provide for them. When he heard about Riebelman, who was rich and involved in so many businesses, it seemed like the ideal place to apply for a position, and hence he had come to Bobiltseve.

The story stirred Ephraim's and Krayne's sympathies. They even promised to put in a word with Riebelman through an acquaintance of theirs, warning, however, that the effort would almost certainly be in vain. Riebelman was already known to have a surfeit of employees.

"On the way here, the young man sharing my wagon tried to persuade me to become a tutor, to teach children to read and write Russian. He said I could easily grow rich. . . . What do you think of that?" he concluded with a chuckle.

"That's Borukh Leyzer-Ber," explained Krayne to her husband. "He's got crazy ideas."

"Maybe he's right. Teaching might pay very well," Krantz said earnestly, but with obvious reluctance. "On the other hand, what sort of work is it for a decent boy of good family? Why should I go crawling in the mud before I've been tripped? To tell you the truth, I don't think I'm really suited for it. I may know ten times as much about reading and writing as the greatest teacher, but nowadays that's not what people are looking for. They want a teacher to be a freethinker, and I don't know what else besides. That's not for me!"

His hosts expressed their sympathy. Letting a few moments pass, he then added in a strained voice, as if to himself, "But what shall I do, with a sick mother and two sisters to support? I can't let them be thrown out into the street."

The question hung in the air, the answer seeming only too self-evident.

Before retiring, Krayne came to Krantz with a request: could he write out an address for her? She handed him a crumpled letter and said, "This is where Hillel lives. Tomorrow I'll give you five rubles and ask you to address the envelope so that I can send him the money."

Krantz glanced at the letter. The return address was given as: Kovadle's house, c/o Joseph Krantz, for Shekhtl.

"This is the wrong address," he said, erasing his own name and putting down the name of Braines in its stead. (Money could not be sent directly to Shekhtl because he lacked a proper residence permit.)

"What luck!" Krayne exclaimed happily. "If not for you, the money would certainly have been lost!"

9

That night, Krantz lay awake for a long time in a state of high excitement, like an actor after a particularly brilliant performance. Going over in his mind the many incidents and conversations of the day, he buried his head in the pillow and giggled madly. Had anyone told him that in fact he had spent the day cheating and lying with more malice and treachery than a thief, Krantz would simply have been incredulous, so intoxicated was he by the artistry of his performance.

The next morning he accompanied Ephraim to the synagogue, deliberately making his first public appearance in the guise of a pious Jew. On the way, he asked detailed questions about what Ephraim was teaching his young pupils, lacing his conversation with enough references to show that he himself was no ignoramus. Several townspeople stopped to ask Ephraim about his companion. He introduced Krantz as a young man from V——, a friend of Hillel's, who had come to town on a matter of business.

There remained before Krantz the prospect of making contact with the underground cell of maskilim. In giving him the password, Shekhtl had told him to approach a certain young man by the name of Leivick, of whom he had provided so perfect a description that Krantz recognized him immediately upon entering the synagogue.

Toward the end of the services, Krantz strolled past Leivick's seat, intoning the indicated verse from the Psalms: "But it was thou, a man mine equal, my companion and my familiar friend. We took sweet counsel together, in the house of God we walked with the throng."

Leivick, without turning his head, nodded acknowledgement, and Krantz went back to his seat beside Ephraim. He waited for a signal, a note, a stealthy message whispered in a corner. But the contact was quite straightforward. After services Leivick came up to Ephraim and, indicating the newcomer, asked who he was.

"This is a young man from V——, a friend of Hillel's in the yeshiva," Ephraim answered.

Leivick greeted him, asked about V—— and about Hillel, and ended by inviting Krantz over to his place for afternoon tea. When he left, Ephraim said, "That's Reb Shmerl, the lumber-dealer's son. A fine young man. Studies day and night. A friend of Hillel's. You should go over for tea if he invited you; his father might be able to put in a word for you with Riebelman."

Krantz was reminded that he still had to play out that particular farce, and right after services he set out for Riebelman's office. The waiting room was full. Several hours passed before he was given an interview with the owner. Bathed in humility, as if he were begging alms, he pleaded for a position. But Riebelman did not even let him finish before waving him from the room. "Leave me alone! I have no positions! I don't have any, and I won't have any, so go home and stop bothering me!"

Krantz did not press the matter.

In the afternoon he went to call on Leivick. The secret free-thinker met him at the door and led him upstairs to his bedroom, shutting the door behind them. It was a large room, with books scattered everywhere.

Leivick was a young man of about twenty, with a drawn, angular face and only the barest trace of a beard. His eyes were dark and piercing, like those of a mouse. There was something dry in his expression, a severity beyond his years, as though he had spent his youth without once having smiled. Even his voice was dry, expressionless, and a little rasping.

Leivick studied his visitor carefully, and asked, almost as a reproach, "What is Hillel doing in V——? Is he at the yeshiva?"

"No. He has thrown off that pretense altogether."

"Pity." Leivick cut him off. "He should have stayed at the yeshiva.

There would have been time enough to jump the fence. . . . Well, and what did you come here for? Lessons?"

"Yes. I'd like to talk to you about it."

Krantz told him his plans and of his deception of Shekhtl's parents. Leivick listened impassively.

"You haven't begun too badly, but where do you go from here? To tell the truth, I don't have much faith in tutoring. . . ."

Krantz was startled: "What do you mean? Why?"

"We've had a few tutors who did more harm than good. They came here, caused a commotion, raised everyone's dander, and left with nothing to show for their stay. . . ."

Krantz was more and more surprised by this attitude, and could only answer lamely that they were probably the wrong kind of people for the job.

"That's not the point," Leivick interrupted, "I just don't trust the big-city maskilim. They love scandal. They want to show off their powers and their wit, to put something over on the pious, but they don't know how to work in the dark, with a steady energy. What's worse, they love to write long, sarcastic letters about everything that ought to be kept secret, and their letters have a habit of falling into the hands of the rabbi or the head of the yeshiva. And they feel a constant need to stuff their pockets with radical pamphlets. . . ."

The scathing irony of this speech cut Krantz to the quick. He got up and said dryly: "You may be right. But I expected something different from our conversation. If you think that tutors can do nothing but harm, then we have nothing more to discuss."

"Now wait a minute," said Leivick impatiently. "You're angry for no good reason. I didn't mean to insult you. I just wanted you to know my opinion. Go ahead. Tell me what you hope to accomplish as a tutor."

"How can you ask? I don't understand you."

"Very simple. A good friend, someone he knows, can more easily open a boy's eyes and expose him to new ideas than a tutor can. The fact that a tutor teaches a couple of boys and girls to read and write doesn't impress me one bit. It's like this: if someone sees the light, he can learn everything there is to know even without a mentor. Take me, for example. In two years, while pretending to sit over the Talmud, I've covered the whole curriculum for the eight grades of high school and college. But if someone is still blind, then knowing how to read and write won't make any difference."

This was a new idea to Krantz, and he found it difficult to disagree.

"I'm not telling you this in order to convince you to give up your plan," Leivick added. "I don't know you, after all, so how can I know what kind of a job you'd do? You're off to a good start, and if it continues as smoothly as before, you'll be able to help us in our work. . . ."

Coming after the previous attack, these words offered Krantz some slight encouragement. "You'll see how well I work!" he assured his host.

"Naturally I'll help you as much as I can. You'll find as many students as you want. Go to see Nahman the dry-goods grocer. We'll see to it that he takes you on for his children—he has a son and a daughter—and others will follow his example. But I'll say it again: work quietly, and without fuss. Bear in mind that when you lead someone off the straight and narrow, it's best if he doesn't even notice the bend in the road."

In coming to call on Leivick, Krantz had been expecting to meet a provincial, someone who would defer to his visitor from the city, listen to him avidly, and follow his advice. Instead he found an independent young man, more mature and better educated than he, who treated him like a disciple. Krantz found himself looking up to Leivick. But he was still eager to meet the other members of the cell, particularly its leader, the butcher's son.

"How do I get in touch with Khayim-Wolf?" he asked of Leivick.

"Who? Who's Khayim-Wolf?"

"What do you mean? Isn't he the leader of your group? Hillel told me that. . . ."

Leivick fixed Krantz with a puzzled stare. "Khayim-Wolf, the butcher's son? Has Hillel gone out of his mind? Was he making fun of you? Khayim-Wolf is one of the greatest fanatics in town. You'd better avoid him like fire."

His tone was so earnest that for a moment Krantz was sure Hillel must have made a mistake. But then he quickly realized that Leivick was simply suspicious. "Don't you trust me?" he asked with injured pride.

Leivick looked at him in bewilderment. "You're the one who doesn't trust me if you don't believe what I tell you. But go ahead, if you like, try to approach Khayim-Wolf. What a story that will make! Listen . . . Hillel was hardly even a member of the group, and he never knew what was going on. What he told you isn't worth a tinker's dam."

By the time he left, Krantz felt humiliated, badly fallen in his own self-esteem. He vowed to take his work so seriously and get so much done that Leivick and his bunch would come and beg him to join them.

10

It didn't take Krantz long to get settled. Shekhtl's parents, out of pity for the supposed condition of his mother and sisters, encouraged him to take up tutoring, and before long his lessons brought him a full twelve rubles a month. He soon found a pretext for moving out, and took up new lodgings at the home of a teamster at the edge of town, thereby freeing himself from Krayne's careful surveillance. But he continued eating his meals at Krayne's, so that his board might ensure the five rubles a month she was sending to her son.

At first it was rather difficult for Krantz to maintain a steady workload, and even more difficult to maintain a rigorous outward piety. But little by little he grew into the part. He singled out some of his most promising students and slowly began to undermine their faith.

Two months went by, and the shtetl grew accustomed to his presence. But the main task he had set for himself did not get off the ground. His conversation with Leivick, and his awareness that a radical cell was operating without his participation, had clipped the wings of his enthusiasm, and eventually undermined his will to work. He was also growing very bored with the monotonous life of the town, the absence of any congenial society or entertainment. He missed the noisy cameraderie of Kovadle's house; even eating in abundance, as he now did, seemed a vulgar habit which could only coarsen the spirit. Heaviest of all was the burden of his disguise, which he could not safely put aside even in the privacy of his room. The daily prayers in the synagogue, the pious bearing, the conversations on matters of observance, were briefly interesting as a test of his artistic skill, but it was hard to walk in these chains for months on end, and after a while it seemed to lack purpose.

Gradually, imperceptibly, Krantz began loosening the bonds, allowing himself greater freedom. In his room he took to sitting bareheaded. When smoking on the Sabbath, he did not always take the necessary measures to avoid detection. Several times he realized too late that he had left Krayne's table without saying the proper blessings. Once, in conversation with a traditional Jew, he inadvertently let fall a skeptical remark. Another time, when the enthusiasm of a Hasid got on his nerves, he permitted himself a scoffing reference to the holy Rebbe. None of this was lost on the townspeople, who now began to watch him closely. Behind his back rumors began to spread about "those freethinkers" and "Berlin Jews." News of his former life—not wholly accurate, but remarkably like the truth—circulated widely. Leivick warned him several times that a storm was gathering over his head, and that he must be more cautious. But by then it was too late; inevitably, the storm broke. On a Sabbath morning, as a very tardy Krantz hurried to the synagogue, he was stopped in a quiet lane by an unfamiliar young man who said nervously: "Don't go to the synagogue. They're out for your blood. Last night, through a crack in the shutters, you were seen smoking."

Krantz returned to his room to await further developments. Luckily for him, the incident came to nothing. Krantz's landlord, a simple teamster who believed that his tenant was a pious young man, unaccountably swore that he had been sitting with Krantz after supper until late into the night. When it was pointed out to the landlord that Krantz might have smoked later, as he was going to bed, the landlord flew into a rage, threatened to crack the skull of anyone who dared to make such suggestions, and tried to drag the rabbi to his home to prove that there were no cracks in his shutters wide enough to see through. The teamster's protestations convinced no one, but peace was temporarily restored.

Thereafter, the attitude of Shekhtl's parents to their guest noticeably changed. Ephraim, who had formerly prattled freely on matters of learning or told endless tales of his Rebbe, now kept a sullen silence. He avoided Krantz's eye, limiting himself to occasional muttered remarks about the weather or household matters, and these only to preserve the amenities. Krayne now hardly ever mentioned her son. Often Krantz would feel her suspicious, probing stare on his face, and he was convinced that both husband and wife had lost faith in him completely.

Before leaving V——, Krantz had been warned by Shekhtl not to rely on the local postman. Since the warning was later repeated by Leivick, Krantz took to handling his mail directly through the post office. One day, he was asked to deliver a card addressed to Shekhtl's parents. The card had on it only several lines of writing—the conventional salutation, and the following message: "Your query came as a surprise. There is no Hillel ben Ephraim at the yeshiva, nor has anyone by that name ever been registered here. You would do well to find out if some misfortune, God forbid, may not have befallen your son." The signature was illegible, but just above it was the title: "Director of the Yeshiva at V——." Clearly, Shekhtl's parents had sent an inquiry about their son—just as Krantz had once suggested they do. He would have had a jolly time of it had the card ever reached its destination . . . which, of course, it never did.

11

One day, not long after the furor over smoking, Krayne approached Krantz with a request:

"I'd like some advice. It's been almost two years since Hillel went off on his own. We invited him home for the holidays, but he said that his studies were too important to be interrupted. I know that he's right, but I'm only a mother, and I'd like to see him. So I've decided to go to V——. It's hard for me to undertake such a long journey, and it'll cost me a pretty penny, but somehow I'll find the strength. What do you think? Is it a good idea? Do you think I should go?"

Krantz realized that he was being tested. For a moment he was shaken, but quickly regaining his composure he answered coldly that it had nothing whatever to do with him. "Why shouldn't you go if you can manage it? See for yourself what his life there is like. As a matter of fact," he added with what he hoped was utter nonchalance, "if you do go, I'd ask you to bring back a small parcel of my clothes. . . ."

Apparently he had carried his assumed indifference a little too far. A smile crept over Krayne's face, and ignoring his last remark she said as if in mockery, "Thank you so very much for your kind advice. I will indeed go to V——. How does the saying go? . . . Your own eyes are the trustiest witnesses. A stranger can be deceived, but a mother's eye sees everything."

"Quite right! You ought to go!" Krantz exclaimed, barely able to keep his fury in check.

Though still uncertain whether or not Krayne would undertake the arduous trip, Krantz wrote to Shekhtl and Braines the very same day warning them of the impending danger, and advising that they take all the necessary precautions to prevent Krayne from learning the truth.

Two days later, Krayne set out for V—— without even bidding him good-bye.

Krantz realized he was on very shaky ground, and awaited her return with less than perfect composure. It was hard to believe that once in V—— she would fail to discover the truth about her son.

A few days later, Leivick, who received mail for Krantz at his own address, sent over his brother with a letter from Braines containing the following ominous words: "As soon as you receive this letter, gather up your few belongings and get you gone from Bobiltseve. We have failed miserably, and the fearsome witch is now on her way home breathing fire and eager to wreak her vengeance on thee."

There followed a detailed account of what had transpired between Krayne and her son. Immediately upon receipt of Krantz's letter, Braines and Shekhtl had gone to work, removing everything of an "un-Jewish" nature, and filling the bookshelves with dozens of talmudic volumes and other religious books. Their friends were told not to show their faces for several days. Shekhtl and Braines borrowed long coats, tassled undergarments, and skullcaps, and wore them during those hours of the day when Krayne could be expected to arrive by train. And in fact, when Krayne did come upon them they were poring over the texts, swaying back and forth and chanting aloud. But it was no use. As soon as she had arrived in V—— and located the gentile section, Krayne set out to find her son. Not far from Kovadle's house, she stopped at a little Jewish shop to make inquiries. When the shopkeeper's wife heard Krayne mention Kovadle's house, and the dark young man with the curly hair, she slapped her hands together and launched into a tale of horror: the inhabitants fed on swine, smoked on the Sabbath, acted like out-and-out gentiles.

"Tear your son away from that house of iniquity and drag him home by force! Otherwise he is lost forever!"

The woman then went on to tell about the ringleader of the group, a rabbi's son who was now gone off somewhere to become a tutor. So accurately did she describe the vile heretic that Krayne instantly recognized her boarder.

She burst into Kovadle's house with a wild lamenting shriek, grabbed hold of Shekhtl by the lapels, and began tugging at him and screaming: "Murderer! Home with you!" Her eyes were so wild that Braines, as he himself wrote, shook like a leaf. Shekhtl tore free from his mother's grasp and fled into hiding. For two days Krayne turned the city inside out looking for him; she went to the rabbi, to the director of the yeshiva, to the leading citizens, wailing and begging for help. Ten times at least she burst into Shekhtl's room, and finding only Braines, cursed him roundly, threatened to call in the police, and finally threw herself at his feet, pleading with him to yield up her son. She pushed a ten-ruble note into his hand for "the gang" if only they would "give her back her child." After two more days of scouring the city in vain, she left for home.

Krantz's first reaction was panic. But soon the prospect of the impending battle filled him with a surge of energy: let it come! Krantz would not flee the battlefield. He would throw off his mask entirely and launch an open attack on the town. Leivick and his group might disapprove, but Krantz could no longer bother himself over those sleepy spirits.

The letter from Braines arrived Friday morning, while Krantz was still in bed. He was certain that Krayne would arrive in time for the Sabbath, and determined to take his dinner there, as usual: he would meet the enemy head-on.

He sat down to a glass of tea and began to map out his strategy.

12

Footsteps sounded in the passageway. Slowly, the door to Krantz's room opened and Krayne's voice was heard from the hall. "Is it all right to come in?"

"Come right in!" Krantz shouted, louder than was necessary. He was startled by her sudden appearance. That Krayne would come to him was something he hadn't anticipated.

She came in slowly, closed the door behind her, took several steps forward, and gave a friendly nod: "Good morning."

Her face was pale and drawn, but expressionless, as always. A demure, good-natured smile was on her lips. Only the gray eyes admitted something secretive and quizzical. It would have been impossible to guess from her appearance the purpose of her visit.

Krantz quickly saw that Krayne was determined to play cat and mouse with him and was looking to catch him off guard. He too played dumb, and replied with a friendly smile, "Ah! Welcome! Back so soon?"

"As you can see. . . ."

"Have a seat!"

"Thank you." She seated herself on the edge of the chair.

"Will you have a glass of tea?"

"Thank you, but I've just had one. . . ."

Even as she spoke, Krantz noticed that her lips were parched and she had to keep moistening them with the tip of her tongue.

"Well, I've traveled far, and seen a lot . . . visited with my son Hillel, may he live and be well," she launched into her account calmly, in a contented singsong. "I'm satisfied, thanks be to His Holy Name, completely satisfied!"

"There you are! What did I tell you?" responded Krantz, with no less satisfaction.

"Yes, you were quite right," she agreed, "but what can you do with a foolish woman? She always imagines the worst . . . a mother after all."

There was a brief pause, after which she resumed in a lively tone, "I don't regret having made the trip. So much to see. So many people. I met Hillel's friends. By the way, what's the name of the boy he shares a room with? The tall one, with the goatee? He seemed like a very fine boy. You must know him."

"Yes, I know him. His name is Braines. He really is a nice chap."

He stole a sidelong glance at Krayne. The calm voice, the polite smile and bashful reticence made her seem like a panther stalking its prey. He braced himself for her pounce; but Krayne was in no hurry.

"I met some of my son's other friends. I heard a lot of fine things about you as well. . . ."

Her voice was caught by a momentary spasm, but she soon regained control.

"I didn't know that you were so well descended, the son of a rabbi. . . . And I had no idea how much help you've been to my son. . . ."

Suddenly she erupted from her seat, red in the face, her eyes glaring in savage hatred. She banged her fist down on the table and cried, "Apostate! Sit down this very moment and write to my son, whom you've murdered, to come home at once! Do you hear me, you blasphemer of Israel? This very instant! Otherwise you won't get out of this place alive. I'll light a funeral pyre under you! I know everything, everything! Sit down and write!"

She threw on the table a sheet of paper and an envelope which Krantz had failed to notice in her hand. What Krantz might have done had the ambush been sprung unexpectedly, it would be difficult to guess; but prepared as he was, he simply rose to his feet and said deliberately, "I will write no letters to your son!"

"You'll write! You'll change your tune!" Krayne shouted with savage conviction. "If not, I'll stir up the whole town against you!

They'll tear you to shreds! Jews will take my part for the blood you've shed."

"You won't do it," Krantz retorted with a calm smile.

"Why not? Why won't I do it?" she cried in bewilderment.

Krantz advanced on her and spoke in a menacing voice. "Listen to me, Krayne! If you dare to say one word against me to anyone, I'll write to Hillel at once and order him to be baptized! Do you hear me? Baptized! You can be sure that if I give the command, Hillel will obey it. You know very well that I'm the highest-ranking member of the group, and a leader is obeyed! I'll say no more. You can do as you please."

Krayne blanched and staggered. Dizzy, she held on to the chair to steady herself. For a while she stood motionless, biting her lips and muttering. Then a suppliant smile, a mixture of entreaty and hatred, appeared on her face. At length she gathered up enough strength to say in a trembling voice: "There's no need to get angry with me. . . . You must understand that it wasn't I who shouted at you, but the pain crying out from inside me. Of course, I won't mention a word about you to anyone—what would I stand to gain? Why drag my own good name through the mud? Well, if you don't want to write him, you don't have to. It happens, sometimes, that a son may die. . . ."

"Now that's the way to talk!" Krantz exploded triumphantly.

Stifling a deep sigh, Krayne added a final plea. "I must ask that this remain between the two of us. The old man must never find out. It would be unbearable for him."

Before leaving, she paused at the door to ask: "Are you coming for supper?"

"Of course I'll come. Why not?"

When Krayne had gone, Krantz paced his room excitedly, rubbing his hands together in satisfaction. He had not anticipated so decisive and glorious a victory. The idea of threatening her with Hillel's conversion was a last-minute brainstorm, inspired by Krayne's scream of "Apostate!" As he remembered his exact words, that if he ordered Hillel to be baptized the command would be promptly obeyed, he burst into a fit of laughter. He was only sorry that he had not made Krayne swear to go on sending Hillel the five rubles each month.

In the evening Krantz went over for the Sabbath meal. In speaking of Hillel, Krayne used the same tone she had earlier assumed with Krantz. But several times she stopped short, as if forgetting her train of thought, and stared blankly ahead of her. Ephraim sat dejectedly, without a word. He sensed that something was wrong, that something was being withheld from him, but unable to get at the truth he simply looked at Krayne and Krantz in despair.

Several days later, Krantz stopped taking his meals at their house and made ready to leave Bobiltseve. It seemed that Krayne had kept her lips sealed, as she had promised, but the atmosphere had grown so heavy around him he could hardly breathe, and there was nothing to be accomplished by staying.

13

About a week after Krantz stopped eating at Krayne's, he happened to be passing the house and noticed her sitting in the window. When she saw him, she motioned him over.

Krayne was greatly altered. Her drawn face had lost its stolidity, and was now more agile and expressive. There was a new expression, a kind of rapturous passion, in her eyes. As Krantz drew nearer she greeted him with a smile of savage pleasure, as if preparing to spring at him—either to embrace him or to sink her teeth into his throat. She began prattling very rapidly, as if sharing a merry confidence that would have to remain a secret between the two of them. "Listen, outcast. It's just your luck that you stopped coming to eat at my home. I was prepared to poison you like a mad dog! With rat poison!"

She gave a soft little chuckle.

It was so unexpected and awkward that Krantz could not keep from laughing. "You would have been deported to Siberia," he protested.

"I? Because of you? Who would have informed on me? What Jew would have taken your part? They would have buried you like carrion, behind the fence—and that would have been the end of you!" And she gave another pleased little chuckle.

But suddenly her head shot up and the eyes that she fixed on Krantz were wide open in stark, indescribable terror. Her gaze so astonished him that he sprang back and almost fled. For the rest of the day he was haunted by the horror of her eyes, with their heaven-piercing agony. . . .

The next morning there were rumors that Krayne had gone mad.

1909 (Translated by Abraham Igelfeld and Ruth R. Wisse)

GO TALK TO A GOY!

▼

1

A few years before the war, during the heat of the reactionary period in Russia. I was traveling by train between Vilna and Warsaw when I met an old acquaintance whom I hadn't seen for seven or eight years. In the old days he called himself Afanasi and always behaved as if he were in the midst of a conspiracy; he was clean-shaven then and used to wear Russian peasant blouses. Now he was dressed in a European-style suit and had a dignified beard—and he had reverted back to his Jewish name. Moshe Silberzweig.

In Switzerland we used to see each other often, though we were never good friends. We belonged to different, conflicting political parties. Since we were both the "speakers" as well as the "active delegates" of our respective parties, we considered ourselves implacable opponents and often exchanged sharp words, sarcastic comments, biting remarks, and sometimes even imprecations.

Now, seeing each other after such a long time, we forgot all about our past rivalry; we were like old friends who had suffered through a difficult emigration together, who had been baked in the same kiln, and we were overjoyed to be together again.

We talked and talked about the past, recalling old party strifes and fiery debates with the special tenderness and loving irony reserved for childhood reminiscences. Both of us had grown old too soon; yet despite our many disappointments and the loss of our youthful enthusiasm and ardor, we felt that those years had been the best and happiest of our lives.

As we sat together into the early hours of the morning and recounted our latest trials and tribulations, I observed Silberzweig carefully; it was clear that he had embraced Judaism once again, that he had undergone a conversion of sorts. We exchanged news about old friends—some were in Siberia, others in prison, all now scattered far and wide. Then I was reminded of yet another person in our group, a passionate young man who thought of himself as an ardent revolutionary.

"Ah, don't ask me about him," said Silberzweig with a wave of his hand, "he's a nothing, a renegade. He became a big businessman and is almost a millionaire by now. And what's even worse, he's become one of 'them.' "

In the past, Silberzweig's use of "them" could only have meant one thing: the "Socialist-Revolutionaries."[1] There had been no other distinction between "us" and "them" for him in those days. Now it was clear to me that he meant something else.

"What do you mean he joined 'them'?"

"I mean that he made use of the only advantage which Jews have over Christians—the privilege to convert."

An elderly Jewish man traveling in our compartment, a doctor who practiced in a small town, overheard our conversation and spoke up after Silberzweig's last statement:

"You're absolutely right! Conversion *is* a privilege, and there are financial benefits, too; some people have made good money from it."

"From converting?"

"Yes, from converting! At the time of the mass expulsions from Moscow," the doctor continued, "hundreds of Jews converted.[2] Then one resourceful Jew figured out a way of turning conversions into a profitable business for himself: he went through the conversion ceremony for others. Obviously no one wanted to study the catechism and be baptized by the priest and all the rest of it, so this Jew did the whole thing for them—for a stiff fee, of course. On a given day he would bring his client's identity papers to the priest of one district of the city and be converted, and on another day he would bring another client's identity papers to the priest in a different district of the city. When he had been converted in this way by all the priests in Moscow, he began to travel through the surrounding cities. All in all, he went through fifty-five conversions and earned hundreds of rubles—and he always managed to come home for the High Holidays, too. You see, converting for others was only his way of making a living; he remained a Jew."

No one seemed interested in whether this was a true story or a joke—and no one felt like laughing.

"I'll tell you something else," said Silberzweig. "Christians are not adaptable enough to take advantage of the privilege of conversion even on the rare occasion when it is offered to them."

"What do you mean by a Christian being given the privilege of converting? Is such a thing possible," I asked, amazed.

"Here in Russia anything is possible. I was once involved in a situation in which a young Christian woman, a genuine Slav from a religious family, I believe, was about to convert. It was absolutely essential for her to go through with the ceremony, and by a stroke of luck the opportunity to do so presented itself, yet she refused— go talk to a goy! If you're interested I'll tell you the story."

"Please, please, do tell us," I begged, bursting with curiosity.

2

"Do you remember a student in Berne by the name of Stephanova," Silberzweig began. "Her full name was Anastasia Stephanova. She was short and blond, and she always had a solemn expression on her face, like a nun. You must have met her many times. She came to every meeting."

"Yes, yes. I remember her very well," I answered.

"She was a fanatical Social Democrat,[3] devoted to the party heart and soul. Her father was a general: he used to send her over four hundred rubles a month, most of which she handed over to the party while she herself went hungry. They considered her one of the most diligent and dedicated workers in the movement.

"Once, after the arrest of a large number of party members in St. Petersburg, I received orders from the central committee in that city to come immediately and to bring Stephanova with me; two-thirds of St. Petersburg's central committee members had been arrested. Those were the stormy days of strikes, demonstrations, and the war with the Socialists-Revolutionaries. And the party itself was plagued by internal dissension and disunity. There was no time to lose.

"Stephanova had just finished her studies at the university and was in the midst of final examinations. But as soon as she heard about the central committee's order, she discontinued her tests and was ready to leave a few hours later. And then the question of passports came up. Being an immigrant I had to have a completely legal passport. Stephanova was, in fact, a legal resident, but she had so many offenses on her record that they would surely have arrested her at the border; so she needed a new passport, too. We explored every possible avenue and finally came up with two passports, one suitable for each of us, thank God. They were legal, but they had some defects. My passport made me fifteen years younger; Stephanova's made her ten years older. But this was nothing compared to the really serious flaws. It was just our luck that on our certificates I was classified as a non-Jew while Stephanova was identified as a Jewess.

"The truth is that Stephanova could pass for a Jewish woman: she had a certain Jewish look, a sadness in her eyes, a longing. On the other hand, as you can see for yourself, my face with the long nose and the black, curly hair didn't in the least match the name I was given, 'Kelim Trifonovitch Soloviev, peasant from the province of Kaluga.' But we had no choice. All we could do was to trust to our wits.

"And we were lucky! We crossed the border, arrived in St. Petersburg, and found the man we were looking for—all without incident. It couldn't have gone more smoothly. Stephanova spent the night with some acquaintances, liberal people who sympathized with our cause. In the morning, when her host asked to see her passport—Gevalt! Catastrophe! Disaster!—a Jewish passport, issued to Hannah Henia Floigelman![4] Within twenty-four hours her entrance papers would be stamped, and then she might be arrested and sent off to prison. What to do?

"We began to scour the town for someone to help us and found a Jew who was an expert in these things. For twenty-five rubles he arranged a 'right of residence' certificate as well as a power of attorney from a timber merchant. For another five rubles the passport was authorized. Everything was correct and kosher.

"Stephanova found a place to live and started to work. After a week she, Hannah Henia that is, was summoned to the police station. Nothing serious! The clerk wanted to know only a few things—how was Hannah Henia's business doing, to whom was she selling her timber, what price was she getting for it? The answer to the question was a three-ruble note. This satisfied him and everything was fine once again. But not for long! He had many children, poor things, so he often found reasons to inquire about Hannah Henia's business. And the police officer, too, was consumed with curiosity about her business. And so was the police commissioner. When Stephanova left town for a few days, they signed her out; but when she returned, the entire procedure was repeated all over again.

"She tried switching apartments and transferring to another police district, but the new passport officer had a large family, too. To make a long story short, Stephanova had no peace. Not a week went by without her being called into the police station. Just picture the situation: a young woman, without a drop of Jewish blood in her veins but living in the city with Jewish papers, is involved over her head in revolutionary activities. Her room is full of illicit brochures and proclamations, and she is constantly harassed by the police! No wonder my poor Stephanova became bitter and depressed."

3

Silberzweig continued. "One day we had a visit from a member of the provincial committee, a Jew, and while we were discussing party matters I happened to mention Stephanova's Jewish passport and the troubles it caused her. Our friend burst into laughter. 'Fools! Are you mad? Why didn't you think of this yourselves?' he shouted. 'She must convert!'

"We laughed, too. The idea is as simple as the Columbus egg trick, but somehow it never occurred to us. You might remember that in those days I was very far removed from Judaism. Nonetheless, I had no use for converts; I considered conversion beneath contempt. In this case, however, I was overjoyed that Jews had been given this great privilege. It's no small thing to rescue a friend from danger, to free her from the necessity of having to deal with the police at every turn, to prevent the failure of a party committee. And how? Simply by having a Christian go through the conversion procedure! I felt relieved and confident that everything would turn out well.

"While walking to Stephanova's apartment a few days later, I laughed out loud every time I thought about her converting. I even wanted to buy her a bouquet of flowers but couldn't find a flower shop on the way. When I arrived, I made a ceremony of congratulating her, asking her how she felt now that she was born again and if she would wear a heavy cross around her neck? Her answer was that she had not gone to see the priest.

"What happened?" I asked, surprised.

"Nothing really. I just couldn't do it," she answered in a whisper.

"Well, don't put it off any longer," I said. "It's very important for you to become a legal resident. You might get into serious trouble if you don't."

Another week went by, and when I met her again, she still hadn't gone to see the priest. This time I was really angry. "You must go to the priest today," I said impatiently. "It's time you finished this business."

She hesitated before talking. Then, with lowered eyes and in a hushed tone, she said, "I don't want to go."

"Why?" I raised my voice, shocked.

"It's disgusting."

"What's disgusting?" I asked, not knowing what to make of her statement.

"The whole business of converting."

"What do you mean?" I blurted out, more confused than ever now. "I could understand your feelings if you were Jewish, but you're Christian, the same as a person who has already converted."

"But it's all a farce."

"And what if it is a farce! What difference does that make to you?"

"That's exactly what disgusts me," she said. "Making a farce of something as serious as religion."

"Watch it." I laughed. "Someone might really take you for a practicing Christian."

"I'm not religious," she protested. "Still, I can't get the thought out of my mind—my action will make a mockery and a sham of the sacred belief of millions of people."

"You sound like a follower of Tolstoy," I countered. "If you think pretense is immoral, why do you constantly deceive the government?"

"A policeman is not someone's God," she replied.

"You're talking nonsense," I shouted at her.

"It might be nonsense," she calmly answered, "but there are sentiments that are stronger than reason."

She sat in silence for a while and then spoke up with conviction, "I want to be truthful with you. I believe that only someone with a godless soul is capable of making a mockery out of another person's religion, or of joking about a God who is holy to His believers."

To the very end, all my arguments fell on deaf ears. She never changed her thinking, and she never converted. What do you think of such a goyish head?

For the first time in my life I felt that it wouldn't be such a bad idea to talk to a goy.

1912 (Translated by Golda Werman)

THE TOWER IN ROME

▼

(Dedicated to the illustrious memory of I. L. Peretz)

Fearsome
and wonderful
story of an enchanted
tower with four gates, of an iron
crown, and of blades of grass that did not wither.

1

From the earliest times there stood in Rome, the capital of the land of Edom, a great tower of indescribable beauty. In the tower there were four gates, facing each of the four sides of the world. All the gates were blocked and bolted with iron bolts and locked with locks so that no living soul could penetrate into the tower, and no one knew what was inside it. From ancient times there was a custom that each emperor, following his coronation, had to have a new lock attached to each gate; no one knew why this was done, but every emperor observed this strictly because this had been the custom from earliest times, from generation to generation.

And it came to pass one day that the king of Edom died. All the lords, dukes, stargazers and other great people assembled in order to choose a new emperor. In those days there lived in Rome a man of lowly origin who had raised himself up from the dust to the highest station and had become a great lord, and everyone followed his word because he knew how to move men's hearts. When they assembled to choose a new emperor, all agreed to seat the man of lowly origin on the throne.

The dukes, lords, and stargazers approached the man, bowed before him and said to him, "Long live our lord! We have chosen you to be emperor over us."

And the man answered, "I will give my consent to be emperor

over you only on condition that you promise me, and certify with your signatures and your seals, that you will fulfill what I demand of you."

They said to him, "Let our lord tell us his wish, what he will demand of us."

The man again said to them, "I swear by your heads that I will not open my lips until you give your word, certified with your signatures and seals, that you will fulfill the request that I will make of you."

They consented, and they seated the man on the throne, placed a golden crown on his head, knelt and bowed before him, and cried out, "Long live the emperor!" And they made a great feast, and they ate, drank, and were merry.

The next day the emperor summoned all the dukes, lords, and stargazers and said to them, "It is my wish to know what is in the tower with the four locked gates. I therefore order you to open the gates for me so that I may enter the tower and see what is there."

The dukes, lords, and stargazers were greatly frightened by these words, and they all answered with one voice, "We fear greatly to fulfill our sovereign's desire! Since earliest times no one has dared open the gates of the tower; rather, each emperor has hung new locks upon them. If we now disregard the command of our ancestors, we will bring the greatest misfortunes upon ourselves and our country."

When the emperor heard these words, he became angry and cried out, "Did you not yourselves pledge and certify with your signatures and seals that you would do everything I required of you? If you do not fulfill my desire, your blood will be on your heads!"

When they saw that the emperor remained steadfast in his wish, the dukes, lords, and stargazers replied with great deference, "May it be done according to the word of our sovereign!"

And they summoned experienced locksmiths and directed them to remove the bolts and to take away the locks from one gate of the tower. When this was done, the emperor with his courtiers and servants went to the tower, opened up the gate, and began to enter the tower. But when the emperor stepped over the threshold of the tower, the gate closed with a loud noise. None of those who had come with the emperor could enter, and he remained alone in the tower.

He raised his eyes and saw before him a great garden in full bloom, like a Garden of Eden, with many trees pleasant to the sight and good for food.[1]

The emperor proceeded further and saw in the middle of the garden a pool consisting of a thick red liquid, and he understood that this was not water but blood. He saw that in the middle of the pool an iron crown lay upon the surface, and from all sides human hands reached out from the earth toward the crown, so many that they looked like a young forest, and many of the hands were intertwined with one another like the roots of an old oak tree. The emperor walked around the pool and marveled at what he saw, for he did not understand the meaning of the hands that reached out and were intertwined, or how the iron crown remained on the surface of the pool without sinking to the bottom as an iron object should.

He returned to the gate and wished to leave the tower, but the gate did not open. The emperor cried out angrily to the gate, "I, the king of Rome, order you to open up immediately!"

The gate opened up, and the emperor left the tower and returned to the royal palace, but he told no one what he had seen.

The next day the emperor again assembled the dukes and lords and stargazers, and ordered them to open the second gate for him. They persisted in their fear, and the emperor again spoke with great firmness; and they fulfilled his desire.

The emperor entered the tower through the second gate, but he could not see what was happening around him because of the thick darkness there, like the plague of darkness in Egypt. When he took his first step, the emperor felt human bodies under his feet. He bent over to touch them, and he could feel that they had not yet lost their warmth. The bodies lay one next to the other wherever he placed his feet. He was amazed that the bodies which had lain there for so many years were warm and gave forth no foul odor as corpses do.

He waited to see what would happen. After a short while many candles were suddenly illuminated, and it became as bright as day. The emperor saw that he was in a temple of wonderful splendor whose dome reached to the heavens, and he understood that this was a temple of the Jewish God. As soon as it became light, the bodies, which had lain as though dead, awakened and quickly stood upon their feet and began to pray with great intensity. The emperor listened and understood that they were praying to the Jewish God. From their great fervor and ardor, the faces of the people began to blaze and sparks flew from their lips, and by the middle of the prayers lightning began to fly and the dome opened and the emperor saw angels hovering under the heavens, gradually descending to the temple. He saw further that the angels carried on their wings a splendid man in white garments, with a brightly shining face.[2] When the prayers drew to a close and there remained only to pronounce the final "Amen," the people fell to the earth as though dead, the dome closed, the candles went out, and darkness once again prevailed. When the time came for the evening prayers, everything that had occurred during the earlier prayers happened again. And in the morning it happened once more. The emperor did not wait for the end of the prayers; since it was still light, he left the tower.

On the third day the emperor ordered that the third gate be opened, and he went in. He saw a circular chamber whose walls were covered with black stones and in the middle stood a golden chest of such wonderful craftsmanship that its like had never been seen by human eyes. The emperor wanted to open it, but it would not open. The emperor cried out, "I, Emperor of Rome, order you to open!"

The cover of the chest raised itself up, and the emperor saw that the chest was filled with all kinds of grass, ripped out by the roots. The blades of grass were green and fragrant, and their roots were fresh and succulent. All the blades of grass were bound in bundles of ten. The emperor counted them and found that there were sixty thousand bundles. He did not know what it meant that the uprooted blades of grass had not lost their greenness, their fragrance, or their succulence over all the years, and he was greatly amazed. He left the tower.

On the fourth day the emperor ordered the fourth gate opened. He went in and saw a palace of red marble, which he entered. Inside, there were rooms adorned with gold and silver, pearls and precious stones. The emperor went through six chambers and entered the seventh, which was the most beautiful of all. In the place of honor there stood a throne carved from a single sapphire stone. In the middle of the chamber stood silver tables covered with golden tablecloths. And on the tables were set out the best foods and the choicest wines, but there was not a living soul to be found in the palace. But when the sun set, a loud noise was suddenly heard, and a blowing of trumpets and shouts of rejoicing, and the noise of footsteps and the hoofbeats of horsemen. The emperor understood that many people were coming, and he concealed himself behind the throne in order to see, unobserved, what would happen.

The doors of the palace opened up and a large number of soldiers entered, and generals and dukes, all armed and in uniforms embroidered in gold. In the lead went a man in royal clothing with a crown on his head. Everyone showed him great honor and called him emperor. They entered the seventh chamber, sat down at the tables, and ate, drank, and were merry. After the meal, the emperor, who had just entered, sat on the throne, and all fell on their faces before him and cried out loudly, "Long live our god, the emperor of the entire world!" Everything the emperor commanded was carried out with great dispatch and deference.

When it had become midnight, the emperor rose from his throne and called out in a loud voice, "I order you to bring the iron crown and place it upon my head!"

No sooner had he spoken these words than the soldiers and generals and dukes threw themselves upon him and dragged him down from the throne, ripped his royal garments from him, and tore his body itself into pieces. And in that moment the soldiers and the dukes and the pieces of the tattered emperor all disappeared.

The emperor left his hiding place and was amazed at what he had seen, for he did not understand what it meant. He left the tower.

2

After all these things had occurred, the emperor summoned all the magicians and stargazers and other sages, and told them everything he had seen in the four parts of the tower. He said to them, "My wish is that you explain to me the meaning of everything I have seen. And if you do not fulfill my command, I will deliver all of you to the executioner!"

The stargazers and magicians and sages all bowed before the emperor and answered him, "Long live the emperor! We are prepared to fulfill your wish, but what we have seen in the tower is full of wonder. It represents deeds from ancient times, and it will be difficult for us to find the solution to all of them immediately. Thus we ask you to give us thirty days in order that we have time to work our enchantments, inquire of our gods, study the stars, and divine with animal entrails."

The emperor consented and said, "It shall be as you have said. I grant you thirty days, and at the end of that period if you have not revealed the secret of the tower to me, your blood will be on your own heads."

The stargazers and the magicians and the sages left the emperor and went to their temples and inquired of their gods, worked their enchantments, calculated according to the stars and the constellations, and divined with the entrails of wild and domestic animals; but the secret of the tower was not revealed to them. And when the thirty days were exhausted, the magicians, stargazers, and sages went to the temples of their idols, wept and cried and rent their clothing and covered their heads with ashes, for they saw that terrible wrath had been vented upon them and that their end was near.

In those days there lived in Rome an old stargazer who had seven sons, all of them magicians and stargazers. It was their custom that each day one of them would come to their father to visit him and wait upon him. On the final day of the thirty days, none of the sons came to visit their old father. He was greatly surprised. With his waning strength, he went on his crutches to see his eldest son. He arrived at his house and asked him: "How is this day different from all other days of the year? Why has none of my sons come to visit me today and taken care of my needs, as you always do?"

And the eldest son answered his father and said to him: "Oh, Father! A terrible misfortune has been vented upon the heads of your sons. Know that before the sun completes its daily course, the thread of their lives will be cut short. In order not to grieve your heart with bitter sighs, none of us has come to you today as we always do."

And he told his father everything that had happened to them. His father listened to his son's words and said to him, "Grief has distracted the thoughts of my sons, and the desire to render honor to their old father has blinded their vision. Have you then forgotten that I also am a stargazer? And like the others I must present myself before the emperor? This is my paternal command: Tomorrow you must take me with you to the emperor and include me in your numbers. Who knows what the coming day will bring? Perhaps we will be fortunate and I will turn the sword away from your necks and change your grief into rejoicing and your sighs into singing."

His son answered with great respect, "It will be as our father has commanded."

And in the morning, when the morning star had risen and there had assembled at the royal court the stargazers, magicians, and sages together with the dukes and lords of Rome and many of the people, there also came the seven sons of the old stargazer, carrying their father on their shoulders.

The emperor went out to those who had come and said, "The thirty days that I granted you for stargazing and enchantments have

become exhausted with the ascent of the morning star. Now you must reveal to me the secret of the marvels that I saw in the tower."

The greatest of the stargazers stepped forward, fell on his face before the emperor, and said, "Long live the emperor! Your servants the magicians and stargazers have forfeited their heads to you. We have worked our enchantments, inquired of our gods, conjured with the stars, and divined with animal entrails. But we did not succeed in removing the veil from the secret of the tower. And now, do with us that which seems good in your eyes."

And the anger of the emperor blazed up and he cried out, "I swear by my head that your eyes shall not again see the stars over which you have no power, and your lips will utter no more conjurations which mean nothing. Before the evening star rises, your bodies will be devoured by wild animals and picked at by bloodthirsty birds!"

Then the old stargazer stepped forward. He bowed before the emperor and said, "Oh, omnipotent Emperor of Rome! May the blazing of your anger be stilled and may the sword you have borne over your servants' heads be stayed. The stargazers and magicians are not to blame for their ignorance. Know, Emperor, that the tower with the four gates was built by the greatest sorceror who ever knew the course of time. In order to conceal his enchantments from the stars and the spirits, he constructed the tower in those moments when day unto day utters speech and night unto night whispers its dreams.[3] In those moments the rays of the stars are extinguished and the rule of the spirits over the world is weakened, and everything done at that time remains concealed from the wisest magicians and stargazers."

When the emperor had finished listening to the words of the old stargazer, he said, "Old man! Your words demonstrate that you have more understanding than all the other magicians, and you know things that are concealed from their eyes. If the secret of the tower is revealed to you, you must know who built it and what is concealed in its stony entrails."

The old stargazer answered, "Oh, omnipotent Emperor of Rome! With your great wisdom, you have foreseen that secrets hidden from the eyes of others are known to me. Know, then, that from oldest times the secret of the enchanted tower has been entrusted to only one stargazer. And when the time of his death approaches, he hands down the secret to the most respected person in his circle. Exactly one hundred years ago an old stargazer from the desert, as he was dying, handed the secret of the tower down to me. Now the time of

my own passing away has come, and I select you to be the guardian of the secret until you hand it down to another. Therefore, command, Emperor, that all who stand here and who are in your palace remove themselves a distance from your throne that they may not hear. Then I will open my lips."

The emperor ordered all those who stood before his throne and who were in the royal court to remove themselves a distance. When that had happened, the old man began to tell the story.

3

"Let it be known to you, King of Rome, that the tower with the four gates was built by Emperor Nimrod, and not by human hands but with the power of enchantment. When Nimrod had subjugated the entire world and had become ruler over all creatures, he said in his heart, 'I am God.' Everyone knelt and bowed before him and brought sacrifices to him. Fearing that after his death another would rule the earth and would destroy the altars that had been raised for him, and would blot out the name of Nimrod from human memory, he put the entire power and might of his universal rule into his iron crown. After this it became so heavy that the strongest man was unable to move it even a hairsbreadth. And Nimrod had a tower erected around the crown and had four gates made in the tower facing each of the four sides of the world, in order that the tower be open before everyone and in order that anyone who stepped over the threshold of one gate could not say, 'I went into the tower and it belongs to me.' But in order to shield the iron crown from the gaze of many persons, he worked enchantments so that the gates would open only for kings and rulers of nations. When Nimrod died, the rumor spread in all countries that whosoever lifted Nimrod's iron crown and placed it on his own head would become ruler over the entire world. Kings and rulers of every country began to come to Rome, and with great covetousness each one grasped the crown in order to lift it. But none of them had the strength to move it from its place, and because of their great exertion, each one of them who had tried to lift the crown began to sink into the earth, at first to their ankles, then to their waists, and finally above their heads so that there remained above the earth only their hands, which did not cease in their covetousness to reach out toward the crown and to snatch at its edges. And thus much time went by and many

kings and rulers perished, but there was nevertheless no decrease in the number who reached out toward the iron crown.

"And it came to pass one day that the emperor of the land of Edom was a strong-willed and merciless man named Nero. He too went to the tower as the others did, in order to lift the iron crown. But seeing the many hands reaching out from the earth around the crown, he understood with his great wisdom that the crown could not be lifted merely by strength of hand. He summoned the greatest magicians from the land of Egypt, presented them with the most beautiful gifts, and asked them to reveal to him with what kind of power the iron crown could be lifted.

"The magicians cast their spells and answered Emperor Nero thus: 'Through our spells we have learned that Nimrod concealed the secret of the iron crown from the stars and the spirits and hid it inside a rock. He recorded the secret on a tablet, and flying to the highest peak of the Mountains of Darkness, he hewed out a hole in a stone of the mountain and placed the tablet in it, and with enchantment rolled the heaviest stone in the world upon it. And in order that no one be able to remove the rock from the tablet, he placed the strongest wind in a cave and through enchantment prevented its leaving, so that the wind could not escape and carry away the stone from the tablet.'

"When Nero had finished listening to their words, he cried out, 'I must obtain the tablet and learn the secret that is recorded on it.'

"And the magicians said to him, 'There is only one way to obtain the tablet. Command that an eagle from the high mountains be captured. Prepare strong ropes and a long stick. Have a man who has been condemned to death brought in, and order his head cut off. Afterward, sit atop the eagle between his wings, fasten the severed head to the end of the stick, and reach the stick out in front of you so that the eagle always has before it the eyes of the severed head. Wanting to peck them out, it will fly after the head, and you steer its flight to the highest peak of the Mountains of Darkness. When you arrive there, do not release the eagle but keep him with you. When you come to the middle of the mountaintop, you will see a cave that is blocked up by an enchanted door. The wind is confined there. Tie yourself to the top of a rock with the rope so that the wind will not carry you away, and with the conjurations that we will give you, undo the enchantment of the cave door. This will release the wind that is rooted in the mountain, and it will carry the stone away from the tablet. You take the tablet, seat yourself on the eagle, and with the stick and the severed head steer its flight back to earth.'

"Emperor Nero followed the magicians' counsel and did as they told him, and he obtained the tablet. And when he returned to the imperial palace, he took out the tablet and there found, recorded in the Babylonian language, the following words: 'From me, the god of all creatures and the omnipotent ruler of the entire world, Nimrod, to Emperor Nero of the Land of Edom, greetings!

'Know, Emperor Nero, that it is possible to lift my crown not with the power of the hand and not with the power of the sword, but with duplicity, fraud, and deceit. In order to obtain my iron crown, dispatch envoys to the kings and rulers of all seventy peoples and nations in the world. Write each one flattering letters praising their might and wisdom. Propose to each king that, together with you but unknown to all other kings in the world, he lift the iron crown so that the two of you will divide the kingdom of the earth between you. Do this with great wisdom and secrecy so that no one king will learn that you are sending your envoys to the other kings. When the rulers of all seventy nations come to you, lead each one separately into the tower, and lead each one by a different path to the iron crown. And when all seventy kings and rulers come together suddenly, instead of lifting the crown they will fall upon one another and they will smite one another with the sword so that all will fall dead. From the blood they have spilled, a pool of blood will form around the crown, and the crown will float upon the surface. At that time you will reach out your hand and with no effort lift the crown and place it upon your head and become the ruler of the entire world.'

"When Emperor Nero had finished reading what was on the tablet, he fulfilled everything that was said on it, and he did everything with great wisdom and deception. And when all the kings and rulers had gathered in the tower and each had smitten another with the sword so that a pool was formed from their spilled blood and the crown floated upon the surface, Emperor Nero entered the tower and reached his hand toward the crown. But he could not move it from its place because even on the surface of the pool of blood, it lay as though welded there and it had not lost its heaviness."

4

"Emperor Nero again assembled the sorcerers of Egypt and asked them why what was written on Nimrod's tablet had not been fulfilled and the iron crown had remained as heavy as before and would not move from its place.

"The magicians cast their spells and answered Emperor Nero thus, 'Know, Emperor, that you yourself are to blame that the crown did not lose its weight, because you did not fulfill everything that was written on the tablet.'

"Emperor Nero was amazed and asked, 'What did I omit that was written on the tablet? Tell me, and I will correct my error.'

"And the magicians answered, 'You were instructed to assemble the rulers of all seventy nations and peoples of the world. But you omitted one people, and you did not address yourself to its ruler.'

"Emperor Nero looked into this, and he found recorded that kings and rulers from sixty-nine nations and peoples had been summoned. When he had them counted up, he learned that the people of Israel had been omitted.

"Emperor Nero assembled the magicians and said to them, 'The words from your lips were just. In truth, I did not assemble all the kings and rulers, and I omitted the people of Israel. But how could I have summoned the ruler of that people when it does not have its own land and wanders among other nations without its own king?'

"And the magicians answered him: 'Know, Emperor, that even today the people of Israel is still ruled by the House of King David. Therefore, we counsel you as follows: Assemble ten men descended from the House of David and lead them to the crown in the tower. As soon as they reach out their hands to it, the crown will lose its weight, because the required number of seventy nations and peoples of the world will be fulfilled.'

"Emperor Nero commanded that ten men be sought who were descended from the House of David, and they were found and brought before the emperor. Nero spoke to them in the same flattering speech he had used when writing to the rulers of the other peoples, and he sought to persuade them to raise the iron crown together with him.

"But the ten men all answered him with one voice. 'On account of our sins we were driven from our land and removed from our soil. And now we turn with our heart and soul to our omnipotent God and pray that he send us the Messiah, who will reestablish the greatness of the House of Jacob. Our soul does not yearn for a crown of sovereignty over the world but rather for peace and goodwill between men and nations. Therefore, Emperor, we will not enter the tower and we will not reach out our hands toward the iron crown.'

"Emperor Nero tried with flattering words to persuade them to follow him. But when he saw that they remained steadfast in their position, he became angry and had them taken by force into the tower, where they were put in copper chains by the pool of blood, since he hoped that when they saw the crown before them, their desire would be aroused and they would reach out their hands toward it.

"But, instead, the men of the House of David rubbed through their chains and removed themselves to the western side of the tower and began to pray for the Messiah to come. They prayed with great fervor and ardor, and because of their great fervor, there were created around the ten men first the walls and then the dome of a temple similar to the Temple in Jerusalem. This synagogue was adorned with great beauty, and many candles illuminated it. And when the middle of the prayers was reached, the dome opened up and the heavens opposite it opened, and angels hovered and sang songs of praise. The angels flew to the Messiah and, surrounding him, carried him on their wings to the open dome of the temple. But since the Messiah's hour had not yet arrived, at the final "Amen" the men who were praying fell to the earth as though dead, the dome closed up, the candles went out, and the Messiah returned to his solitude. But when next the hour came for prayers, the men of the House of David awoke, and everything happened again as at the first time. And from then on, this has occurred three times a day.

"Emperor Nero waited a while, and then entered the tower to see whether the stiff-necked men of the House of David had succumbed. And when he saw that instead of reaching out their hands toward the crown, they had enclosed themselves within the walls of a temple and were absorbed in fervent prayer, he became enraged."

5

"Emperor Nero again assembled the Egyptian magicians and asked them to show him how to break the wills of the men from the House of David.

"And the magicians answered him, 'There are no means of overcoming the children of that nation, for they are greatly stiff-necked. Therefore, hear our counsel. Instead of compelling the men from the House of David to reach out their hands toward the iron crown, in order that the number of nations and peoples of the world be completed at seventy, it were better to annihilate this nation to the last person so that no remnant shall survive. There will then remain the sixty-nine nations who have submitted to your order, and the iron crown will then lose its weight before your hands.'

"The counsel of the magicians found favor in Emperor Nero's eyes, and he asked, 'With what kind of power can that nation be annihilated to the last person?'

"And the magicians answered, 'The secret of how to annihilate the people of Israel can be revealed to you only by someone who is himself descended from that people. Know, Emperor, that in the eastern portion of your empire there is a country whose inhabitants bow down to the severed head of a Jew. They search in all the distant countries for a Jew who is both of priestly stock and the eldest son of an eldest son for seven generations, and with sweet speech and sundry promises they entice him to their country, where they cut off his head and insert magical writings under his tongue. The severed head lives on for seventy years and prophesies, and the inhabitants of that country bow down to the head, bring it sacrificial offerings, and burn incense before it. When the seventy years are exhausted, the head loses its power, and the inhabitants of that country, finding another Jew of priestly stock and a firstborn unto the seventh generation, throw the head to their dogs. And this is our counsel to you, Emperor: Go to that eastern country, bring a sacrificial offering to the severed head, and ask it to tell you how to annihilate the nation of Israel to the last person.'

"Emperor Nero accepted the counsel of the magicians and went to the eastern country. He found the temple where the severed head was placed on a platform, and he brought it a sacrificial offering and asked it to prophesy.

"And the lips of the severed head opened up and began to prophecy:[4]

> 'Behold, a man has come from Edom,
> A mighty emperor from the city of Rome,
> He came to seek out my words,
> To hear out my prophecy,
> How to annihilate the House of Jacob,
> How to destroy the people of Israel.
> How can I be silent,
> When the conjuration under my tongue is not silent?
> How can I conceal,

When my lips speak against my will?
Hear my words, son of the Land of Edom,
Listen to my prophecy, man from Mount Seir.
Behold, the people of Israel is before you,
Spread among foreign peoples.
It is compared to sprouting blades of grass,
That cover the face of the earth.
There is no limit to their spreading,
And no end to their race;
They grow, flourish, and wither,
But when the sun rises,
They revive and flourish again. . . .
But know, son of Edom,
Incline your ear to my words, Emperor of Rome. . . .'

"And the severed head said further, 'Each of the children of the
people of Israel has his blade of grass in the world, and as long as
the blade of grass grows and is green and has its fragrance, the
person that is bound together with it lives and is healthy. But when
the roots of the blade of grass begin to dry up and its stem bends
over and becomes yellow, and the blade of grass loses its fragrance
and succulence, in that same hour the body of that person loses its
vitality, and it is compared to dust. And know further, Emperor of
Rome, that the blades of grass of the Children of Israel have a
different appearance, which sets them apart from all other blades of
grass. In order to annihilate the people of Israel to the last person,
you must seek out the blades of grass of the life of their children:
seek them out in high places and low, in fruitful fields and in desolate
deserts, on mountain peaks and in the crevices of rocks, and when
you have found them, rip them out by the roots, gather them, and
keep a count of their number. When you have picked six hundred
thousand blades of grass, know that the number is complete, for
this is also the number of the Children of Israel, and know that all
the blades of grass will wither and turn yellow and the succulence
of their roots will dry up. Then there will be an end to the House
of Jacob and a disappearance of the Tribes of Israel.'

"When Emperor Nero heard the prophecy of the severed head,
he returned to his country and dispatched his servants experienced
in wild plants to the four corners of the earth, and ordered them to
find and uproot the grass of life of the Children of Israel. He
transmitted to them the signs of how to recognize these blades of
grass. And after a certain period of time had passed, the servants

returned with heaps and heaps of grass. Emperor Nero began to count the blades of grass, but he could not count them all.

"But suddenly the blades of grass themselves began to approach one another, and thin threads went out from them, and they bound themselves in bundles of ten. Emperor Nero rejoiced that it would now be easier to count them. And when he counted sixty thousand bundles, he knew he had uprooted the life roots of the people of Israel to the last one. He had brought the most beautiful and costly golden chest from the royal treasury, put in the blades of grass, and carried the chest into the tower. He returned happy and in good spirits, for he was confident of the destruction of the people of Israel and of attaining universal sovereignty in the near future.

"He waited for a year. And the year ended, and he went to the tower to see the withered grass. But when he opened the chest, he saw that all the blades of grass were fragrant and their roots had not lost their succulence—just as though they had not been ripped from the soil.

"When he saw this, he cried out in blazing anger, 'I now see that the severed head spoke false prophecy, and I swear by my soul that I will annihilate the people of Israel with my sword so that not even a memory will remain!'

"He sent forth his armies over the land of Edom and over all other countries of the world and ordered them to destroy the Children of Israel to the last one—men, women, and children—and to give over their property to plunder. And their annihilation began, and heaps of them fell, and they melted like wax before fire.

"And when the destruction of the people of Israel was already near, there appeared before the throne of Emperor Nero multitudes—multitudes of spirits in the shapes of troops and generals and princes. With a great sounding of trumpets, they announced to Emperor Nero that his wish had been fulfilled, for they had conquered the entire world for him. They led him with great honor to the tower to a red marble palace that they had erected. They brought him into the last chamber, where a banquet had been prepared and there stood a throne carved from a single sapphire stone. They ate and drank and praised Nero, emperor of the entire world. Afterward, they placed him on the throne and rendered him divine respect and cried, 'Long live Emperor Nero, the ruler of the world!'

"Since it had become midnight, Emperor Nero rose from his throne and cried out, 'I order you to bring me my iron crown and set it upon my head!'

"Immediately, all the soldiers and generals and princes threw themselves at him, dragged him down from the throne, ripped the royal garments from him, and tore his body into small pieces. And then they all disappeared.

"And this is repeated every night. . . .

"And it came to pass, when the princes and lords from Nero's court saw that the emperor had gone to the tower and did not return, they understood that some misfortune had befallen him. To prevent the same thing from happening to subsequent emperors, they decided to lock all four gates of the tower, and they further decided that each new emperor should affix a new lock to each gate. The magicians and stargazers, reading Nimrod's tablet, decided that in the future the secret of the tower and of everything that had happened to Emperor Nero would be known to only one magician, who would transmit it before his death to the most important of his colleagues. And thus it was done."

6

When the old sorcerer had told the entire story to the emperor of Rome and finished his narration, he fell asleep and his life began to pass away. But the emperor of Rome turned to him, began to revive him, and asked him to reveal why the grass of life of the people of Israel, even after it was ripped out by the roots, remained fresh and succulent, and what must be done to make it wither and dry up.

The old stargazer opened his lips with great pain, and with an effort murmured, "The blades of grass did not lose their greenness and their succulence because they were bound together in bundles. . . . If Emperor Nero had scattered them one by one. . . ." And with these words the old man spent his strength and died.

The emperor of Rome hurried down from his throne and went quickly to the tower through the third gate, approached the golden chest, and opened it and reached out his hand toward the grass.

And it came to pass, when he began to rip apart the threads with which the bundles of grass were bound, a two-headed calf of dreadful appearance quickly sprang out of the chest. Fixing a burning gaze on the emperor of Rome, the calf let out a resounding roar, like the roar of a lion. From this roar the emperor of Rome fell dead, the tower filled with smoke, the pool of blood began to rock with noisy waves, and the iron crown was overturned and sank to the bottom. And from the temple of the Children of the House of David there was heard the final "Amen."

End of the story of the tower
with the four gates in
the city of
Rome.

1916–1918 (Translated by Michael Stern)

▲

The Destruction
of Galicia:
Excerpts from a
Diary, 1914–17

August–November 1914

The plight of the defenseless Jewish population of Galicia and their horrendous treatment at the hands of the invading Russian army, especially the Cossacks and the Circassians, became known to us right at the beginning of the war [1914] through snatches of information that reached us. The occupation was swift; Galicia was overrun all the way to Prague in the west and to Hungary in the south within two or three months. A large part of Brody was burned, the Jews were robbed and some were killed—all in response to a provocateur's shot. Belz and Husiatyn were completely destroyed. A bloody pogrom in Lemberg left many casualties, and scores of other towns and villages suffered the same fate. Furthermore, the Jews in the conquered region were starving; they were ruined economically and cut off from their own land as well as from Russia.

The most frightening thing about the dispatches we received, which arrived only erratically, was their precise information. A letter from the front, for example, said that a wounded soldier, A.D.G., had been evacuated—nothing more. All other means of obtaining news were closed; civilians were forbidden to enter or to leave Galicia. Even those letters and messages which managed to reach us were more like cries of desperation than systematic reports of the facts.

"My hands shake and my eyes fill up with tears when I think of the fearful events which I witnessed in Galicia, when I remember the cruel things the Cossacks and the other soldiers did to the Jews," wrote a Jewish soldier. "They murdered, they plundered, they raped young women in the streets and cut off the breasts of old women, leaving them to die a slow death."

Another [Jewish] soldier wrote: "We came to a Jewish shtetl in Galicia. The soldiers discovered a wine cellar, which they looted; they soon became drunk. I drank, too, and got drunk right along with them. But when I came up from the cellar and saw what was going on in the shtetl, what the soldiers were doing to the Jews, I sobered up right away. . . ."

A third letter was from a [Jewish] soldier who became insane as a result of what he had seen in Galicia: "When the soldiers arrived in a town the Christians put icons in the windows and on the doors. Wherever there were no icons, that is to say, in a Jewish home, they were free to loot and plunder. Our company came to a certain village, and one of the soldiers noticed a house on a distant hill. He told the officer that he thought it was a Jewish house and was given permission to investigate. When he returned with the news that Jews lived there the officer ordered the company to go to the house. Inside there were about twenty Jews, half dead with fear. They drove them out and the officer gave the order: Stab them! Hack them to pieces! I didn't stay to see what happened after that—I just ran and ran until I fell down, exhausted."

The human mind simply cannot grasp the horror of the events described in these and scores of other frantic letters. A region in which only yesterday a million Jews enjoyed human and civil rights was suddenly enclosed within a ring of fire, blood, and steel; they were cut off and at the mercy of frenzied and violent soldiers and Cossacks who attacked them like packs of wild animals. Many people believed that the entire Jewish population of Galicia was about to be destroyed.

Our most urgent problem was to make contact and to bring them whatever material help we could. This would be difficult, but not impossible. During the first months of the war our philanthropists wouldn't hear of organizing any extensive activity to help the Jewish war victims. They had discharged their obligations by donating large sums of money to the general war charity, they felt, and argued that Jews shouldn't set up a separate organization; it might be considered unpatriotic. Obviously, these super-patriots weren't interested in the plight of the Galician Jews. When a high Russian official asked a millionaire from Kiev, a man with a reputation for doing good works, why he didn't help his Jewish brothers who were dying of hunger in Galicia, his answer was: "Your Excellency, we don't consider the Galician Jews our brothers; they are our enemies—we are at war with them."

But I must admit that this attitude toward the Galician Jewish war victims soon changed.

When the reports from Galicia no longer left any doubt that a disaster was in progress, I decided I had to get there at once and see for myself the extent of the destruction in the shtetls. I wanted to assess the amount of help needed so that I could appear with the facts in hand and request specific sums for the Jews of Galicia, rather than make a general appeal for aid.

Carrying out my plan was no easy task. It took three full months of knocking on doors to make all the necessary legal arrangements for my trip. At first I had hoped to get a merchant's visa and cross into Galicia in one of the wagons of flour or sugar that was being sent by Brodsky.[1] When that didn't work out I turned to Count Ivan Ivanovich Tolstoy, the mayor of St. Petersburg, and asked him to allow me to accompany a medical team going to Galicia.

Tolstoy, a true friend of the Jews, made every effort to fulfill my request. But as there was no detachment leaving just then from St. Petersburg to Galicia, he gave me a letter to the mayor of Moscow, M. V. Chelnokov, the head of the Union of Cities. Chelnokov gave me a letter to the head of the Union of Zemstva, Prince George Evgenevich Lvov.[2] He couldn't help me either, so he sent me back to Count Tolstoy to ask for a letter to Guchkov,[3] who was then in Warsaw and in a position to give me a special pass into Galicia. When I returned to St. Petersburg I received a telegram informing me that Prince P. D. Dolgorukov was organizing a detachment which would soon leave for Galicia and that I would be included in the group. I returned to Moscow only to discover that Dolgorukov had gotten orders to go to Riga, not to Galicia. Another detachment was organized by Konovalov, but for bureaucratic reasons he couldn't take me along. In short, everyone displayed great sympathy for my problems and a readiness to help—and then sent me on to someone else.

Finally I decided to go to Galicia via Warsaw. With a letter from Count Tolstoy to Guchkov, as well as a recommendation from Prince Lvov to the chief of the Warsaw branch of the Union of Zemstva, V. V. Virubov, I left for Warsaw on the twenty-first of November, 1914.

2

The Jewish population was in a state of shock, incapable of defending itself against the brutality and the murders and powerless to repudiate even the most shameful libels. The people resorted to the old Jewish method of finding strength and comfort in weaving tales out of their sighs and tears. It was whispered that "the rebbe is writing a *megillah* on the war which will surpass everything that has been written until now, and when he finishes it, redemption will come to the Jews." Others said that the end of the Jewish exile would surely come soon; they had studied the ancient tomes and calculated that the days of the Messiah were at hand.

But mostly they spun tales about accusations of espionage which, in the popular mind, recalled the blood libels of old and were retold in exactly the same way. In both types of stories, it was assumed that these were not fictional crimes but actual crimes perpetrated by others in order to frame the Jews. Like all folktales, they were suffused with a deep-rooted optimism, with the belief that in the end the truth will win out.

The most widespread libel had to do with secret telephones that the Jews purportedly used to pass information to the enemy. This inspired a whole string of tales in which the town of Zamosc was often the chosen setting. One version simply told of how a number of Jews were hanged as a result of the telephone libel; other Jews would have been hanged too, were it not for a priest, carrying a cross, who appeared before the judge and testified that it was the Poles who were guilty. The priest's evidence proved to be correct; all the Jews were immediately freed and the Poles were hanged instead—sixteen in all.

A second, more literary folk legend, concerned a libel against some Jews of Zamosc who were arrested for aiding the enemy. Just when the trial judges were at the point of passing the death sentence, two Russians entered, a woman teacher and a district magistrate; they fell to their knees and begged to be heard, and the judges agreed. "The Jews are innocent," they testified. "Come with us if you want to know who the guilty party really is." The judges were taken to the Count's courtyard and from there into a deep cellar where they found the Countess Zamoiska talking by telephone to the Austrians. She was hanged on the spot.

I heard this folktale in Minsk. A similar one, which I heard in Lublin, ended as follows: When they went down to the Countess Zamoiska's cellar they found a group of Jews with long earlocks, wearing caftans and skullcaps, speaking to the Austrians by telephone. The judges were astounded. This proved that just the opposite was true—the Jews were indeed the guilty ones. The district magistrate took them in for questioning and discovered that they were really Poles. The masquerade was intended to cast blame on the Jews in the event that they were arrested.

Another tale told of a Pole who convinced a German spy to dress up like a Jew and stay near the trenches; then he informed against him. When they came to arrest him they found that he had a German passport and he confessed that he wasn't Jewish.

A similar tale concerned six Jews who delivered to the army a shipment of oats which killed all the horses that ate it. The Jews were arrested and sentenced to death. Five were hanged immediately and the sixth, who was arrested later, was to be hanged, too. He appealed to the authorities: "Why hurry? I beg of you, before you hang me, send for some oats from the Polish nobleman's middle granary."

They sent several cavalrymen to the nobleman, who was very polite and showed them oats from every granary but the middle one. "What about those oats?" they asked. "Those are of very poor quality," he answered. But they insisted that he open the granary and when they removed some oats and tested them they proved to be poisoned. The Jew was freed and the nobleman was hanged.

The most popular folktale among Jews was about two soldiers who confronted each other on the battlefield. As one stabbed the other, he was shocked to hear the dying soldier cry out, "*Shma Yisroel*, Hear O Israel."

Before the war I had traveled through Volhynia and Podolia to collect folklore and repeatedly heard a legend about a bride and groom who were killed by Chmielnicki just as they were being led to the bridal canopy; in at least fifteen or sixteen shtetls I was taken to a grave near the synagogue where the bride and groom were supposed to have been buried. This is perhaps the only folktale from the time of Chmielnicki which is still widely known. During the massacres of 1648 the very existence of the Jewish people was threatened, and there was a real danger that all the Jews would be killed. This danger was symbolized in the legend of the bride and groom who were murdered at the moment of their union and prevented from perpetuating the family and the people. It symbolized a tree cut down just when it was beginning to blossom.

This war was not perceived as a threat to the continued existence of the people, but it was marked by one of the greatest tragedies that can happen to a nation: brothers fighting against brothers. The people dwelled on this tragedy from the very beginning and expressed it symbolically in the legend of the "*Shma Yisroel*, Hear O Israel."

I heard many different variants of this folktale in at least eight or ten different localities—St. Petersburg, Moscow, Minsk, Kiev, Warsaw, in short, every place where there were homeless Jews or soldiers.

Most people thought that this was a factual account about real people, not a folktale.

3

January 1915

Galicia is certainly one of the poorest if not the poorest area of central Europe. The land has few natural resources and almost no mineral deposits, and the ground, which is not distinguished for its fruitfulness, is cultivated in the most primitive manner. Furthermore, industry is not at all developed and neither are manufacture or trade. The local population, especially the Ruthenians of eastern Galicia, are very backward intellectually and economically; even the Russian peasants are more advanced than they. Obviously this has had an effect on the economic and to a certain extent even on the cultural condition of Galician Jewry, which numbered between 900,000 to 1,000,000 before the war. Despite the fact that the Jews of the Austrian Empire enjoyed equal rights along with the general population and were free to pursue any profession, the Galician Jews were very poor and unsophisticated. This is indicated by two objective statistical facts: they have the highest mortality rate of any Jewish group, and they have the highest rate of immigration to America.

In a cultural sense, too, the Jews of Galicia were more backward than other Jewish groups. It is true that Galicia was not left out of the stormy ideological wars among the Jews. Along with other countries it experienced the crises of the false Messiah, Hasidism, the period of enlightenment, the movement toward assimilation, revolution, nationalism, and Zionism. Many important personalities in all these areas came from Galicia. But not in a single one of these movements did Galicia play a central part or create something reflecting its unique character.[4] Galicia was distinguished from other Jewish regions only in that such movements were more extreme and more impassioned. The hasidic movement became very degenerate there; the struggle between orthodoxy and the Enlightenment was extremely bitter and often became violent; and the movement toward assimilation was expressed in a form that was almost a caricature of itself.

Furthermore, although the Jews of Galicia enjoyed equality and civil rights in the Austrian Empire, their political situation was complicated. In the never-ending struggle for national expression among the nations which comprised the empire, the Jews had no national political identity; they slid back and forth between the fighting camps. Because of this, every national group, whether it was the politically reigning Germans, or the Poles, or the Ruthenians—all of whom considered themselves the only legitimate heirs to the country—thought of the Jews as their subjects alone and expected them to be loyal and faithful only to them. Not having their own political identity, the Jews mainly sided with the ruling majority. (Until 1866 they sided with the Austrians, after that with the Poles, and in more recent years with the Ruthenians.) In such circumstances the other nations resented the Jews, viewing their behavior as subverting their own interests.

But at the same time the political situation of the Galician Jews made them feel important and gave them a sense of worth as well as a strong awareness of their civic responsibility. Austrian patriotism was so strongly developed among them that their loyalty to the old emperor Franz Josef was almost a cult. They loved him and obeyed him as their protector and helper. At the beginning of the war, when the Austrian Poles played a two-sided role, siding first with one party and then with the other, and the Ruthenians did the same, the Jews remained firmly on the side of Austria, openly displaying their loyalty even in the most difficult times, regardless of the consequences. The self-sacrifice which the Jews exhibited was extraordinary. I saw Jews crying bitterly when they heard that Przemysl fell. Jews couldn't hide their joy when the Russians suffered a defeat, and bravely announced to the occupation forces that as Austrian citizens they were completely loyal to their government. It reached the point that in some places the local Jews behaved coolly, sometimes even with open hostility, toward Dr. Lander and me, viewing us as representatives of an enemy country.[5]

Notwithstanding the fact that Galician Jewry, both the orthodox and the emancipated sectors, drew its inspiration from the Jews of Russia and was closely tied to them, the two national groups had been alienated from one another until the war. They felt they were strangers, even adversaries to a certain extent; there were certainly no warm feelings between them. Galician Jews regarded the enslaved, disenfranchised Jews of Russia with a certain amount of disdain, and couldn't understand how they were able to live and breathe in an atmosphere of constant pogroms and persecutions. Furthermore, in Russian Jewry orthodox Galician Jews saw the source of apostasy and ungodliness. And on their side the Russian Jews were contemptuous of the Galician Jews, whom they viewed as backward, removed from the world of culture and having no cultural aspirations of their own.

This alienation and lack of understanding had existed for a century, and it took a terrible catastrophe and a sea of blood and tears for the Russian Jews to draw closer to their Galician brothers. This war will forge a closer spiritual tie between the previously separated groups in Judaism.

4

For almost a hundred years the two shtetls, Radziwillov and Brody, were like enemy camps that faced each other. Each of them was armed with a strong defense system and they were separated by ropes, custom houses, barriers, and wooden border gates. And yet they had close relations and were heavily dependent on one another—their physical separation united them and was the source of their economic well-being, for the main trade route between Russia and Austria ran through the borders of both shtetls. As soon as the first shot was heard in the warring camps, the fence separating them was demolished, the border posts were torn down, and there were no longer any barriers to crossing from one side to the other. This ruined the two shtetls; they lost not only their source of income but also their raison d'être.

The two shtetls are only seven viorsts apart, and my train ride from Radziwillov to Brody lasted less than a quarter of an hour. But during that brief period I felt very uncomfortable. In Kiev, and before that in Moscow, I saw for myself what strict military arrangements had been made to prevent Jews from crossing into Galicia. In Kiev they told me that David Feinberg, the well-known St. Petersburg businessman and personal friend of the governor of Galicia, Count Bobrinski, was refused a travel permit to Lemberg (though afterward I heard that he did finally get to Galicia).

Will they let me through? The document which I carried, an authorization from the Committee of the Members of the Imperial Duma to bring two wagons of medicine to Tarnow, was not confirmed by any military agency and didn't even have my photograph attached. It did, however, clearly display my Jewish name and that of my father. I was sure that when they checked the passes at the former border they would make me get off; it certainly would not be an easy crossing.

But I was mistaken. The officer, who was accompanied by two policemen as he walked through the train to check the passes, didn't even look at my authorization; he just made a mark on it with his pencil and handed it back to me.

Later I had several occasions to cross the Galician border, and although it was strictly forbidden for Jews to do so, I never encountered any problems with my authorizations and always managed to cross freely. More than that—during the year and a half in which I traveled through Galicia and visited scores of towns, I often had to talk to members of the military staff and never once was asked to show my documents.

Private citizens generally have great difficulty in gaining access to military camps in countries at war because of the many guard posts set up to examine documents. In Russia they took care of this problem in a very original way. The military rulers arranged for all authorized personnel of the Red Cross and other social agencies, generally private citizens, to wear uniforms with special insignia and to carry swords. This meant that authorized personnel could go wherever officers went without attracting the attention of those whose duty it was to prevent espionage. It was not easy to become a member of one of the social agencies which were given the privilege of wearing military uniforms, but there must have been many German spies among the tens of thousands of social workers who walked about undisturbed in the military camps, seeing and hearing everything. When it later emerged that the enemy knew all the Russian military secrets, they accused the Jews of being spies; this was their catchall solution and it suited everyone very well.

Brody's large railway station had been burned down at the very beginning of the war. A buffet had been set up in one of the rooms of the ruined building, and when I arrived it was full of officers standing around the buffet and sitting at the small tables, enjoying Russian borsht. I noticed that all the plates had "mazel tov" written across them; they had been stolen from a Jewish hotel where weddings used to take place.

My traveling companion Dr. Ratner and I went to the center of town, which was a few viorsts from the station. It was dawn and we could see burned houses on both sides of the road and, in the distance, a field burned to the ground. We could make out the town in the gray early morning mist; it was completely destroyed. From both sides, as far as the eye could see, there were broken chimneys and burned walls. Everything was covered with downy snow. The ruins were overgrown with moss and looked very old, like another ancient Pompeii. A phrase inscribed over the door of a burned synagogue caught my eye: "How awesome is this place"—ironically appropriate words for both the synagogue and the area as a whole.

I noticed a small, undamaged brick house half sunk into the ground amidst the ruins, as if it had attempted to save itself during the fire by hiding underground. An old Jew was standing nearby, as poor and bent as the small house itself. As soon as he saw us in our uniforms he took off his hat and bowed low. I walked toward him and asked in Yiddish: "How is it that your house didn't burn during the fire?"

The old man looked at me for a while, thinking. Then he gave a shudder and said, sighing: "It's probably a miracle; it was fated that we would have a house in which to die of hunger." I gave him a ruble and he was so overwhelmed that he forgot to thank me and just stood there staring.

We walked around in the ruins for quite a while and I noticed something odd: In every corner of the burnt street, on the walls and on the destroyed houses, there were newly affixed signs on which street names were written in Russian letters. The Russians had given all the streets new, highly literary names: Pushkin Street, Gogol Street, Lermontov Street, I think there was a Turgenev Street, too. Apparently the victors didn't understand how cynical it was to call the horribly disfigured, fire-gutted streets after the greatest representatives of Russian culture, nor did they think it insulting to the memory of the great writers. The street signs left me with the same feeling as did the icons which the Christians put in their windows during the pogroms.

5

May 1915

On the sixth of May [1915] I traveled from Kiev to Lemberg. This time I did not go through Brody, where the track was filled with military cars, but through Woloczysk and Tarnopol. The entire area was annexed by the Russians almost without a struggle, and there were no signs of war along the way—no burnt villages or destroyed fortifications, no abandoned wire fences. I passed intact villages, churches, fields piled high with hay and grazing animals; even the few wounds which the earth had received, the graves, were covered and overgrown by the healing power of the spring sun. The peasants contributed their share to this bucolic scene—they plowed the fields, they built the houses, they brought the produce from country to town. Who would believe, seeing this, that a bloody slaughter was taking place only 100 or 150 viorsts from here and that the storms of war would soon come to these tranquil fields and villages?

But while the mood of spring and the plenitude of nature reigned on both sides of the road, the movement on the long, narrow tracks was agitated. Crowded military trains were constantly riding by, and all the stations were crowded with soldiers. Our courier train, scheduled to arrive in Lemberg at one o'clock in the afternoon, arrived at nine in the evening. We had to wait for hours at almost every station to let trains filled with soldiers and cannons through. Traveling in the opposite direction were trains filled with wounded soldiers, prisoners of war, and deserters. A medical train went by and bandaged heads, arms, and bodies could be seen through every window; the serious, pale, suffering faces stared out in a sadly curious way, all drawn toward the spring sun.

A freight train filled with prisoners of war went by; it was so crowded that the prisoners seemed to be sitting on top of one another. Some even sat on the roof. No one guarded them, either because they were sure that they wouldn't try to escape or because they didn't care. The prisoners were mostly barefoot, ragged, unshaven, but they appeared to be sanguine and calm. They carried on animated conversations and laughed a lot, so unlike the frightened, shrunken, dejected prisoners whom I had met several months ago. Perhaps it was because of the weather; then it was winter and freezing cold and now it was spring and warm and the sun cheered everyone. Or perhaps it was because then the Russians were conquering town after town, and now their side was winning and the Russians were retreating. The prisoners felt self-confident and looked upon their captors with disdain, behaving as if they were the conquerors because they knew that the Russians would soon be totally defeated. But the most likely explanation was that the prisoners were not Slavs but Hungarians. Everyone said that they were cruel and unrestrained—but they looked to me like strong, healthy peasants with proud, open faces.

Approaching one of the railroad cars, I attempted to start a conversation in German, Russian, French—but they didn't understand and shook their heads.

"Hungarian?" I asked.

They shook their heads brightly and answered me with pride: "Yes, Hungarian."

The long, long trains came one after another, filled with fleeing Ruthenians, mainly women and children, packed tightly together like chickens in cages. Some trains were entirely filled with children, others with students. There was no luggage at all to be seen—either it had been stored in a different train or the fugitives had had no time to pack. But no sighs were heard and no despair could be seen on their faces.

"Where do you come from?" I asked someone.

"We come from Turkey."

"Why did you leave?"

"They forced us to."

"We were afraid of the Hungarians," said someone else. "They always take the young, healthy people with them and shoot the rest."

"What will you do in Russia?"

"What do you mean what will we do? We'll farm."

I thought: tens of thousands, even hundreds of thousands of refugees will come to Russia and spread over countless fields in greater Russia, the Ukraine, and Siberia. And with them, spreading over the same fields, will be hundreds of thousands of prisoners from all the fronts—Slavs, Hungarians, Germans, Turks. They will meet the Russian peasants, and all of the former opponents, all the bloody enemies, will work hard together to earn their bread on the vast fields which stretch on forever. They will walk behind the same plow, eat from the same dish, drink from the same pitcher, express their sadness and longing with the same universal sigh. And when they have sobered up from the bloody drunkenness which engulfed the world they will find it hard to understand how they ever fought each other like bloodthirsty animals. They will become friends and will talk intimately with one another and will find that they have a lot in common—a lot of suffering and joy. And then they will be reminded of their Jewish neighbors, who did not make war with either of them and did not kill anyone—and they will agree that it was the Jew who was responsible for all their misfortune.

Meanwhile, here on the bloody battlefields where the hatred between different nations is still burning, there is already an alarming unanimity about the Jew. All of them—the local Pole with his insincere smile, the naïve Ruthenian refugee, the Austro-German prisoner of war, the Hungarian, the Russian soldier—are at one in their hatred of the Jews; all repeat the same libels and baseless accusations against them. And this unanimity is found even among the higher, more cultured strata which in every other respect has nothing in common with the masses and the ordinary soldiers. The highest military circles still talk of Jewish espionage and Jewish treason, even though Myasoedev's betrayal and the recent defeat in the Carpathians made it clear who was really responsible for all the disasters suffered by the Russian army since the beginning of the war.[6]

A group of officers, consisting of Count Bobrinski, an adjutant with epaulets, a colonel with a long gray beard, a lieutenant colonel with two medals on his chest, and a military doctor were standing near my seat in the train, discussing the war. They expressed great sympathy for the suffering of the poor, ruined peasants, whose troubles they blame on the Jews: "They suffer mainly because the Zhids inform on them. It is the Zhids who are responsible for their misfortune."

And then they began to exchange anecdotes about various incidents of brutality which they had witnessed against Jews with so much pleasure and with such vindictive joy that I was overcome with revulsion—not just anger and outrage but overwhelming disgust. I wanted to vomit. I tried to shut out their conversation by getting involved in my book but I couldn't help hearing their stories. One was about a respectable Jew who was suspected of informing the Austrians about the approach of Russian artillery; his entire estate was doused with gasoline and set on fire in his presence. Another was about a Jew who was caught talking on the phone; the general winked, giving his men to understand that there was no point in taking him to headquarters. The soldiers took him into the woods and hanged him.

The officers laughed with pleasure.

"Now we do things better," said the lieutenant colonel. "When we capture a place the first thing we do is drive all the Zhids out, toward the enemy. It's the best way."

"It makes good sense," said the adjutant. "It's impossible to put up with their espionage. It was a big mistake to open the area to Jews—they came in droves."

"And so many physicians came," interrupted the doctor. "In our medical corps the twelve senior physicians are Jews! It's really disgusting."

"It's not surprising that they side with the Austrians," the colonel added. "With us they work like dogs but in Austria they are officers, judges, public prosecutors. They fill the best positions."

A few days later when I was traveling back to Lemberg I heard the same discussions. A tall, big-boned, drunken Cossack officer, cheerful and good-natured, cursed the Jews from the moment I entered the train. He laughed heartily as he recounted how his division robbed and destroyed an estate owned by a Jewish baron, which they happened to pass on their way to Sokol; when they saw the baron sitting in one of the ten carriages in his courtyard, ready to drive off, they pulled him out and threw him into the mud. Later on, when this officer saw the death notice of a well-known man with a Jewish name in a newpaper he was reading, he shouted out gleefully: "Another Jew dead. One less in the world, thank God."

Opposite him sat another Cossack officer, a doctor, who had not said a word until now: "Everyone attacks the Jews. What do they want from them?"

Such a sentence coming from an officer, and a Cossack at that, was rare indeed, so I went closer to hear more of what he was saying.

"They are the basest, vilest people," said the first officer.

"Let it be. We could take an example from their excellent behavior. For example, if you come to a Jewish village you'll never find a young woman who is available for your pleasure. Their families are strict. They are as pure as silk. Children are married off at fifteen."

"But everything bad stems from them. Wherever they can they take over. Ten years ago they were at the forefront of the revolution. I was in Minsk at the time."

"And I was in a place where there wasn't a single Jew and there were strikes and upheavals there nonetheless. No, it's simply a habit to blame the Jews for everything, without even thinking."

"But they are our enemies, our blood rivals."

"And why should they love us? Because we persecute them, curse them, hang them? But I don't care whether they love me or hate me. The main thing is—what do they do to us? I don't see that they harm us in any way. There are hundreds of thousands of Jews in the army. And how do we thank them? By blaming them for everything that goes wrong. I say that the Poles are guilty; they avenge themselves against Jews by spreading false information against them. The truth is that the Poles are our enemies to a far greater extent than the Jews. You know yourself that we just captured four or five hundred Polish Sokols. Why don't you have anything to say about that?"

"There are a lot of Jews among the Sokols."[7]

"But the organization is Polish. What have the Jews done against us as Jews?"

"They are spies."

"That's preposterous—all Jews are spies? How can you accuse a whole people of such a thing?"

"Well, you might find one decent Jew among a thousand—but the rest are all traitors."

"And have you ever met a Jewish spy?"

"There are so many you can't count them."

"Tell me about some."

"Well, they caught a Zhid walking and carrying a few geese on his shoulders."

"I don't see any great crime in that."

"They searched him and found a letter which he was carrying to another Zhid."

"And what was the letter about?"

"The devil knows! They probably found something if they took the Zhid to headquarters."

"Your 'probably' doesn't mean much. I was there when seven Jews were brought to headquarters with a letter saying that they should be hanged as spies. Fortunately the director was a decent person and instead of hanging them he initiated an investigation; the Jews were found to be completely innocent."

The Cossack who defended the Jews so passionately fascinated me. Never before had I come across an officer who spoke this way. Once I did meet an army doctor in a train who strongly defended Jews and argued that they were innocent of the libels of which they were accused. I fairly glowed with happiness at his liberalism. But when we were ready to part and I asked my fellow traveler what his name was, he replied: "Epstein." Then I told him my family name, and we both laughed.

But this time the lover of Israel was no Epstein but a genuine Cossack, Rozsenikov. I introduced myself and we had a long talk. I didn't speak to the other Cossack officer, but he apparently understood that I was a Jew and said to me later, somewhat embarrassed: "Don't take my babbling against the Jews seriously. Deep down in my heart I understand that they are human, just like me. They want to live, too, and they are helpless. Everyone insults them and makes trouble for them. I really feel sorry for them."

This is typical Russian anti-Semitic talk.

I didn't say a word.

6

May 1915

The trip to Brody took twelve hours instead of the usual two and a half. Our train had to stop at every station for several hours to let military transit through; there were endless lines of trains taking soldiers to the front, including several units from the Caucasus which were rushing through.

In Brody I met a Mr. Mass of Radziwillov who went from one Galician shtetl to another distributing aid after his father died. His pass had become invalid, and so this rich man, who was prepared to donate thousands to needy Jews, had no way to get the money into the shtetls where Jews were dying of hunger.

"Today Jews who were deported from Galicia came through Brody," Mass told me, "and I asked the stationmaster if I could bring them some food. He wouldn't permit it. He would only permit me to send them money, but through an intermediary—not directly to them."

In Vilna I had to wait eight hours for the courier train, so I went into town. There I learned some facts about the horrible expulsion from the province of Kovno. Some of those who were expelled, between one and two thousand, remained in shtetls in the province of Vilna. There were seven thousand refugees in Vilna itself; no more were permitted to remain. The others were sent to the provinces of Yekaterinoslav and Chernigov.

They raised eighty thousand rubles for the refugees on the first day in Vilna. The ministerial council let it be known that they were firmly against the mass expulsions, and that had an effect. The commander-in-chief telegraphed: "Stop expulsions. Punish the guilty. The remainder to be permitted to return." The military commander of the Vilna district interpreted the telegram very strangely: the people who had been expelled should be allowed to return on the condition that they have guarantors who would be responsible for them. Those who were expelled refused the honor.

They told me that in some villages the peasants brought out free bread and milk for the expelled Jews and cried at their plight. In other villages the peasants viewed the expulsions in a different light entirely: "The Jews get the best care," they grumbled among themselves. "They're taken away from the dangerous war areas while we're left behind."

ministerial council spoke out unanimously against expulsion, calling it "not permitted" in a report to the emperor, and that the emperor had written "agreed" in his review of it. When the emperor was in Kovno and asked why the town was so deadly silent he was told about the expulsion of the Jews. This made him very angry: "Why didn't they consult me about this?" he asked.

Even in military circles there was great dissatisfaction with the Kovno expulsion. The Kovno commandant and several officers let it be known that since the Jews had been expelled it had become almost impossible to house the army properly—the peasants would not quarter the soldiers. The commandant of the fourth army, [General G. D.] Danilov, seeing the refugees crowding into Dvinsk, spoke up harshly against the expulsion, too, as did many others.

All of this appears to have had an effect. The madman Nikolai Nikolaievich apparently understood that he had exceeded the limits and tried to justify himself. On several occasions he said that it all was done against his will. It was significant that the finance minister, Bark, went especially to military high command to discuss the Jewish question; and it was even more significant that Nikolai Nikolaievich began to defend himself on the question of the Kovno expulsion, when a few months previously he wouldn't even discuss the subject of Jews with Sazonov.

After the discussion between Bark and the Grand Prince, the following announcement was made: Bark is convinced that the mass expulsions serve only to turn the civilized world against them and that this will destroy the country. Nikolai Nikolaievich responded to this by saying that he never intended such mass expulsions, that his orders were misinterpreted, and that no more expulsions would take place. Instead, they would take only hostages. Bark was adamant: "Even that is not desirable," he said.

"Well, it's a small matter," answered Nikolai Nikolaievich. "You can talk to Ianushkevich about it."

Nikolai Nikolaievich also declared that he was no anti-Semite. His evidence for this was that he did not agree to the expulsion of Jews from Warsaw. And he also said that though some Jews were involved in espionage, the great majority were loyal. Ianushkevich was more dogmatically biased against Jews, but even he promised Bark that there would be no more expulsions.

As important proof of the government's new policy toward Jews, they pointed to the following fact: the St. Petersburg Welfare Committee turned to the government with a request for help for the Jewish refugees, and the government dedicated half a million rubles for this purpose. Of course, this was nothing compared to the hundred million rubles given to the Poles for the same purpose, but symbolically it was significant.

When the Welfare Committee discussed the current situation of the Jews of Galicia, they agreed that it was important for a representative of the Jewish community with access to Count Bobrinski to go to Lemberg.

7

June 1915

The situation that developed after the Russian army quit Galicia, and Lemberg in particular, upset all my plans. There was no point in talking about a plan of action to help the Galician Jews when it was impossible to know in advance where one would be permitted to go. Under these circumstances, it was not clear that any purpose was being served in traveling to Galicia. The Kiev Committee was strongly for my going, however. Hundreds of towns and shtetls remained under Russian rule. These shtetls, which could not be reached with aid from Lemberg and which might remain under Russian control for a long time, had to be helped somehow. And if a travel route could not be worked out in advance, then I would simply go wherever I could. Every shtetl was in need of material support and, perhaps even more, moral support at this critical time when the Russian army was leaving the area.

I agreed to travel to any Galician town or shtetl I could get to by joining Demidov's or Komisarov's divisions, or with an authorization from them. And since Dr. Kozhenevsky agreed to organize Demidov's division in Sokol, I went there via Kowel.

In Kowel I met with the members of the Central Jewish Relief Committee and its able and dedicated chairwoman, Dr. Feinstein. Their most important function was to provide food for the hundreds and thousands of Jewish refugees who were being transported through Kowel and to fight the officials of the railroad who tried to deny them contact.

At the railroad station I met scores of refugees from Galicia sitting on the ground. Some were in prayer shawls and phylacteries. The conductor would not let me get near them.

"Where are you from," I called to someone.

"From Sokol. There are thirty-five of us."

"What happened there?"

"They beat up the Jews and robbed their stalls."

"Why?"

"The commander ordered the Jewish stalls to be dismantled. They didn't touch any that didn't belong to Jews."

"Are you sure that the commander ordered it?"

"Yes, your excellency, I know it for a fact."

With a great deal of trouble and persistence I finally got permission to bring food to the Jewish refugees.

At the Central Jewish Relief Committee they told me that when the commander of the southwest regiment, Ivanov, was in Chelm he met with a delegation of four rabbis who brought him a Torah scroll. Very moved, he kissed the rabbis and presented the oldest among them with a silver tobacco case. After the meeting he asked them to return and gave them six hundred rubles for Jewish poor people. This story is similar to the many legends concerning Ivanov. The Jews were convinced that Ivanov had Jewish roots, that either he or his father was captured for military service as a child—he and his father were called Yudovich.

In Kowel I met Nadiezhdin, a member of Komisarov's division, who told me that they were stationed in Krystanopol, seventeen viorsts from Kowel. He invited me to join them and we traveled together.

8

Komisarov wasn't in Krystanopol when I arrived, but he was expected to return in the evening.

The shtetl was small and mostly Jewish. Apparently they had not bothered the Jews lately—all the small shops were open but the tension and anxiety were palpable. The streets were filled with incoming soldiers. I went into one of the shops and talked to the owner, an elderly Jew with an intelligent face. Hearing that I came from the Lemberg Committee he told me what had happened: "Ten months ago the Russians invaded and they pillaged and destroyed the town. They killed five Jews (three were shot and two were slaughtered). They raped eight girls and twenty women right in front of their fiancés and husbands. The massacre and destruction were indescribable. When it was over everyone was left penniless.

They forbade us to leave the shtetl, even to buy flour. People actually died of hunger. And there was no help from anywhere. Now more trouble is in store for us, and more suffering. Only God knows how it will end!"

At my behest the grocer called four people, members of the shtetl's community council, into a back room. I discussed the present situation with them and gave them five hundred rubles for the poor. One of the men took me to the synagogue which was filled with boxes and baskets. Jews from all over the shtetl had brought their valuables there, thinking it the safest place. Among the objects were many brass chandeliers. I suggested that all the boxes be brought up to the attic, and that the tall ladders be chopped into pieces. I also proposed that every house prepare a barrel of water to be used in case of fire, which would doubtlessly be set. Everyone tried to guess what town or village had been set on fire when they saw the daily pillars of black smoke rising from every direction. Was it Welki Mosti? Was it Belz?

Komisarov came in the evening and told us that the Russian army had quit Welki Mosti but the Cossacks had managed to make a terrible pogrom before leaving, and that the town was being bombarded and set aflame. The medical division, under the management of Dr. Shapira, remained in the village of Porchatch, nine viorsts from Krystanopol; Dr. Shapira and her devoted nurse continued to work while the village was under siege, performing operations and bandaging wounds. However, at two in the morning they arrived in Krystanopol; the Austrians were approaching Porchatch, and while the rearguard was holding the enemy back it would be imperative to leave that night, or in the morning at the latest.

I went to the railroad station. It was a ruin. Everyone was gone and the last train had left. The tracks leading west to Lemberg were destroyed, the rails removed and the ties torn out and cut up for kindling wood.

At night the ring of fire from the burning towns came closer. As I lay down to sleep I saw a huge flame approaching the railroad station, and I went there with Nadiezhdin. The wooden planks were burning. The night was clear—a full moon shone in the starry sky. As we turned to go we saw a fantastic sight: hundreds of tall stones, red and glowing, with flaming Jewish letters on them appeared in the distance. At first I didn't understand what it was—and then I realized that we were looking at a Jewish cemetery. The burning flames were reflected on the headstones, making them look as if they were on fire. It was an extraordinary sight; generation upon generation appeared to have come out on this mystic night of the full moon to gaze with fiery looks at the horror that was all around and that was fast approaching this spot.

We stood there a long time, spellbound. Then we talked about the present and meditated on the future of mankind—what would it be like after the nightmare of war was over, after the last river of blood had dried and the horrible red fires were doused. It was dawn when we returned to the shtetl.

Not a soul was in the street. Everything was deadly quiet, except for the regular cannon shots. I didn't sleep long, however. By eight a corpsman was bending over me: "There's a pogrom in the shtetl," he cried. "A couple of hours ago Cossacks came and robbed everyone, broke down stalls, beat Jews." I ran to the window. The street was like a boiling cauldron. Women screamed and groups of older Jews were running back and forth. Broken and torn goods had been thrown around many of the shops, and circles of people stood nearby, but no soldiers or Cossacks.

When I went into the street I learned that a division of Cossacks had come at six in the morning and immediately began a pogrom; within two hours the city was in ruins and half the shops were robbed. Now only individual soldiers and Cossacks were there, taking whatever was left in the shops. Peasants from the village walked with them, carrying sacks full of goods.

I went into several shops where the soldiers were stealing and drove them out. From one cellar, I pulled a Cossack out by the ears and threatened to shoot him; he was as white as a sheet and shook the pilfered goods out of his pockets. The Jews were very impressed with what I was doing to the robbers and I could hear shouts from all sides: "Come to me! Have pity on me! They're robbing me!"

Gradually things quieted down. I reconvened the members of the ad-hoc relief committee. They arrived, shaken and tearful. We made an attempt to ascertain the extent of the damage and found that during the past several hours about a hundred households had become impoverished, totally ruined. I left another eight hundred rubles for the victims of the pogrom, on the condition that an exact accounting would be sent to the Lemberg Committee after the Russians left.

While the committee was discussing these problems, someone came to inform us that the commandant had ordered one of the most respected members of the Jewish community to appear before him. He wanted to know whether the man should go and I advised that someone else be sent to speak to the commandant first.

An even greater predicament for the Jewish community was a directive that had been sent around during the pogrom stating that all males between eighteen and fifty would be deported; in contrast to the Lemberg directive, it stated explicitly "not excluding Jews."

Around noon there was another disturbance: people stood in groups in the street again, frightened and crying, while a Cossack officer and two soldiers searched all the shops for weapons and noted the amount of flour, sugar, gasoline, candles, and other provisions that remained on the shelves. Everything was to be requisitioned.

The shopowners stood by helplessly, pale as ghosts, wringing their hands. A Jewish woman, her eyes following the soldiers' moves nervously and her face white with fear, joined the circle. Twisting her hands she said anxiously: "Oh—oh, I'm done for! They're coming to my shop and going into my storage basement."

"At this point they're not taking anything, they're only listing the goods," I told her, trying to reassure her. "They won't have time to carry out their threats."

"Oh—but you don't know what I have in my basement," she cried, growing more and more upset by the minute. "I'm lost."

"What do you have?" I asked, getting nervous myself.

"You're better off not knowing. Oh—it's all over."

"Tell me what you have. Weapons?"

"What weapons? I have several hundred rubles hidden there as well as my widowed sister's jewels, which are also worth a few hundred rubles. That's all we have in the world. They're sure to find it all and keep it."

A few hours later there was another commotion. Thirty Jews were in the marketplace; they had been told that they were being rounded up in the streets and taken from their homes to be sent to forced labor, but they were to be used as hostages, instead. Among those who were arrested was a pale, sick young man. I was successful in convincing the guards to let him free. And as soon as they freed him I saw some men begin to whisper to the guards, offering money, bargaining, and one by one buying themselves off.

The cannon shots came closer. As the last divisions left the shtetl a medic came by to tell me that our group was leaving at six o'clock and that I must join them. Dr. Shapira and several of her assistants would remain to take care of as many wounded as possible; they had an automobile at their disposal and, as before, would leave at the last moment—just before the Austrians arrived.

Several Jews came to me, pleading that I remain a little longer. I was prepared to do so but Dr. Shapira informed me that there was no place in her automobile. So I told the Jews to go to her with their problems, asking her to take care of them until she left; I offered to leave a hundred rubles in case of emergency. She wasn't at all pleased with my suggestion—she didn't feel it was appropriate for her to deal with specifically Jewish problems. This intelligent woman, who exhibited the most remarkable bravery in operating under fire, didn't have the courage to declare herself a Jewess and to defend her persecuted brothers. And she wasn't the only one who exhibited this weakness.

When I was already in the car ready to leave, a Jew with blood oozing out of his head ran toward me. He had been accosted by a soldier who demanded money. When he didn't give him any, the soldier hit him on the head with the butt end of his gun and tore his purse away from him; it contained the last four rubles he had in the world.

9

Late June 1915

On the morning after I came from Luck I traveled to the shtetl of Torczyn, to which many refugees from Horochov and other places had come. It was an old, poor shtetl that had only one long street and a few small, wretched shops. Women and children were outside, as if the overcrowded houses couldn't contain them. And it was very nearly true. Every household had taken in at least one newly arrived family and some had taken several. All the granaries and the animal stalls had been turned into living quarters for the refugees, too.

There had been about two thousand Jews out of a total population of four thousand in the shtetl before the war. They made their living by selling produce abroad. Now with trade at a standstill, the loan company no longer functioned and even the agricultural school was closed. All the wealthier residents had left.

Poryck had suffered a pogrom the week before, and the local residents were frightened to death that it would reach them. The mood was a bit calmer now but the underlying fear persisted that the Cossacks might come. They were not much reassured by the military's rumored directive to the Cossacks: "Whatever happened in Galicia happened. But we must not behave the same way with the Jews of Russia. No robbing!"

We suggested that a committee be set up to register the homeless in Torczyn and to help the neediest among them. I gave the committee four hundred rubles to help the many refugees who could not find housing and who slept in storehouses and even under the open sky.

I spent all day Friday in Torczyn and in the evening, just before I left, I stopped at a bakery to buy some rolls. "There aren't any," I was told. Hearing this, a Jewish woman who was standing nearby spoke up: "What do you mean, there are no rolls? Do you know who this officer is? You may not know—but I know! There have to be rolls for him. Give him whatever you have, everything which you prepared for the Sabbath. He deserves it. Oh, if only there were more Jews like him."

This was unexpected and the bakery woman was a little confused. "I'll bring some right away," she said and went into her house. But before she returned, several other women from the neighborhood brought me challahs. I took two and wanted to pay but they wouldn't hear of it. I was very moved, but at the same time I felt uncomfortable with this kind of popularity. Somewhat later I heard a Jew who didn't know who I was say: "In a godforsaken village there is a Jewish officer who talks to everyone in Yiddish; he gives candy to the children and distributes money to the needy. He gave one woman who was traveling with her children five rubles; she didn't need the money and gave it to someone else. No one knows who he is."

A rumor went around in Torczyn that the Russians had won a great victory and had recaptured Lemberg; also that two Japanese artillery divisions had arrived. These kinds of false rumors were repeated during the entire trip back.

10

December 1916–March 1917

In Chorostkow I met two Jews, Reb Frenkel of Husiatyn and Reb Lipe Shvager; both dealt in Jewish religious books, especially ancient Hebrew books and manuscripts. They had the largest business of the kind in Galicia. During the pogrom and the fire which followed, their business was completely destroyed. They were able to rescue only a few of the manuscripts and old books, some of which I took to the museum in Petrograd for safekeeping.

Reb Lipe Shvager, an intimate of the Kopyczynecer Rebbe, told me a wonderful story which was very like a mystical, symbolic legend. It has since been accepted into the treasury of hasidic wonder tales. The story goes as follows: When the war broke out the Kopyczynecer Rebbe was in Hamburg, taking the cure. The entire family was with him and Lipe Shvager, too. When the Russians invaded Galicia the Rebbe summoned Shvager and said to him: "I want you to know that I have two letters which were written by the holy Baal Shem himself. They might be destroyed in the war, God forbid. Please go to Kopyczynec and save the letters; if you can't get back here, keep them in a safe place. You know that the dangers are great. You might be shot on the road, or someone may make a false accusation about you, may Heaven protect us. Don't permit the danger to deter you from completing the sacred mission of saving the letters."

Shvager agreed at once, but he asked: "Rebbe, what about your gold and silver and the many precious objects which are in your court and are worth millions?"

"I don't care what happens to them," answered the Rebbe calmly, "but the Baal Shem Tov's letter must be saved."

Shvager arrived in Kopyczynec just a few hours before the Russians entered. There was no possibility of getting back, but he did have time to get the letters and hide them. He put them in a metal box and buried them two meters deep in a wall of a cellar in the Rebbe's courtyard; he also buried part of his gold and silver in the same place. For three or four months he couldn't get near the cellar. He narrowly missed death on several occasions and was actually arrested on suspicion of spying. Finally, when he was able to get to the cellar, he couldn't find a single one of the precious objects which he had buried there; everything had been stolen. Furthermore, the wall in which the metal box with the letters had been placed was demolished and the box was gone.

Shvager was beside himself—he wanted to die. But a few days later, when he dug around the wall again, he found the box untouched and whole. Upon opening it he was astonished to find that all the writing had disappeared from the letter which had been written by the Baal Shem himself (the second letter was only signed by him); the paper was completely blank.

The truth is that I didn't believe the story; I thought it was one of the typical legends invented in times of turmoil. I asked Shvager to let me see the letters. They were hidden in a secret place in

Kopyczynec and Shvager didn't want to show them to me. But when I saw him a few weeks later I insisted so vigorously that he reluctantly agreed. He brought the letters, wrapped in several layers of paper, into the synagogue. Shvager reverently unwrapped the letters, taking care not to touch them. There were two very old sheets of paper, one completely covered on both sides in a narrow, spare script— that of Reb Gershon Kitever, according to Shvager (the letter had been published).[9] On the back, at the very edge, was the barely discernible signature written in long, wide characters: Yisroel Baal Shem. The second sheet, which had partially disintegrated (both letters had been written in 1753), was completely blank, without a trace of ink; the only marks on it were spots caused by either dampness or tears.

Shvager gazed at the letter with a look of mystic contemplation and said quietly: "They say that dampness has erased the characters and that they can be restored by treating the paper with chemicals. But we Hasidim think otherwise."

Looking at the page from which the words had "flown away" I was reminded of a piece of stone which I found in the despoiled synagogue in Dembica; it had broken off the tablets of the Ten Commandments which hung on the wall, and contained only the words "kill" and "commit adultery".[10] These occurrences melded together in my mind into the rabbinic phrase: "broken tablets and flying letters." To me they symbolized the life of Galician Jewry.

On my first journey through Galicia in 1915, I followed closely on the path of the war; I tramped over smoldering fires and saw fresh traces of the most horrible pogroms. The fear of death was everywhere. Every shtetl, every house, every object was marked with drama; and the people who had survived the threat of death were steeped in even greater tragedy. They were shattered and almost crazed with despair. To me these people were like broken tablets, bleeding from every crevice. Yet at that time the tragedy was still external, a result of the war. Hundreds and thousands of lives were cut off, fortunes lost, great cultural treasures despoiled, but the storm had not yet touched the depth of the soul, had not yet destroyed the sense of human worth.

But when the wealthy and respected members of the community suddenly found themselves without bread, their greatest tragedy was that they could not bring themselves to beg. Many preferred to starve rather than stretch out their hands for help. The suffering of the bloodied, ruined, and degraded Jewish people was very great then, but I also saw a harsh beauty in their sorrow and pain which raised their torment to the level of an epic folk tragedy.

Now, in my travels through those still relatively intact towns and shtetls I no longer saw the drama as beautiful and uplifting. The former tragedies had become banal, everyday occurrences; the former heroes of the folk epic had become professional beggars. The past was forgotten and the future too terrible to contemplate; life revolved around the petty concerns of a beggarly existence—the struggle for a crust of bread or a handful of groats. People had grown used to a constant state of hunger, to covering their bodies in rags, to spending hours in line at the food stations; they were apathetic, silent, lost in despair, indifferent to the terrible conditions of their lives. The few intellectuals who survived had grown used to being cut off from all cultural, social, or intellectual pleasures. These living dead no longer projected an image of "broken tablets"; they were tablets whose letters had "flown," which had been stripped of all grace and dignity.

11

From Tlusti I was supposed to travel to Bukovina—Sniatyn, Zaleszczyki and Czernowitz. But I happened to meet Homelski who suggested that I go with him to Buczacz where he had to attend to something. I agreed.

The Carpathian mountains and valleys begin in this area. From a distance, about halfway to our destination, we saw a very large and beautiful building on the top of a mountain; as we came closer we realized that it was an ancient ruin of which only the walls remained. Later we learned that it was an old monastery.

I kept thinking: why is it that ancient ruins which might be hundreds of years old have a majestic and dramatic beauty about them, while newly destroyed buildings are quite the opposite—undramatic, even repellent? Perhaps it is because there are always parts of a recent ruin that survive the destruction and create a glaring disharmony obscuring the inherent drama. Ancient ruins preserve only those parts that are indestructible and can withstand the ravages of time and of nature.

The same is true of human tragedy. While one is in the midst of a misfortune, the elements of pettiness and wailing numb the senses and veil the essential mystery of the tragedy. Only with time, when all the trivia and inessentials, all that is ephemeral and unimportant are forgotten, does the tragedy crystallize into the splendid, unalloyed truth that is used by artists to create the immortal epics of the world.

As we crossed over the mountain we saw a terrible scene—a dead town in the valley. It was a big town, with many streets and houses; but all the houses were burnt and demolished. They looked like shattered, stony corpses—a veritable Pompeii. I have seen many razed towns, but I've never seen a picture of total destruction like that before.

We stood there for a while. What town was this? None of us knew of a large town on our route. Could it be that we erred in reckoning the distance and we were already in Buczacz—a destroyed Buczacz? Homelski, who had been to Buczacz before, looked around and thought he recognized it: Yes—it must be Buczacz.

There was not a living soul in sight. But once in the town, we saw two soldiers coming out of a small, half-collapsed house which looked like a cave at the bottom of the mountain. We stopped them and asked the name of the town.

"Jaslowiec," they replied, and seeing us staring at the ruins, they added, "fierce battles were fought here. When we retreated, our artillery demolished the town."

"And the little house you just left, what's in there?"

"A shop."

We went into the tiny house, which had a low ceiling and an earthen floor. A Jew and five or six members of his family were in one room; the other room was a kind of shop where soldiers bought cigarettes, rolls, and other items.

"Do you have something to eat?" we asked. At first the shopowner said that he had only rolls, but when he found out that we were Jewish he invited us into the other room. It was Friday evening and his wife was about to light the Sabbath candles.

"We have a pot of sour cream," she said, "and we'll give you half. You have to eat, too."

We were about to refuse but when we saw that the bowl was as big as the head of the giant Og, king of Bashan, we no longer felt awkward about it. The shopkeeper came in while we were eating.

"Are there a lot of Jews in this town?" I asked.

"There is only one Jewish family—mine," he answered. "All the Jews ran away when they bombed the town and set it to flames. Now they won't allow them to return. They did me a favor and let me settle here—this place is considered outside of the town proper. We live here, and I earn my bread in the shop."

"And the soldiers—don't they harm you?"

"No—on the contrary. They are only too happy to have a place to buy things. The town is a ghost-town."

Through the little window of the house I could see part of the shtetl, and among the ruins I recognized the remains of a large, splendid stone synagogue, its roof and windows destroyed by fire.

"Was the synagogue set to flames, too?" I asked the storekeeper mechanically.

"Yes," he answered with a sigh. "All the holy books were burned. And what a synagogue it was!" He was quiet for a time and then continued, "It was six hundred years old. They say that it wasn't constructed but was found fully built under the ground."

In Volhynia and in other places, too, I had already heard the legend about finding an old, complete synagogue under the ground. But this man added a new element: "When they dug it up and entered they saw an old man with a gray beard which reached down to his waist, sitting and poring over a holy book."

We reached Buczacz late at night and found a scene like that in Jaslowiec—street after destroyed street and houses burned to the ground.[11] The few houses that remained standing were occupied by the military staff and infirmaries. They were lit by large electric lamps which added an even greater air of tragedy to the dead city.

Some Jewish families remained in town, where they lived in cellars. I didn't have the time to interrogate them because I was due to return early in the morning. But in the evening, on my way to the military infirmary where I was spending the night, I met an elderly Jew and stopped to ask him a few questions.

"What a disaster!" I said, expressing my sympathy.

"Everything is called a disaster," he responded, sighing. "What you see here is not the half of it."

"What else is there?"

"What else? They destroyed the cemetery, they shattered headstones that were six hundred years old and carried them away, they set the tombs of the greatest scholars on fire. The *Oreh Hayyim* is buried in our synagogue."[12]

I felt that for him the desecration of the cemetery was a greater tragedy than the destruction of the town.

12

Sadigure had long been the residence of a hasidic family stemming from Reb Ber of Miedzyczec, the Baal Shem Tov's most outstanding student. The founder of the Sadigure dynasty was Reb Ber's grandson, Reb Sholem Shakhne of Pogrebishtsh—a great kabbalist and a unique personality. He dressed in European clothes and enjoyed the aristocratic life of the Polish magnates of the time. His son, the well-known Reb Yisroel of Rizhin, was the first of the dynasty to settle in Sadigure and is said to have surpassed his father both in his personal qualities and in his life-style. Many legends about the Rizhiner Rebbe claim that he was given the Baal Shem's soul, and his rich and expansive life-style is a never-ending source of wonder in the legends. His court was like that of an emperor: a band of twenty-four musicians played at his table, and his carriage was driven by a team of six horses in tandem. His son and grandson adopted the same life-style, and the court of Sadigure achieved renown as the richest and most genteel of the rabbinical courts.

The war, which destroyed so many Jewish treasures, also annihilated the court of Sadigure—its unique way of life as well as its antiquities. It brought to an end the material and spiritual wealth of generations of believers.

Before the war there were about ten thousand people living in Sadigure, three-quarters of whom were Jewish. They suffered a horrible pogrom when the Russian army occupied Sadigure for the first time, in September 1914; all the Jewish houses and shops were robbed and many Jews were murdered or wounded. The chairman of the local Jewish community, a rich and respected man, and three other Jews were killed for shielding their wives and daughters from rapists. Except for one hundred Jewish women who were hidden by the pharmacist in his cellar, where they remained for three days without food and water, all the women in the town, young and old alike, were raped. In the same area an officer took Elyokum Gastanter's two daughters away; Weissenberger's daughter was also taken. They returned them a few days later, I was told.

Soon afterward the Russians left. When they returned, in December of the same year, almost all the Jews fled, mainly to Czernowitz. They left all their worldly possessions behind and the local peasants stole everything. The few Jews who remained were tormented and falsely accused of disloyalty.

The libel against two Jews, Yitskhok Shmatnik and Shmuel Zagrebelski (a Russian subject), was interesting. They were living in a storeroom in the Rebbe's court and were arrested because a telephone was discovered there; later it transpired that the phone had been flung there by soldiers. The story is as follows: When the first military division arrived they found a telephone in the Rebbe's house which was connected to Czernowitz. They cut the wires and threw the apparatus into the storeroom. When a second division of soldiers arrived at a later date, they found the telephone and accused Shmatnik and Zagrebelski of divulging military secrets to the Austrians, who were then in Czernowitz. Both men were handed over to a military tribunal. This was their verdict:

"May 16, 1915. By order of His Majesty, the Emperor, a military tribunal has been established which include: Chairman: Commander of the horse brigade, Colonel Drozdovski; Members: Staff Officer on assignment from the commissary corps, Captain Czekerulkush; Chief Officer on assignment from the commissary corps, Captain Zhuriari; officer in charge of managing the infirmary of the twenty-ninth brigade, Captain Shechovuyev; the senior adjutant of the staff-corps, Porutshik Ametistov; and executive officer Fraporshtshik Zusman. Concerning the criminal charges against Izak Shmatnik and Shmuel Zagrebelski of the crimes listed in the thirteenth bylaw in the *Book of Court Martials*, in the second section of paragraph 241, volume 22 of *Field Ordinances*, 1869, 4th edition, they have been found *not guilty* of contacting the enemy at the end of April, in the year 1915, at the time of the Russo-Austrian War, through a telephone which was found in their residence and was connected to Czernowitz where Austrian troops were stationed, and of divulging information of the size and position of Russian military troops—because the charge was not proven.

"And therefore, according to paragraph 1309 of supplement VIII and paragraphs 1376 and 676 of supplement 24 in the *Book of Military Court Martials*, 1869, the judgment is as follows: The accused Izak Shmatnik and Shmuel Zagrebelski are acknowledged free, under the law.

"Signed: Chairman, Colonel Drozdovski; Members, Captain Czekerulkush, Zhuriari, Shechovuyev, Ametistov."

Nonetheless, despite having been acquitted and judged *not guilty*, they were sent to Russia—Zagrebelski to prison in Kiev and Shmatnik to Siberia.

The scene of a town laid waste appeared from a distance as soon as I left Czernowitz. An entire field of tall, smoking chimneys, skeletons of burned houses, caved-in walls and holes for windows and doors, mountains of bricks, pieces of clay and burned, twisted metal. Sadigure itself was unrecognizable—it was even impossible to tell where the streets had once been located. Everything seemed to have melted together into one large ruin.

I went through the entire town without seeing one Jew. The few Jewish houses which had not been entirely destroyed and the shops in the marketplace had been taken over by local and newly arrived Christians who didn't allow any Jews into the town. The shops, on which the Jewish names still appeared, were open and run by Christian women; a tailor shop had been turned into a bakery and a dress store was selling pork.

I traveled to Sadigure in a military car with Dr. Ratni, a Jewish physician working at a hospital in Czernowitz. I also took along a Jewish teacher from Sadigure who was now living in Czernowitz; he was afraid of the soldiers and the local non-Jewish population and didn't dare to return to his home. He proposed that I buy some rare, old books from him which he had hidden in Sadigure. His house, which was at the edge of town, had not been burned, and he was sure that his books were safe. "I hid them so well that the devil himself couldn't find them," he boasted.

He was correct about his house—it was still standing, but had no door or windows. Inside we found straw and horse manure. The Jew looked bewildered—he could barely recognize the little house.

"Where are your books hidden?" I asked.

"In the attic," he answered, his voice breaking.

We found a ladder and climbed up to the attic. Where were the books? Gone—everything had been taken, even the chimney bricks.

The Jew looked like a broken man as he stared at the corner where his books had been hidden. He had covered them with bricks and was certain that no one would find them. In a state of shock he returned to Czernowitz on foot.

I went to the Rebbe's court, which was at the end of town. It consisted of two medieval, Moorish-style castles with rounded turrets at the sides and ornamental cornices; its massive doors resembled gates. Both buildings were painted red and were identical in structure and size. One had been the Rebbe's residence, the other the synagogue.

The shells of both buildings were intact, but almost all the contents had been plundered and what remained was filthy. The buildings served as military infirmaries for typhus patients.

A characteristically Russian incident took place there. As soon as

Dr. Ratni and I stepped out of the military vehicle in front of the Rebbe's court, two military doctors and several nurses and orderlies greeted us. They were very anxious to please and most deferential, especially toward me. I was confused by this, but when we left Dr. Ratni burst out laughing: "Guess what! They mistook you for the new general of the division and thought you had come to inspect the hospital. I was told so by the senior doctor just before we left."

The confusion occurred because my epaulets resembled those of a general; that's why they showed me around and explained everything. We went into the building that had been the Rebbe's home and I shuddered at the destruction that confronted me: empty, muddied rooms and cracked walls covered with spittle. Bunks had been placed against the walls of the largest rooms for sick Romanian soldiers who had just been brought from the front. They were emaciated, filthy, miserable—mere shadows of men—hunched over, shivering feverishly, and moaning on their bunks as they sat or lay, wrapped in torn, muddy, wet coats. Some were barefoot. In another room the wounded were being bandaged and the men with typhus were being shaved. In a third room a bath had been installed in which a huge vat was being heated, and dozens of naked, gaunt, sick soldiers were walking about in the heavy steam. The stench was terrible.

As we were standing in the first room containing the recently evacuated sick soldiers, the senior doctor pointed to them and with an ingratiating smile said to me: "What do you think of these heroes, our brave friends? Ha, ha! They probably thought that war is as simple as making music in a Romanian café." And then, whispering, he added: "Do you know what the emperor said about Romania? He said that Romania is not a nation, it's a profession. Ha, ha! That's brilliant."

Outside, the doctor pointed to the buildings: "Look at these! Marvelous architecture—genuine palaces. They belonged to a great Jewish rabbi, something like an archbishop, whom the Jews worship. He was very wealthy, a millionaire—and he got all of his money out to Austria. It's a historic building. The well-known Beilis trial which shook the world took place here."[13]

"What do you mean that the Beilis trial took place here?" I asked, astounded.

"Here, in this very place," he said with the knowing smile of a man who has a secret.

"What are you talking about? The trial took place in Kiev."

"Kiev was just the showplace," he said, and lifting his hands, he continued, "it was here that they pulled the strings that controlled the puppets in Kiev—this was where the real trial was."

I began to be interested in what he had to say. "Tell me more!"

"The greatest Jewish rabbis and the richest bankers in the world assembled here, and under the chairmanship of the local bishop they directed the entire procedure—they worked out all the details and paid all the expenses. Then they sent their directives and orders to Kiev, and whatever was decided here was accepted there."

He told me the story with so much assurance that I was convinced that the old Russian doctor and intellectual actually believed this fantastic legend.

"The second building was their house of worship," he said, pointing to the synagogue. "We set up an infirmary of eighty beds there." I went into the large synagogue and saw rows and rows of bunks on which the sick and dying lay, covered by their coats. I was shocked. The air was heavy, choking, and the soldiers stared at us with suffering, pitiful expressions, pleading for help. Some of them stared at us coldly; they had lost hope and had turned in on themselves.

The walls were filthy, but some of the traditional pictures of lions and leopards and musical instruments were still recognizable. A broken chandelier hung from the ceiling. My glance fell on the eastern wall and I trembled at what I saw. The rich ornaments which surrounded the Holy Ark and the tablets of the Ten Commandments above it were unharmed. But in the middle of the empty Ark a large icon had been placed.

"An idol in the sanctuary" flashed through my mind.[14] Somehow I was more shocked by this than by the ruins of the pogroms that I saw. My heart was filled with the ancient mourning for the destruction of the Temple. I couldn't tear my eyes from the sight of this terrible sacrilege, this desecration of both religions. The brutal hand of a crazed soldier had exacted the same revenge from God that he had from man. I didn't hear what the doctor said to me after that.

On returning to Czernowitz I met a hasidic Jew from Sadigure and told him what I saw in the Rebbe's synagogue. He wasn't at all surprised by my story; his embittered face retained the same cool, stony expression as before.

"What was done to the synagogue was nothing compared to what they did to his grave," he told me, sighing.

"What happened to the grave?"

"Don't you know? They destroyed the entire cemetery and

smashed all the gravestones. They pulled down the Rizhiner Rebbe's tomb, dug open the grave, and flung his bones everywhere. Someone told them that Jews bury money in the graves and they were looking for it."

What I heard and saw in the court of Sadigure reminded me of a legend about Reb Yisroel of Rizhin. It is well known that the Rizhiner Rebbe was arrested on the false charge of ordering two Jewish informers to be put to death—and when he continued to be persecuted after his release from prison he moved to Austria. The Russian government demanded his extradition, and it took a lot of pressure and the help of Metternich himself to convince the Austrian government not to return him.

This inspired a legend about a mighty battle between the Rizhiner Rebbe and Czar Nicholas I. According to the legend, Nicholas was a bitter personal enemy of the Rizhiner Rebbe and constantly pursued him. The Russian ministers couldn't understand this and finally asked him outright: "Why do you hound the Rebbe? Is it seemly for a mighty monarch like you to chase after a contemptible little Jew?"

Nicholas jumped up, furious, and shouted: "You say contemptible little Jew, but all my life has been devoted to bending the world one way—and he bends it the opposite way. And I cannot vanquish him."

Reb Yisroel of Rizhin used to say: "I was born on the same day as he, but three hours later—and I cannot seize hold of him. If I had only been born a quarter of an hour earlier I would be victorious."

While Nicholas was emperor the Rizhiner Rebbe refused to reveal himself as the zaddik, the righteous hasidic leader. The condition was—either Nicholas or I, not both! This led to an upheaval among the heavenly hosts; Nicholas was about to be deposed from his throne when his protecting angel protested: "What is this? Is there no law and no judge? If both of them were about to be seated on the throne at the same time, there might have been room for debate about who would have to abdicate. But since Nicholas is already the emperor he cannot be deposed."

So the heavenly court decreed that Nicholas should retain the throne and that the Rizhiner Rebbe should reveal himself as the zaddik. In compensation the Rebbe was to be invited to take whatever he wanted from the heavenly kingdom. He chose the most beautiful melody from the music of the spheres.

Nicholas is long in his grave, but the war between him and his opponent has not ceased. His dead hand reached across three generations of czars and destroyed the Rizhiner's court, defiled his synagogue, and desecrated his grave. The evil deeds of dead hands are even more terrible than those of the living.

1917–20 (Translated by Golda Werman)

Bibliographical Note

▼

The Dybbuk: First published as *Tsvishn tsvey veltn (Der dibek): a dramatishe legende in fir aktn* in Sh. An-ski, *Dramen, Gezamlte shriftn* (Vilna-Warsaw-New York, 1920–1925), vol. 2, pp. 1–105.

"In the Tavern": Published in Russian as "V kabak" in S. A. An-ski, *Rasskazy* (St. Petersburg, 1905), pp. 69–145; here translated from "V Omute (ocherk s naturi)" (dated 1883–1886) in S. A. An-ski, *Sobranie sochinenii* (St. Petersburg, [1913], vol. 5, pp. 25–59. For a Yiddish translation by Yitskhok Daytsher, see "In shenk," in *Noveln, Gezamlte shriftn*, vol. 7, pp. 192–222.

"The Sins of Youth": First published as "Grekhi molodosti i grekhi starosti" in *Evreiski Mir* No. 10 (1910), pp. 7–10; No. 11 (1910), pp. 9–13. The Yiddish version, *"Khatos neurim,"* first appeared in *Lite* 2 (Vilna, 1919) and was reprinted in *Gezamlte shriftn*, vol. 10, pp. 5–16. Translated from the Yiddish as "I Enlighten a Shtetl" in Lucy S. Dawidowicz, ed., *The Golden Tradition: Jewish Life and Thought in Eastern Europe* (New York: Holt, Rinehart and Winston, 1967; paperback: Schocken Books, 1985), pp. 306–11.

"Hunger": Published as "V dvadtsat let (ocherk)" in S. A. An-ski, *Rasskazy*, pp. 255–81, and dated 1892. Here translated from "Der hungeriker (skitse)" in *Noveln, Gezamlte shriftn*, vol. 14, pp. 71–100.

"Mendl Turk": First published as "Mendl Turok" in *Voskhod* (December 1902), pp. 3–34, but consistently dated 1892 in the Russian editions of his writings. Here translated from "Mendl Terk" in *Noveln, Gezamlte shriftn*, vol. 7, pp. 61–102.

"Behind a Mask": First published as "Pod Maskoj (rasskaz starogo 'maskila')" in *Evreiski Mir* (June 1909), pp. 64–98. Translated by Abraham Igelfeld and Ruth R. Wisse in *A Shtetl and Other Yiddish Novellas* (Detroit: Wayne State University Press, 1986), pp. 218–47, from "Unter a maske (ertseylung fun der haskole-epokhe)" in *Noveln, Gezamlte shriftn*, vol. 14, pp. 7–54.

"Go Talk to a Goy!": First published as "A goyisher kop" in *Di yidishe velt* (February 1912), pp. 13–20; reprinted in Sh. An-ski, *Noveln, Gezamlte shriftn*, vol. 14, pp. 127–35. Ansky changed the first line when revising the story.

Bibliographical Note

"The Tower in Rome": First published as "Der turem in Roym" in *Vayter-bukh* [Memorial Volume for A. Vayter], ed. Sh. Niger & Zalmen Reisen (Vilna, 1920); here translated from *Fun eybikn kval, Gezamlte shriftn,* vol. 1, pp. 61–90, where it is dated 1916. A Russian version, dated 1918 and dedicated to Russian symbolist·writer Fyodor Sologub, can be found in the Central State Archives for Literature and Art in Moscow.

The Destruction of Galicia: From *Khurbn Galitsye: der yidisher khurbn fun Poyln, Galitsye un Bokovine, fun togbukh 1914–1917, Gezamlte shriftn,* vol. 4, pp. 13–17, 38–42, 123–31; vol. 5, pp. 5–14, 40–47, 93–96, 100–106, 127–29; vol. 6, pp. 58–63, 88–93, 126–37.

Notes

▼

INTRODUCTION

1 / A fully documented account of Ansky's reidentification as a Jew appears in my essay "S. Ansky and the Paradigm of Return" in Jack Wertheimer, ed., *The Uses of Tradition: Jewish Continuity in the Modern Era* (New York & Cambridge: Jewish Theological Seminary & Harvard University Press, 1992).

2 / Jonathan Frankel, *Prophecy and Politics: Socialism, Nationalism, and the Russian Jews, 1862–1917* (Cambridge: Cambridge University Press, 1981), pp. 133–363.

3 / For a lively portrait of this cultural renaissance, see Mikhail Beizer, *The Jews of St. Petersburg: Excursions Through a Noble Past*, ed. Martin Gilbert (Philadelphia: Jewish Publication Society, 1989). Ansky's activities are described on pp. 92–122.

4 / As quoted by Lucy S. Dawidowicz, *The Golden Tradition: Jewish Life and Thought in Eastern Europe* (New York: Holt, Rinehart and Winston, 1967; paperback: Schocken Books, 1985), p. 305. For the full text of his remarks, translated into Yiddish, see Moyshe Shalit, "Sh. An-ski loyt zayn bukh fun di tsaytungs-oysshnitn," *Fun noentn over* 1 (Warsaw, 1937–38): 229–31.

5 / Ansky published his programmatic essay on Jewish ethnopoetry in the inaugural issue of *Perezhitoe* (St. Petersburg, 1908), the journal of the Historic-Ethnographic Society, and a somewhat different version in Chaim Zhitlowsky's New York–based journal *Dos naye lebn* 1 (1909): 224–40. Volume 15 of Ansky's *Gezamlte shriftn*, which brings together most of his ethnographic studies, includes a Yiddish translation of the *Perezhitoe* essay by Zalmen Reisen.

6 / S. An-ski, *Dos yidishe etnografishe program*, ed. L. I. Shternberg, vol. 1: *Man* (Petrograd, 1914), pp. 10–11. Translation here by Golda Werman.

7 / See S. Ansky, "Death in Jewish Folk Belief" (in Yiddish) *Filologishe shriftn fun YIVO* 3 (1929): 90–100. The original edition of the questionnaire, only one volume of which ever appeared, was already a collector's item in 1929. Though attributed to Ansky and written in Yiddish, the question-naire was compiled with the active collaboration of L. I. Shternberg, a noted Russian-Jewish anthropologist.

8 / Some of the minutes, now housed in the YIVO Archives, New York, have been translated from Russian into Hebrew by Isaiah Trunk in the journal *Gal-Ed* 6 (1982): 229–45. The quote is on p. 236.

9 / M. Vanvild [pen name of Moses Joseph Dickstein], *Pseydo-kunst un pseydo-kritik* (Lodz, 1921). Vanvild was otherwise a great admirer of Ansky and dedicated his own remarkable anthology of underworld and underground Yiddish folklore, *Bay unz yidn* (Warsaw, 1923), to Ansky's memory.

10 / *Mishpat "Ha-dybbuk"* [The Trial of *The Dybbuk*: a transcript of the public tribunals at Bet Ha'am in Tel Aviv on 24 Sivan and 4 Tammuz 5686] (Tel Aviv, 1926). Witnesses for the prosecution included expressionist poet Isaac Lamdan and symbolist poet Abraham Shlonsky; Zalman Rubashov (later Shazar) was one of three who formed the defense. The bill of indictment was drawn up by Eliezer Steinman.

11 / The version that survived was reconstructed by Ansky from a Hebrew translation of the play done by Hayyim Nahman Bialik. On this whole complex of linguistic and stylistic issues, see Shmuel Werses, "S. An-ski's 'Tsvishn tsvey veltn (Der Dybbuk)'/'Beyn Shney Olamot (Hadybbuk)'/ 'Between Two Worlds (The Dybbuk)': A Textual History," *Studies in Yiddish Literature and Folklore* (Jerusalem: The Hebrew University, 1986), pp. 99 –185.

12 / Though the critics were quick to recognize that the Messenger owed more to Leonid Andreev's *The Life of Man* (1906 and 1908) than to Jewish legend, they differed in their evaluation. Hillel Zeitlin, the major exponent of Hasidism among secular Jews, defended the Messenger as both voice of fate and moral voice who explained and justified the harsh decrees of heaven ("Der lebnsveg fun Sh. An-ski," *Almanakh "Moment"* [Warsaw, 1920], p. 49). The prosecution at the *Dybbuk*'s trial in 1926, however, rejected the Messenger outright as a foreign accretion.

13 / Sara Zfatman-Biller, " 'Tale of an Exorcism in Koretz': A New Stage in the Development of a Folk-Literary Genre" (in Hebrew), *Jerusalem Studies in Jewish Folklore* 2 (1982): 17–34.

14 / The growing skepticism concerning dybbuks is amply illustrated in Beatrice Silverman Weinreich's collection of *Yiddish Folktales*, translated by Leonard Wolf (New York: Pantheon Books, 1988), nos. 174, 178. These tales were collected by A. Litwin at precisely the time of Ansky's expedition.

15 / Ansky kept the time-frame of *The Dybbuk* deliberately vague. In act 1, the study house regulars swap stories about the great hasidic masters, one of whom, the Talner Rebbe, died as late as 1882. But the original prologue to the play (published in 1918 and then scrapped) opened on a generational conflict between a *contemporary* father and daughter. It ended with the elderly father placating his wayward daughter with the tale of a dybbuk that he once heard in his youth.

16 / Gershon Shaked, "The Play: gateway to cultural dialogue," in Hannah Scolnicov & Peter Holland, eds., *The Play Out of Context: Transferring Plays from Culture to Culture* (Cambridge: Cambridge University Press, 1989), pp. 11–12, 18–20.

17 / Sefer Zerubbabel has now been made accessible by Martha Himmelfarb in David Stern & Mark Jay Mirsky, eds., *Rabbinic Fantasies: Imaginative Narratives from Classical Hebrew Literature* (Philadelphia: Jewish Publication Society, 1990), pp. 67–90.

18 / The original diaries (written in Russian) have recently been located in the Central State Archives for Literature and Art in Moscow (the TSGALI, in Soviet parlance). From the preliminary investigation done by my student, Michael Krutikov, it appears that the diaries and the published memoir are two independent works.

THE DYBBUK

1 / Shmelke of Nikolsburg (1726–1778), Zushe of Annipol (d. 1800), Yisroel of Rizhin (Israel Friedman, 1797–1850), and the Talner Rebbe (David of Talnoye, 1808–1882) were all important hasidic figures. Many legends were associated with Reb Shmelke's name. The Rizhiner and Talner "courts" were known for their opulence. For a different set of legends on the Rizhiner Rebbe, see chapter 11 of *The Destruction of Galicia.*

2 / Chariot of the Lord is a reference to the *merkavah*, the chariot that took Elijah to heaven and that inspired early Jewish mysticism.

3 / The Primordial Serpent is first mentioned in the Babylonian Talmud (Sanhedrin 29a) in conjunction with the Garden of Eden; in kabbalistic lore, it is the primal source of evil.

4 / "Blessed is the man" is the beginning of Psalms.

5 / Tosefta Hagigah 2:3; Talmud Hagigah 14b; and elsewhere. "Entering Paradise" here means engaging in esoteric philosophy. Aher (lit. "another person") is the rabbinic name for Elisha ben Avuyah, a leading second-century rabbi who became an apostate. There are conflicting traditions as to the nature of his heresy.

6 / The *Book of Raziel the Angel* is a compilation of Jewish mysticism, cosmology, and magic, first printed in Amsterdam in 1701 and richly illustrated. Ansky plays on the name by calling his wonder-working rebbe "Azriel."

7 / The Cossack Revolt under Bogdan Chmielnicki (pronounced *Khmel-nits-ky*) began in 1648. For Ansky's discussion of these legendary graves, see chapter 2 of *The Destruction of Galicia*.

8 / A great-grandson of the Baal Shem Tov, founder of Hasidism, Reb Nahman (1772–1810) was the author of mystical tales unique in the annals of hasidic literature. The quoted passage comes from the third of the "Seven Beggars." The best available translation of the tales is by Arnold J. Band, *Nahman of Bratslav: The Tales* (Mahwah, N.J.: Paulist Press, 1978).

9 / "This is the feast of King David the Messiah" is an Aramaic formula chanted by male Hasidim before their Melaveh Malka, the festive Saturday evening meal.

10 / The source of this passage on the ascending order of holiness is Mishnah Kelim 1:6–9.

11 / Throughout these ritual proceedings, a person is identified by first name and mother's name, in line with standard hasidic practice. Thus: Azriel son of Hadas (= Hadassah); Leah the daughter of Hannah.

12 / The *shofar* is generally sounded only during the High Holy Days and the preceding month of Elul. Judges may also blow it to pronounce an excommunication (Sanhedrin 7b; Avodah Zarah 40a; and elsewhere).

13 / Ansky is careful to distinguish between the zaddik's charismatic powers and the rabbinic authority vested in the rabbi, Reb Shimshon. The latter has sole jurisdiction over matters pertaining to Halachah (Jewish law), but at a critical moment abdicates authority to the zaddik.

　　　Yiddish speakers address a hasidic leader as *rebbe*, a rabbi as *rov*, and any male Jew as *reb* (Mr.). In act 2, Menashe also addresses his teacher as *rebbe*.

14 / Through the recitation of set formulae, all evil omens will be removed from his dream. Act 4 begins with this formulaic rite.

THE SINS OF YOUTH

1 / Hattot Ne'urim (1876) is a confessional autobiography by Moshe Leib Lilienblum that turned one man's life into an indictment of traditional Jewish society.

2 / Zerubavel is a posthumous work by Isaac Baer Levinsohn (1788–1860), a founder of the Hebrew Enlightenment in Russia. It was written in defense of rabbinic Judaism. Abraham Mapu's *Ahavat Zion* ("The Love of Zion," 1853) is the first Hebrew novel, written in a pseudo-biblical language and set in the times of the prophet Isaiah. Peretz Smolenskin's *Kevurat Hamor* ("A Donkey's Burial," 1873) is a satiric novel in Hebrew.

3 / Ansky had already fictionalized this episode in *The First Swallow* (1904). For a Yiddish translation, see *Pionern* ["Pioneers: A Chronicle of the Seventies"], *Gezamlte shriftn*, vol. 12.

4 / Following the assassination of Czar Alexander II on March 1, 1881, rumors spread that the Jews were responsible. On October 15, the fourth day of Easter Week according to the Orthodox calendar, an anti-Jewish riot broke out in the Ukrainian city of Elizavetgrad. Soon the rioting spread throughout the south—but never reached as far north as Lithuania, where Ansky was then situated.

5 / Hebrew poet, essayist and occasional prose writer, Judah Leib Gordon was the towering figure of the Hebrew Haskalah. "Two Days and a Night in the Inn" (1859) was his first short story and was published in 1870.

6 / Shomer was the pen name of Nokhem-Meyer Shaykevitsh (1849–1905), the author of dime novels and potboilers that were read mostly by women. Once the rabbis were already burning Hebrew heretical books, they threw Yiddish popular fiction in for good measure.

MENDL TURK

1 / Halevanon was a Hebrew newspaper published intermittently from 1863 to 1886 and based in Jerusalem, Paris, Mainz, and then London.

2 / Lord Beaconsfield, i.e., Benjamin Disraeli.

3 / Described in Ezekiel 38, the visionary battle of Gog and Magog fed the Jewish apocalyptic imagination for millennia.

4 / Psalm 115:5–6, also recited in the Hallel service on festivals.

5 / "Hurko" is General I. V. Gurko (as his name is spelled in Russian), who commanded the Russian cavalry during the Russo-Turkish War and was instrumental in the capture of Shipka and Plevne.

6 / Notarikon is an acrostic, used both as a mnemonic device and as a method of uncovering the hidden meanings of Scripture. Here Ansky is tapping Jewish folk responses to war and historical catastrophe.

GO TALK TO A GOY!

1 / Founded in 1902, the Socialist-Revolutionary Party believed that Russia would pass directly from feudalism to socialism, without going through a capitalist phase. Drawing on an anarchist tradition, they supported the use of terrorism to achieve their ends.

2 / From Passover, 1891, through the winter of 1892, some 30,000 Jews were summarily expelled from Moscow, leaving 5,000 behind.

3 / Founded in 1898 and reconstituted in 1903, the Social Democrats were orthodox Marxists who believed that a capitalist stage had to usher in the Russian Revolution.

4 / St. Petersburg was one of several cities in the Russian part of the realm barred to all but a few categories of privileged Jews. Having a Jewish name on her internal passport was therefore a distinct liability for the heroine. (Ansky too lived in St. Petersburg without a right-of-residence. The requirement was not abolished until 1916.)

THE TOWER IN ROME

1 / Genesis 2:9. All biblical allusions in this work were identified by the translator, Michael Stern.

2 / Possibly a reference to Daniel 10:5–6.

3 / An ironic reference to Psalm 19:3.

4 / Ansky is here imitating Balaam's famous prophecies, Numbers 23–24.

THE DESTRUCTION OF GALICIA

1 / Lev Brodsky (1852–1923), Jewish industrialist and philanthropist.

2 / The All-Russian Union of Zemstva [Provincial Councils] and Municipal Councils was created in August 1915 to assist the war effort on the home front. The Union adopted the red cross as its emblem.

3 / Alexander Guchkov, minister of war in the First Provisional Government.

4 / Historian Jacob Shatzky later faulted Ansky for this hypercritical view of Galician Jewry.

5 / Dr. Lander was a Jewish physician from St. Petersburg who worked with Ansky in Galicia on behalf of the EKOPO [Central Jewish Committee for the Relief of Victims of War].

6 / Colonel Myasoedev, chief of railroad police on the border between Russia and Austria, was arrested and tried for espionage in 1912 but was acquitted and reinstated thanks to the personal intervention of General Sukhomlinov, the minister of war. In 1915, when his protector lost his office due to the massive Russian losses on the front, Myasoedev was rearrested, convicted, and hanged as a spy.

7 / Founded in 1867 as the Polish Sporting Society, in 1914 Sokol became a paramilitary organization that fought for Poland's independence.

8 / Pavel Milyukov, a leading Russian liberal and founder of the Constitutional Democratic Party (Cadets).

9 / Gershon Kitever (Rabbi Gershon of Kuty) was the Baal Shem Tov's brother-in-law. He lived in the Holy Land from 1747 to 1757.

10 / The shards of these Ten Commandments were found among Ansky's possessions when he died.

11 / The destruction of Buczacz in World War I forms the backdrop for S. Y. Agnon's novel *A Guest for the Night* (1938).

12 / Abraham David ben Asher Anshl Buczacz (1770–1840) served as rabbi of Buczacz from 1813 until his death. Among his works was *Eshel Avraham* (1885), annotations on the *Shulhan Arukh, Oreh Hayyim*.

13 / The infamous ritual murder case against Mendl Beilis was tried in Kiev in 1913. Notwithstanding immense pressure brought on it by the bureaucracy and the church, the court acquitted Beilis.

14 / Mishnah Ta'anit 4:6. For more on the significance of placing an idol in a sanctuary, see my book *Against the Apocalypse: Responses to Catastrophe in Modern Jewish Culture* (Cambridge, Mass.: Harvard University Press, 1989), pp. 16–17.

Glossary

▼

BAAL SHEM TOV: "Master of the Good Name"; Israel ben Eliezer (1700–1760) was a healer and mystic whose teachings became the focus of a religious revival movement in Jewish Eastern Europe known as Hasidism.

BESMEDRESH: A study house, sometimes attached to or serving as a synagogue.

DYBBUK: The soul of a sinner that, after death, transmigrates into the body of a living person.

EIGHTEEN BENEDICTIONS: Recited in silent devotion at each of the daily services, also known as *Shimenesere* or *Shmona-esreh*.

GEMARA: Here referring to the Babylonian Talmud as a whole.

HABAD: Acronym of *Hokhma Bina Da'at*, a movement founded by Schneur Zalman of Lyadi (1747–1812) to combine Hasidism and talmudic learning. Better known today as Lubavitch.

HASIDISM: A religious revival movement in Eastern Europe that traced its beginnings to the figure of the Baal Shem Tov. It centered on a charismatic leader called a zaddik, or rebbe, and placed great emphasis on religious enthusiasm and knowledge of God. Continues to flourish in present-day Israel, North America, and pockets of Western Europe.

HASKALAH: The Jewish Enlightenment that upheld western European culture as an ideal for Jews to emulate. Flourished in the nineteenth century.

HAVDALAH: A brief ceremony that marks the close of the Sabbath.

HEDER (literally "room"): A Jewish elementary school for boys, often convened in the teacher's home.

HEREM: A ban, or excommunication, pronounced by rabbinical authorities.

KABBALAH ("Tradition"): A term referring to the tradition of Jewish mysticism. Among its other characteristics, the Kabbalah developed a system of symbols to try to describe the mystery of creation as a reflection of the mysteries of divine life. Its major text is the Zohar, "The Book of Splendor."

KADDISH: The mourner's prayer.

MASKIL(IM): A follower of the Haskalah.

MELAMED (pl. MELAMDIM): A teacher in the heder.

NIGGUN(IM): Here referring to a contemplative melody sung by male Hasidim.

PRAYER SHAWL: A garment in the four corners of which fringes have been knotted, worn during morning prayers by observant Jewish males over the age of thirteen.

RAMBAM: Moses Maimonides (1135–1204), the greatest Jewish philosopher and rabbinic authority of the Middle Ages.

REB: Mister, traditional title prefixed to a man's first name.

REBBE: The term for a hasidic leader.

SFIRES: In Kabbalah, the emanations of the Godhead.

SHEMA (YISROEL): The declaration of God's unity and providence. Deut. 6:4–9.

SHTETL: Any Eastern European market town inhabited by Jews.

SHTIBL: A small hasidic prayer house.

SIMCHAS TORAH: A holiday that follows Sukkoth, celebrating the completion of the year's reading cycle of the Torah.

TZIMMES: A stew of fruits and vegetables.

YESHIVA: An institute of talmudic learning.

YORTSAYT: Anniversary of death.

ZADDIK: The leader of a hasidic community, also called *rebbe*.

ZHID (Russian): Pejorative name for a Jew.